Rediscovering CONFESSION

DAVID A. STEERE

Rediscovering CONFESSION

The Practice of Forgiveness and Where it Leads

Routledge
Taylor & Francis Group
New York   London

The figures in this book were used with the permission of HarperCollins Publishers.

Routledge
Taylor & Francis Group
270 Madison Avenue
New York, NY 10016

Routledge
Taylor & Francis Group
2 Park Square
Milton Park, Abingdon
Oxon OX14 4RN

© 2009 by Taylor & Francis Group, LLC
Routledge is an imprint of Taylor & Francis Group, an Informa business

Printed in the United States of America on acid-free paper
10 9 8 7 6 5 4 3 2 1

International Standard Book Number-13: 978-0-415-99746-1 (Hardcover)

Library of Congress Cataloging-in-Publication Data

Steere, David A., 1931-
    Rediscovering confession : the practice of forgiveness and where it leads / by David
A. Steere.
        p. cm.
    Includes bibliographical references and index.
    ISBN 978-0-415-99746-1 (hardbound : alk. paper)
    1. Forgiveness. 2. Confession. 3. Psychotherapy. I. Title.

    RC489.F67S74 2009
    616.89'14--dc22

                                                                            2008050572

Visit the Taylor & Francis Web site at
http://www.taylorandfrancis.com

and the Routledge Web site at
http://www.routledge.com

Contents

Acknowledgments

I am indebted to my wife Margaret for her encouragement and thoughtful reading of this manuscript. Conversations with my sons Andrew Steere and Tevis Steere, have been beneficial. Sarah Brown has proven invaluable in her careful editing and consultation as an English professor without peer. Her husband and my old roommate from college, Jim Brown, has been a source of support, always telling me I am smarter than I am. And my daughter, Elizabeth Monroy, who showed her courage and creativity in organizing a school for filmmaking in Florence, Italy after losing her physician husband at midlife, remains a source of inspiration and encouragement.

My good friend Louis Weeks has looked over the manuscript several times, making helpful suggestions. Tom Knepshield has been of great assistance in dealing with computer problems and preparing the graphics. John Lentz, who is doing some fine writing these days himself, gave my work a careful reading and shared valuable feedback. I am also indebted to a group of people who read the book, did some of the exercises, and shared their reactions in a most helpful fashion: Sara Foerster, April Gentile, Anne Mason, Deborah Moxley, Bill Sligar, and John Wood. Then there are all the people who have helped me hammer out and refine the ideas in this manuscript, including my clients, students, and colleagues, together with those who have attended my workshops and presentations at various conferences. So many people have had a part in influencing my thinking, and I am grateful to them all.

Preface

At a recent workshop for some 50 psychotherapists, virtually every hand in the room shot up when I asked how many thought that hearing confessions was an important part of their jobs. I doubt a similar gathering of all types of clergy would have come close to matching them. For those who want to introduce spirituality into psychotherapy, confession is the natural place to start. This is a book for professionals and their clients who look for a way to introduce spiritual concerns into their work, or, better said, respond to the confessional opportunities constantly present. I wrote it with my clients in mind, many of whom were seekers who felt what we were doing touched something in their souls. They wanted to ground our efforts in a viable spiritual practice that would permit them to discover for themselves what is sacred.

Long before there was psychotherapy, there was the spiritual practice of confession. For centuries it served as the only treatment to sustain the religious through whatever troubled them most. This book is about recovering the experience of confession, in danger now of becoming a lost art. It explores our common urge as human beings to share and to deal with what disturbs our well-being, whether we are inside or outside organized religion. Its thesis: What we have traditionally known as confession of sin and confession of faith are inseparable parts of a continuing process that forms the core of vital spiritual experience.

The recent surge of interest in spiritual practices among virtually every school of psychotherapy reflects a hunger for spiritual experience among both professional therapists and their clients. Psychotherapists are encouraged to use religious practices, values, ideas, and influences that fit within their treatment plans. This can prove awkward for clinicians trying to meld beliefs that are psychological with practices that are theological. We need some workable understanding of what we or our clients can do or say that is "spiritual." The narrative character of both psychotherapy and confession serves to provide a cognitive perspective that is capable of integrating both practices.

I wrote this book for the people with whom I work. My practice has always included persons from diverse backgrounds—educationally, culturally, and religiously—including liberal numbers of Protestants, Catholics, Jews, and some Muslims. Most were lay people, although there were significant numbers of professional people in education, law, medicine, and the helping professions. A large portion I would characterize as spiritually homeless, searching for more than simply relief from whatever symptoms they presented. I write with their questions and needs in mind. Out of respect for their diversity, the language in this book is as neutral as possible, language with which the reader would be familiar and comfortable. I have tried to keep at a minimum loaded terms from scientific literature or religious or theological circles. For example, I've used terms like "Presence" and "Creator" as much as I can, rather than God-language or religious terms from any particular faith tradition. I hope any colleague or client, whether religious, humanist, or agnostic, can make use of the confessional practices we consider.

I am sure I write as a Protestant, a Presbyterian minister, and a professor of pastoral care and counseling at Louisville Presbyterian Seminary for 34 years, as well as a practicing psychotherapist since 1966. Some of my own beliefs, predilections, and prejudices will obviously influence my approach and stick out at times. My desire is to embrace human experience in everyday terms. The practice of confession in and of itself engages us in a universally human endeavor. Once we allow ourselves full sway to explore our experience in depth, particularly what distresses us, we discover resources held in common that have been described in many different ways, some religious, some not, but understandable and valid for all. It is for this "all" that I write. At the same time, I have tried not to omit or shy away from the language of spiritual experience when used in various historical expressions of confession. I hope what I've come out with proves plausible and useable to all.

Many other groups may find this material helpful. I can envision professors and teachers studying it with their students, pastors reading it with their parishioners, administrators sharing it with those responsible to them, and anyone else with a twinge of spiritual homelessness who wants to pick it up and listen in. I have in mind anyone who wants to discover how to be "weller than well" without having to be somebody's patient. The audience extends beyond professionals like me to a lot of people I know. Very few of us can make it through life with the faith we were taught as a child.

Confession and the forgiveness it seeks have strong traditions among Christians, Jews, and Muslims, all descendants or "sons of Abraham." All three faiths share common scripture and rituals to preserve their practice in spiritual life. Islam requires the hajj, which annually brings nearly 2 million followers to Mecca. There, the faithful throw pebbles at the pillars to cleanse themselves of their sins. Judaism begins each new year with Rosh Hashana, a time of self-examination and seeking forgiveness that culminates in Yom Kippur, a day of atonement. For centuries, Catholic Christians have gone to the confessional booth to declare their wrongdoing and receive penance and absolution. In public worship all over the world, Catholics and Protestants alike engage in prayers of General Confession and Assurance of Pardon. Yet all these efforts not withstanding, Christians, Jews, and Muslims can't seem to stop killing each other.

Confession and the practice of forgiveness appear notably absent from our public and private life at every level. In a post-9/11 world, our leaders can't seem to stop branding one another with terms like "evildoers," "the Great Satan," or "the Axis of Evil." No one wants to admit guilt or shame openly in public life where apologies or admission of mistakes can end a public career. Maintaining "deniability" and concealing responsibility are commonplace in political and corporate life. An ad on television advertises the services of Alibis, Inc., offering fabricated deceptions for all occasions. For the first time, fewer than half the married couples in our country can forgive each other often enough to stay married. Whether at home, at school, at church, or in the workplace, confession could jeopardize relationships, inviting raised eyebrows and betraying whispers that tend to isolate anyone bold enough or sufficiently open to venture its expression. Rarely can anyone count on some kind of active acceptance from others. And what should we confess anyway? The word "sin," as we shall see, has become virtually unusable. Something is missing at the core of our spiritual life that increasing numbers of persons are restlessly seeking in new and different ways.

Spiritual Homelessness

These are not the worst of times. Neither are they the best of times. But they have the distinct flavor of both. Never before have we lived with such a mixture of unlimited possibilities and sobering disillusionment. A new kind of consciousness is spreading among us. A recent television poll on *The Today Show* indicated that 51 percent of the people interviewed described themselves as "spiritual," while only 26 percent claimed to be "religious." Something major is afoot when this many people disclaim their roots in the organized religion of their traditional faith and identify themselves as "spiritual" instead.

I wrote about the growing sense of spiritual homelessness that marked the second half of the past century in *Spiritual Presence in Psychotherapy: A Guide for Caregivers.** Vast numbers of Americans were no longer "at home" in the church of their childhood. This was evident in the declining membership and vitality of most mainline churches, particularly among the baby boomers. Even among those who remained, many no longer found congregational life the source of spiritual power and influence it once was. Only the religious right seemed to be gaining in influence and power with its evangelical message, fundamentalist theology, and staunch conservatism.

During this time, as a practicing psychotherapist, I listened to any number of people unburden themselves of things that troubled them deeply. Finally, I began to feel that many saw me somewhat like a secular priest— hearing all kinds of confessions from people in all walks of life. Some went to church. Others didn't. The ones who did often told me that their church was not a place where they could talk about their guilt or matters of which they were deeply ashamed. They may have wanted to, but everyone seemed too "tidy" and dressed up for the messy entanglements of their inner turmoil. Often, they had a pastor who counseled them or referred them safely to anonymity away from their home church where no one would be judgmental. But I always felt strangely alienated from my own beliefs when this happened because I also taught in a seminary where we shared a lot of ideas about what the church ought to be like. We were supposed to be the fellowship of the forgiven, for Christ's sake! Why did I have to get outside the congregation of believers to engage in serious conversations with others about what troubled them most?

So many people I saw during those years were spiritually homeless, looking around their worlds in quiet desperation for someone to talk with about what was going on in their lives. They described themselves more as seekers than as the believers around them who seemed so certain and comfortable in their faith. They were on a search for something missing. They were confessing all kinds of things about their lives that troubled them deeply. And once they got started, they wanted a whole new direction, not simply a way out of their current crisis. Many of them stayed on to look for a new pathway with personal meaning for their life. I came to understand spiritual homelessness as an opportunity for spiritual awakening, whether it arose inside or outside the church. Recently, Robert Wuthnow described this phenomenon as a changing pattern away from "a spirituality of dwell-

---

* Steere, David A. *Spiritual Presence in Psychotherapy: A Guide for Caregivers* (New York: Brunner/Mazel, 1997).

ing" to "a spirituality of seeking."* People feel less and less tied to a particular sacred space (e.g., a church or synagogue). Instead, they move between sacred spaces on a pilgrimage that seeks moments experiencing that which is divine.

At the center of this quest is a hunger for confessional conversation that helps us to unburden ourselves of what troubles us most, and a thirst for personal forgiveness that can bring not only a sense of self-acceptance, but also the relief of forgiving others. Slowly I realized that we are in the midst of a conversational crisis in our culture. We no longer talk to one another, listen to one another, or discuss with one another what really matters to us. We relate electronically, not face-to-face. We chatter away on cell phones while walking or driving, or shopping or whatever. We dine side by side watching television. We retire to the privacy of our computers at work or at home after the usual greetings and pastimes. We attend PTA meetings, ball games, church and Sunday school, bazaars, bingo, fashion shows, and social affairs, but we rarely attend to one another's basic experience as a human being with real troubles, wants, needs, and dreams.

The ranks of the spiritually homeless are filled with people who want to talk and to listen to one another. They represent a growing awareness that we are spiritual beings longing for connection and conversation with each other about what is vital to our lives. They present a rather sobering confession that many can no longer believe in the way they once did. Accepting what they have been taught without question no longer satisfies the yearnings of their souls. They must know for themselves, think for themselves, and discover their own faith for themselves. Spiritual awakening arises in self-awareness the clear sense that there is something deep inside that resonates to a larger Presence both within and without, awaiting our discovery.

So "seekers" and "believers" are coming to represent two different mentalities emerging on our current scene. My father used to say, "All generalizations are false, including this one," but well-placed ones help us understand trends or tendencies that operate to shape our common consciousness. Those who identify themselves as spiritual rather than religious are earnest seekers, not simply looking for a sense of Presence on the golf course each weekend. Their quest for spirituality is born from a sense of strong dissatisfaction and disillusionment. The spiritually homeless spawned my interest in confession—for confession originates in the painful self-awareness of a seeker. You have to be disturbed enough, troubled enough, or worried enough to need to talk. Really talk. And know it.

---

* Wuthnow, Robert. *After Heaven: Spirituality in America since the 1950s* (Berkley, CA: University of California Press, 1998).

The Confessional Mind

Confession arises from a heightened experience of self-awareness. Some inner discontent points us toward something else, richer and fuller. We find ourselves thinking, "I feel bad about this," or "I am not what I should be," or "I can do better than this." Often, there comes a commensurate awareness that we are spiritual beings. Or can be. Other thoughts may follow, such as, "I am not what I could be," or "I am not living the life I was meant to live," or "I am not what I want to be." If you have said or are saying one or more of these things to yourself, you are a "seeker." And you already sense the power of honest confession.

Now for some generalizations about what those who call themselves "spiritual" react to and reject. They see their "religious" counterparts on the far right as "true believers," clinging to a mentality marked by certainty and self-assurance, a conservative way of thinking, bent on preserving a faith given for once and for all long ago. Their beliefs are founded upon Scripture, buttressed by inerrancy, and regarded as necessary for salvation in an afterlife. This mentality is committed to conserving its ideas as an infallible guide in the present. It is the "Faith of Our Fathers," incapable of improvement, all encompassing, excluding all others from God's favor and salvation, including members of the other two Abrahamic faiths of Judaism and Islam.

In between the spiritual mentality on the left and the religious right lies a continuum of all kinds of spiritual and religious practice inside and outside organized religion. Distinctions between "seeker" and "believer" fade away in this flow of life. Most of the people I know have to become seekers in order to believe, and have to believe in order to continue seeking. More about this later. Instead of liberal and conservative battles between the religious right and the spiritual left, which continually drain our energies and distract us from the difficult task of living together cooperatively and productively, I am proposing the task of honest confession. It can engage and unite us in sincere self-examination and personal growth. To recover this tried and ancient practice is to reinstate a legitimate and time-honored part of everyone's religious tradition, including all who belong to the three great Abrahamic faiths. It is impossible for me to conceive of anyone who would not benefit the pool of human consciousness through practicing authentic confessional self-awareness.

Instead of doing battle with one another across faith lines or within them, this confessional approach is offered in the belief that we all need one another; ultimately, everyone on the planet needs everyone else. Honest confession is an excellent place to start bringing us together somewhere in the middle. I recently heard Daniel Siegel, M.D., talk about integrating the mental processes of the brain. He described what he called *contingent relationships* in which the developing human being from childhood on experiences *being accurately perceived, understood, and responded to by others.*ʼ Such relationships are essential for us to develop a full sense of selfhood and a resonant compassion for others. Siegel provided the audience with a powerful analogy of interpersonal relationships developing mental capacity. We imagined ourselves standing before a river. On one bank were people singing one note, the same note on and on, over and over. He even provided us a solo demonstration. On the other bank were people singing their own song at their own pace in their own individual way. This he invited us all to do at the same time, producing a chaotic mixture of dissonance. In the middle, he invited members of a choir to sing something together, which they did automatically and in harmony ("You Are My Sunshine"). Consciousness is formed between the Scylla of monotonous self-sameness and the Charybdis of chaotic randomness where interpersonal harmony becomes a human possibility.

Siegel's metaphor of the flowing river is a powerful one for human consciousness, both individual and societal. On the left side of the river is chaos, and recent "chaos theory" holds that all significant novelty and change occur on the brink of chaos, where previously unrelated particles or ideas or processes come together to form something truly new. One step in from chaos on the continuum is creativity. On the extreme right is the kind of lockstep conformity and unanimity of thought and activity and belief that insulates us from any change in our institutions and practices. A few steps in on the continuum are stability, continuity, and the kind of persistent self-sameness that creates habit and identity. Everything in the flow of the river in between is made possible by the increasing complexity of human harmony, mind-to-mind, person-to-person, experience to experience. The flow of life between both banks is sustained by continual relational motion and mutuality. The balance required between constant change and reliable stability is held in place by the polar forces between one bank and the other channeling a workable course of passage in between. More about this later.

As we launch into a discussion of confession, this river metaphor provides a vivid picture of how both negative and positive experiences become intimately connected in the flow of life. The solution to every human predicament is present within the problem itself, pointing in other self-corrective directions. What begins in painful self-awareness, when fully explored, points beyond itself to the restoration of wholeness and balance. When we are carried too close to the left bank of chaos and confusion, our anxiety thrusts our attention toward something more reliable and

---

ʼ See Siegel, Daniel J. *The Developing Mind: Toward a Neurobiology of Interpersonal Experience* (New York: The Guilford Press, 1999).

trustworthy. When we bog down near the banks of mindless conformity and senseless bastions of prejudice or habit, our anger and rebelliousness push our attention in another direction that may lead to a way better balanced and more appropriate.

What we have traditionally thought of as confession of sin and confession of faith merge as inseparable parts of this continuous flow of self-awareness that forms the core of vital spiritual experience. What begins as an acknowledgment of what troubles us most creates a commensurate awareness of what we hold sacred. What originates in the most painful parts of self-knowledge, when excavated, uncovers for us the most powerful and joyful aspects of our selfhood. But I'm getting ahead of myself here. We have a lot to discuss before this becomes plain and plausible. This is the direction in which we will head.

Something else about the development of the human brain is worth noting as we start. Siegel, who is associate clinical professor of psychiatry at the U.C.L.A. School of Medicine and conducts research at the Center for Culture, Brain, and Development, adds another significant picture of the developing brain.* If you fold the fingers of one hand over your thumb, and then lift them up exposing your thumb across the palm of your hand and then put them back, you have a model of how the layered neocortex of your brain develops around something called the hippocampus. The hippocampus (your thumb) forms at about age 2, permitting us to recall explicit memories. This new active circuitry connects the prefrontal cortex with our sensory awareness, creating autobiographical memory. It permits us to develop a sense of self and time. As our minds grow, so does our capacity for self-awareness and self-reflection. And for our purposes, confession among human beings becomes possible.

Good definitions are hard to come by. I have always liked Anton Boisen's notion that confession constitutes the socialization of an otherwise isolating human experience.† Through making a confession, we may break free of whatever renders us painfully alone and out of touch with others. Our capacity for autobiographical memory not only makes this possible, it also dictates the necessity for such sharing. The great confessional writings of the past were all autobiographical self-disclosures of personal struggles with what troubled the confessor most. I remembered St. Augustine's *Confessions*, which I read years ago in seminary, and reread it with greater interest. Then I looked around for others with which I could compare my developing understandings of this ancient practice. Comparable

---

* See Siegel, Daniel J., and Hartzell, Mary. *Parenting from the Inside Out* (New York: Penguin Putnam, 2003).
† Boisen, Anton T. Exploration of the Inner World: *A Study of Mental Disorder and Religious Experience* (New York: Willett, Clarke & Co., 1936), pp.161–162.

autobiographical documents of self-awareness and self-disclosure don't grow on trees. What I found was so fascinating that I want to take you on a similar tour of where my search led. In the process, we can see how contemporary brain research and our religious traditions converge to embrace confession as an essential activity at the center of our growth as human beings. We need desperately to talk to one another about what really matters in our lives.

Practice

This book is designed to stimulate thoughtful conversation. We all have a dialogue inside our heads when we read something new. I hope you will run across many things to mull over with yourself, but I sincerely hope you will not stop there. I also hope you will find yourself wanting to talk to others around you, and to listen to what they have to say. If you do decide to engage someone else in the conversation, here are some things to consider: First of all, confessional conversations are not designed to invade your privacy. They are opportunities to disclose at your own pace and in your own way matters you have decided to share with someone you trust. All of us are entitled to our privacy and solitude. Confession has never been about "telling all" in some compulsive way. We all have the privilege to hold whatever we choose in our own inner world as confidential. Whatever we acknowledge to ourselves is already shared by a larger Presence deep within.

In writing this book, I had to consider how I would manage my own personal life. For me, a central article in teaching is to model or demonstrate the subject matter in the way you present it. I did not set out to write a confession of my own, but how could I write about this kind of autobiographical self-disclosure without occasionally adopting a confessional stance to illustrate what I am talking about? Obviously, this is a book about the practice of confession, not intended to be confessional in nature, but I decided along the way I could do some of what I was encouraging you to do.

A word about how the book is put together. It is laid out roughly as my own research and thought unfolded. At the end of each chapter, I have suggested several levels of exercises or experiences you may choose for yourself. They have to do with various ways you can begin to explore the practice of honest confession in your own life. You may choose to read this book for yourself, by yourself. In the process, you may find yourself wanting to talk about it with others, sharing your experience at some level. The possibilities are as follows:

1. *Self-Awareness and Internal Dialogue.* At the end of each chapter there are several exercises you may elect to expand your self-awareness. They are designed to invite various measures of

self-confrontation that are confessional in nature, inviting internal dialogue, personal growth, and increased self-esteem. If you do no more than complete the book by yourself, there should be ample experiences and activities to engage you in meaningful confessional practice. I anticipate the strong possibility that you may establish some consciousness of companionship with a larger Presence within.

2. *Confessional Partnership.* Forming a confessional partnership with another person is a possibility at any stage. You could select a trusted friend, a family member, someone in your discussion group, or a partner from a confessional group. Your contract or covenant with each other is to hold in confidence whatever is discussed. Remember that the purpose will not be to "tell all." Each of us is entitled to our privacy and our own personal world. Whatever you decide to share with one another is in the comfort and security of assured acceptance. There is no invasion of privacy.

3. *Discussion Group.* The opportunity to exchange views about a new idea, a fresh insight, an old doubt, a growing hope, or an emergent belief can make your reading a much stronger learning experience. Various topics or avenues to explore from the book appear at the conclusion of each chapter. One member of the class could initiate the conversation at each meeting with a few pungent thoughts, observations, and questions.

4. *Confessional Group.* There is no hard-and-fast line to be drawn between an educational group and a confessional group. The difference is in focus. Members of a discussion group often share various aspects of their experience with one another. A confessional group meets for the express purpose of sharing at the confessional level. A contract or covenant of mutual confidentiality and accountability guards conversation. Forthright acceptance of one another is part of a commitment to work together toward personal growth and positive change. The same right to privacy and personal choice in self-disclosure governs the process.

As you have probably guessed, my thought has been greatly influenced by carefully studying points where the clinical processes of psychotherapy intersect with the concerns and practices of the spiritual life. The rich convergence of these two fields constitutes one of the great opportunities of our time. There is so much that each can learn from the other. Erving and Miriam Polster sensed this when they wrote in *Gestalt Therapy Integrated: Contours of Theory and Practice* that psychotherapy had become too rich

an experience to be confined to the mentally ill or emotionally disturbed.*
This investigation of confession is conducted on a constant two-way street
with traffic moving in both directions. We can learn a great deal about
confession from the practice of psychotherapy. By the same token, understanding the time-honored practice of confession can shed a great deal of
light on effective psychotherapy.

One place where our understandings of confession could impact
current treatment is in reconsidering the growing emphasis on Brief/
Solution-Focused approaches. All fix their patients' attention on what
they are doing right instead of what they are doing wrong. Lengthy
explorations of a current crisis or predicament or the connection of
present symptoms to one's personal past often bog down, squandering valuable time and energy. Better we circumvent the presenting
problem wherever possible in search of reaching and strengthening the
patient's practices that are symptom-free and productive. Behavior-
change trumps self-understanding any time, particularly in an age of
managed care. Confession is essentially cathartic and may be necessary,
but only to the point of releasing enough "pent-up emotional steam"
to permit shifting attention to some well-located other endeavor that
brings relief.

Traditional confession, as we shall see, has often worked at this level.
But its richer and deeper expressions have always sought a more thorough
exploration of the human predicament. There is genuine merit in understanding and owning how we participate in the painful processes of our
life. We shall see repeatedly how the predicament itself has served to point
the way to a fuller life. Beyond catharsis, confession involves a purpose-
ful effort to grow as a person. The aim is to become wiser and stronger
and better. Self-awareness and self-knowledge seek to integrate our more
painful experiences into our autobiographical consciousness, which develops a growing sense of selfhood. Confession then becomes a process of
taking responsibility for our choices and responses in life. Possibilities of
forgiving ourselves and others begin to occur. We may not want to skip or
jump over the negatives until we have sufficiently explored them for where
they direct us. This fundamental progression from owning the negatives
to discovering the positives in confessional practice forms the core of vital
spiritual experience.

---

* Polster, Erving and Polster, Miriam (New York: Brunner/Mazel, 1973), pp. 23–27.

CHAPTER 1

Honest Confession

Martha Key was a woman in her mid-forties, attractive, and carefully dressed with a professional touch. She looked like the high school principal she was. Of course, that is not really her name. As with all the characters in this book, it is a pseudonym for the real person. Enough facts about her are altered to protect her confidentiality. But on this day she was real, as real as life itself.

She spoke, gingerly rubbing her right shoulder, which had troubled her unexplainably for several weeks, "I'm here because of the pain that won't go away. My doctor said the MRI showed nothing that could be causing it. He asked me how my life was going. He wanted to know whether I was under stress at work. How about my marriage? Guess he was looking for some emotional cause since all the tests were negative."

Then she paused, leaned forward, and looked me straight in the eye, "I'm really here, Dr. Steere, because I'm a liar. I lied to him when I told him my marriage was fine. It hasn't been for two years now. I lied to him when I said I like my job. I am under so much pressure that I don't even want to go to work anymore. I lied to him when I said things were OK with the family. Mark and I can't agree on anything with the children. Worse than that, I decided I've been lying to myself for years. And it's time to stop."

With that, Martha sat back in her chair, letting out a deep sigh, "There! Honest confession is good for the soul!" And it was, not just for Martha Key, but for me as well. For Martha, it marked the beginning of earnest reflection on her life that led to some significant changes across the months ahead. No longer would she march blindly on into one frustrating personal experience after another, looking the other way and pretending everything was "fine." It became the starting point for dealing with many things that troubled her, some of which she was only beginning to allow into awareness.

For me, Martha's confession served to focus attention upon the truth in that old adage I had not thought about in years: *Honest confession is good for the soul.* I began to think about some of the confessions I had heard as a practicing psychotherapist during the past three decades. There were so many. Some were dramatic disclosures delivered with similar relief. Others came with halting speech, piecemeal and across a number of conversations. Some were blurted out in despair, desperate for acceptance and relief from the shame and guilt that shrouded them. Still others followed the quiet conclusion of a growing awareness that they were missing out on life. As one man put it, "I'm tired of coping. I want to start living." And although they differed greatly in content and context, they all bore the character of confession to me. They all seemed honest. And good for the soul.

Soon I was listening for confessional themes throughout my work, with individuals and families, with couples and groups. I was amazed by the frequency with which they appeared. I also went through many of my records searching for similar themes I may not have recognized as confessions at the time. There were plenty of those, too. So for the past few years what Martha called "honest confession" has occupied my attention. What makes for it? Under what circumstances does it occur? Can we identify some of its characteristics?

A Lost Art

I had always thought of confession as the province of the church. The confession of sin was a regular ritual at the beginning of public worship. Particular acts of confession to a priest or a fellow believer were part of our religious tradition. Yet, I was amazed at how seldom I heard the practice discussed or even mentioned, not in church or in the seminary where I taught, or among the clients I saw day in and day out. I cannot remember a serious discussion of confession among my colleagues in theological education during my thirty-five years of tenure. I looked in vain for some substantial consideration of the subject on the contemporary scene. Surprisingly enough, I finally found one in the magazine *Oprah* quite by chance. Confession was the theme for June 2002.* It provided a good introduction to current understandings of the term outside the venue of organized religion:

> … the idea is own up. Come clean. Get it off your chest. Confession means all that and more. Admitting your sins to a trusted listener is the classic definition, but there's no end to what we are moved to

---

* *Oprah,* June 2002, pp. 32ff.

profess or acknowledge: beliefs, opinions, behavior, quirks, foibles, outright folly. True confession is not tabloid TV (self-exposure merely for titillation). Soul baring is an act of trust. It's whispering your flawed humanity into someone's ear. It's allowing yourself to be all that you are.

The feature article described secrets as living creations in our minds, constantly begging for expression. We become like Coleridge's Ancient Mariner who once killed an albatross, bringing a curse against himself and his shipmates. We carry an inner pain we are compelled to declare to others. It's what Theodor Reik called the compulsion to confess. You may recall the Mariner's shame when the crew hung the dead bird around his neck. Soon thereafter, all 200 died in a shipwreck only he survived. From then on he was driven to tell his story at times and places where he could recover a sense of acceptance and perhaps do others some good.

There followed articles by several writers unburdening themselves of secrets about sex, plastic surgery, lying, and other needling shames. There was even a brief study of persuasive techniques to obtain a confession by interrogating criminal suspects. The final piece was devoted to considering ways the author could atone following a confession of committing verbal violence against her husband. She consulted a philosopher, a Buddhist monk, a rabbi, a priest, a psychologist, and "Mom." Not only is confession no longer the venue of the church, but when Oprah looks for expertise concerning its place in life, the search carries her considerably beyond the boundaries of organized religion.

The experience with Martha Key set me to thinking about the whole role of confession in our lives. The practice is as old as religion itself. I mentioned Anton T. Boisen's description of it as "the act of socializing an otherwise isolating experience." It was my privilege to meet the old gentleman in New York while a graduate student in 1958. I even dug up an article I wrote on him in October of 1969 shortly after his death, entitled "Anton Boisen: Figure of the Future."* He was a Presbyterian minister who, at the age of 44, had an acute psychotic episode following a series of unfortunate incidents centered around an unsuccessful love affair. He wrote confessionally about his experience in this "little-known country" of mental illness. Diagnosed schizophrenic (*dementia praecox* in 1920), he became convinced that the flood of ideas that rushed in upon him were not unlike the mystical experiences of Madame Guyon, Heinrich Suso, George Fox, and the Apostle Paul. His upheaval pointed to a more constructive resolution of his life struggle, which he achieved without benefit of the major tranquilizers that came in the 1950s to still such emotional crises.

---

* Steere, David. "Anton Boisen: Figure of the Future," *Journal of Religion and Health,* 8:359–374, 1969.

Boisen went on to introduce chaplaincy programs to mental hospitals and became known as the "Father of Clinical Pastoral Education." He insisted we needed to study theology in *living human documents*, not just books on the shelf. Perhaps he was right. And I was too. He really is a figure of the future. The urge to tell another about what creates an inner sense of guilt and shame appears to be universal. The pain of concealment from others is fueled by a growing sense of estrangement—not just from others, but from ourselves and our Creator as well. If honest confession is good for the soul, what goes into its making and why has it fallen into such disuse?

Definitions

Whenever I set out to study something, I start with the dictionary. More often than not, I come across some surprise or new awareness that arises in the interconnections of language cultivated by our predecessors to express their experience across the years. The various uses of the term "confession" proved no exception. To make a confession means to acknowledge or reveal something to others, to own or admit it as true. It was spawned in the traditional religious community to describe the act of declaring or acknowledging one's sins to God or someone who represents God or to fellow believers in order to obtain forgiveness. It could also mean admissions of guilt before a court of law in the legal community.

Then I came across the second usage of the term in religious circles. Confession also involves acknowledging our belief in something, as in confessing our faith. It can refer to formal professions of belief or the acceptance of church doctrines upon being admitted to membership. Nothing really new here either. But how and why did those who shaped our faith use the same word to designate both acknowledging our sins and declaring our beliefs? I must confess I had never put the two uses together. Not in all my years in church and seminary had I considered the relationship between confessing our sins and confessing our faith. So this ancient practice of making a confession involves not only an open reflection upon the most negative aspects of our life, but also an equally important task of addressing the most positive aspects of what we really hold as true and sacred.

So what if they really belong together, not just etymologically but dynamically, one following from the other? What if they are actually two parts of one and the same process, each enabling the other to thrive and grow in the human spirit? I had never before put together confessing sins and confessing faith as part and parcel of one continuous process. I began to recognize both elements in many of the confessions I was examining. They all came in narrative form, unfolding against the background of that person's life. Only as we hear this person's story are we able to actively understand and accept what is really happening. Our acceptance does not mean condoning or going along with what someone like Martha Key declares about her life. It means taking her seriously and committing ourselves to helping her explore its implications as an act of seeking something better for herself. The choice to confess and encounter the worst, even the unbearable, in one's life starts to lead beyond itself almost from the beginning.

Some Dimensions of Confession

Not all the confessional experiences I examined showed promise in bringing together these two aspects of confession. But in those that did, there were some common dimensions that I could isolate early on. First, there was a continuing state of *heightened self-awareness* fueled by the pain and discomfort of extended guilt, shame, or anxiety. In Martha Key's case, the choice to stop "lying to herself" began to quench a deeper thirst for honesty and freedom from all the self-deceptions she warily constructed to cover her mounting discontent. It felt good to level with herself and with others; just as it fit for Anton Boisen to hospitalize himself, acknowledging to his friends and family that he was mentally ill. A certain emotional energy is generated by such confessions, enabling one to begin to deal with what has been ignored and denied, and increasingly painful. Often there is a profound sense of relief.

Second, *the predicament points beyond itself.* For Martha, the solution lay in confronting the problem once she became willing to explore it. She had grown up the "parentified" or "hero" child in an alcoholic family and always had to do everything right and pretend all was well even if it was not. It was time to stop deceiving herself and to deal with life as it really was. Any number of choices began to present themselves, once she "faced up" to what she was doing. It was a bit different for Boisen, who became convinced there was a method in his "madness." He began to realize some disorganization deep within his internal world had upset the foundations for ordinary reasoning. His journey to the boundary of chaos made him aware of an intimate connection between his psychotic episode and the experience of creativity shared by spiritual leaders and persons with a touch of genius. What distinguished one from the other was the constructive outcome of the experience through which they passed. Somewhere, in the midst of his illness, Boisen got the idea he was to help break down the barriers between religion and medicine. Soon thereafter, he met a physician named Richard C. Cabot, of the Boston Cabots who "spoke only to God," who became a supporter and benefactor. Cabot continued to fund Boisen's chaplaincy programs liberally, although he denied to his dying day Boisen's belief that there were psychogenic factors in the origin or treatment of mental illness. Years later, Boisen attended a public lecture given by Cabot on "The Wisdom of the Body," in which the famous physician outlined the marvelous devices the body employs in maintaining and restoring health. Afterward, Boisen suggested he was interested in searching for analogous processes in the human mind. Cabot shook his head emphatically and replied that he believed thoroughly in the "wisdom of the body" but not in that of the mind.

A growing *demand for a relevant response* is the third dimension. It is still possible to abort the confessional process at this stage by refusing to search for one. Martha Key had come too far to stop. So had Boisen. However, each had to go through a rather difficult sorting process to decide what for them was right or wrong, true or false, worthy or unworthy, appropriate or inappropriate. Our conscience can be spectacularly untrustworthy at times, the product of overzealous and misguided parenting. Sometimes what troubles us with guilt and shame may prove unwarranted when carefully considered in the light of day. Lengthy discussions exist between psychiatrists about the difference between neurotic guilt and real guilt. More about this later. But in the end, we must all determine whether or not our guilt, or shame, or anxiety is appropriate. For example, one of the things Anton Boisen confessed was a lifelong struggle with the urge to masturbate. He grew up in a time when it was broadly considered sinful and dangerous, the cause of psychological problems. Now with all the research by Kinsey, Masters and Johnson, and others, I doubt it would have troubled him so. Boisen was clear that many of the ideas that engulfed him in the hospital were both distorted and destructive, but others were more fertile and might stand the test of time. The error he and others who were mentally ill shared was to assume that they all carry authority simply because of the way in which they come.

Martha Key faced a similar task of discriminating between past assumptions of how to be and what would fit her present reality. In the process, she decided to let go of a lot of family secrets, both past and present, to press beyond matters of guilt and shame, as we shall see. This relevant response must be different for each person, framed in terms of one's own unique situation in life. No confession reaches this stage without confronting us with a range of options from which to choose. We cannot not respond. Denying, doing nothing, and trying not to think about something are irrelevant responses. A relevant response is one that deals directly with the consequences of our situation. We come to claim our ability to make a meaningful response to our predicament. We make it our responsibility (response-ability) and no one else's.

Finally, this confessional process carries *the potential for spiritual encounter,* which may or may not enter the confessor's awareness. Sometimes it comes much later. This was the case with Martha Key, who months afterward suddenly realized the pain in her shoulder had long since disappeared. She referred to it as "tapping into some kind of healing power deep within." Boisen later wrote about the recurring idea that it was his job to help break down the wall between religion and medicine. He insisted this notion he had been following with some measure of success had been given him by an *intelligence* beyond his own. The spiritual encounters we are talking about come in our own language and symbols, drenched as they are in our own immediate experience. They mark some point where we break free from the radical claim of what was confessed (lying, madness, or whatever). For many they point to what will become their most sacred beliefs, the personal articles of faith they hold most dear. For others, old ways of thinking may be challenged so deeply that new and different understandings emerge in what have been their core beliefs.

Four Levels of Narration

It took me quite a while to realize I had already worked out the relationship between confession of sin and confession of faith in *Spiritual Presence in Psychotherapy.* There I identified four levels of narration evident in clinical practice when people began to talk about their lives. Every recollection is constructed from what Daniel Siegel calls our autobiographical memory. It is the product of the way we integrate our brain. We collect images that are called up by the activities of our mind. They are combined and preserved in original ways in our memory, and get assembled in various combinations and arrangements of meaning. Given the narrative character of our experience, we order our memory of similar events in simple succession to form larger, more encompassing stories. Related events become associated with one another and are strung together as pearls on a string, creating a larger story composed of an ongoing series of smaller ones. Our storied existence can be divided into four levels of narrative expression, each constituting an overarching story constructed from a series of smaller ones standing in intrinsic relationship to one another. They are (a) *the public story,* (b) *the private story,* (c) *the transformational story,* and (d) *the sacred story.* Each is true in its own right. Each possesses its own set of meanings about how we are related to others in significant ways. Each has an independent existence yet is interdependent with the others. All four levels of narrative are equally applicable, not just to our individual stories, but also to the stories that couples, families, groups, institutions, and corporate communities develop about their common life.

---

* Steere, David. *Spiritual Presence in Psychotherapy* (New York: Brunner/Mazel, 1997), pp. 179–199.

The Public Story

The public story is the one we tell everybody—who we are, where we are from, what we do, how many children we have, whom we know, and so on. It is the story that appears on our resumes. It both presents and protects what Jung called "the persona," the face we show openly to the world around us. It is the story from which we choose to be known among friends, acquaintances, co-workers, and the public in general. We tell it on e-Harmony and in letters of application of other kinds. It comes into play when we are "being professional," dating, engaging in pastimes at a cocktail party, or meeting someone for the first time. This story is real and essential to finding our place and establishing ourselves in society.

For the family, our public story is the one that accompanies family albums or is told in the commentaries made while presenting slide shows, home movies, and videotapes. It is in the Christmas letters we annually send to friends and acquaintances. The public story is always constructed for general consumption and, in addition to vital statistics, usually includes an update on important activities of everyone concerned. In institutions and organizations, the public story is found in their promotional literature and other items concerned with presenting an image to the general public. Educational institutions promote their public story on celebrative occasions, brochures, and annuals; religious institutions in public worship, bulletins, newsletters, and so on. Public stories are usually constructed for general consumption by members, friends, potential members, clients, customers, students, and the public in general.

The Private Story

The private story is a secret story concealed from others and told only to a confidant. Our private story as individuals involves our secret dreams, our hidden aspirations, and our strongest unfulfilled longings. It contains the record of our deepest grievances, our most humiliating failures, our secret sins, our lost loves, our lasting disappointments, and our deepest affronts and estrangements from those closest to us. It is the repository of what troubles us most, producing guilt, shame, and anxiety. The dynamics of our private story usually involve repetitive themes of blame, self-defense, competition, and survival. Our private story contains secrets that we keep without telling, often ones we will not deal with, some, perhaps that we do not even know that we know, fearful of disclosing them even to ourselves. It contains what Eric Berne called our life script.

Honest confessions originate around the elements in our private story that we choose to disclose to others. We do so only when we feel assured that we will be accepted and understood. We do so in despair of the isolation and estrangement the private story creates. The private story proves too much for most of us to bear alone. The measure of anxiety (sometimes "dis-ease") guilt, and shame surrounding this story defines and preserves the privacy with which it is guarded. We disclose it reluctantly, sometimes testing those we tell with progressively selected parts and pieces, often revising as we go to render our role as favorably as possible. We are entitled to its privacy, as we have said. Its disclosure should never become a matter for any compulsion to "tell all," as if to purge ourselves in some blindly cathartic effort toward spiritual bulimia. Editorializing in our own interest is often part of a search already begun for a more favorable story.

With families, the private story remains "in-house," reserved for members or for our most intimate acquaintances to learn once they move "inside the family's conversational system." It is composed of the things we learn after we get married, not only about our spouse but also our in-laws and extended family. Ordinarily, it is composed of the series of narratives about secret affronts, coalitions, and long-standing, unresolved conflicts and factions that divide a family, group, or community. The private story contains all "the dirt we sweep under the rug." In institutional life, it involves the things you learn after you have been hired and are on the job. It is the way things really work rather than what the manuals, the catalogs, or the articles of governance say they do. Part of the private story of every organization is the bundle of secrets that permeate it. When we get caught up in the private story, wherever we are, we possess a tunnel vision that fails to see beyond the conflict at hand. At its core, this story protects a demoralizing, sometimes destructive, occasionally devastating gap between our ideals (public story) and our actuality (private story).

The Transformational Story

The transformational story is a story in search of healing and reconciliation. It is a curative story constructed to make right what is wrong in the private story. Transformation can take place in any number of ways through key events or turning points that expand our awareness and open us to change. It contains in one form or another those pearls of personal experience that may be strung together around turning points in our life course that make all the difference. Often they contain some fresh level of understanding previously unknown, such as "the other side of the story." In some way, elements in the private narrative are rearranged so that we may undertake something new and different outside its confines. The transformational story contains a modified, more complete version that we sometimes refer to as "the whole story," leading us to responsibility on the one hand, laying claim to our part in what has gone on, and to reconciliation on the other, once we come to understand more completely the roles and responses of those around us. Such transformations, we shall come to see, form the essence of forgiveness.

Families and social institutions also have their transformational stories. These often involve significant events in common life, such as births, deaths, moves, mergers, marriages, new presidents or leaders, as well as formative events that impinge upon the group from within or from the outside world. Usually, some similar emphasis on healing emerges through concrete efforts of self-consciousness and self-reflection on the part of the group. A family goes to therapy, the company invites a set of consultants to explore positive changes, managers deal with some internal conflict by confronting it openly—and there is reconciliation. Whether we are considering an individual or some larger community of persons, the transformational story is one of renewed responsibility and change in relationships long subjected to the stress and strain of some private narrative they have shared in common.

The Sacred Story

A fourth narrative may be developed through the accumulation of transformational stories. It is the sacred story, a narrative of transformation and triumph. It draws together at the center of consciousness what we have chosen to hold as sacred. It is a story of accumulated meanings constructed in accord with the priorities, values, ideas, and ideals we have acquired in the process of healing and change. It gathers up what we grasp and learn in the torque and twist of transforming our private pain into something overcome, constructing our own convictions about what is more deeply true and more highly good in our common life together.

Not everyone might choose to pursue the confessional process to this fourth level of narration. Often we are grasped much later by some awareness of its continuing presence in whatever has made our life rich and worth living. Many are content to take whatever growth and healing comes at times of transformation without any attempt to weave its meaning into a larger fabric of relevance to the purpose of life itself. Most of us, however, do this quietly, if not consciously, in the way we look back upon significant events in life, remembering them through some overarching narrative that frames them as valuable and worthwhile in their telling and retelling. With repetition comes some sense of what we hold sacred. Families also do this, not only in their stories but in the rituals, customs, or traditions they form around birthdays, anniversaries, seasons, or holidays. Institutions and organizations of all kinds preserve their values in narratives of various sorts about founders, expansions, products, slogans, and length of service. Religious bodies canonize sacred scripture and accumulate collections of sacred stories, interpretive literature, liturgy, and other modes of corporate celebration of that which is most meaningful.

A Full Confessional Experience

A full confessional experience originates in a heightened state of self-awareness that carries us into significant reflection on some aspect of our *private story*. Whatever the problem, the process of self-encounter serves to point beyond the immediate predicament to choices we can make to move beyond its grasp. A *relevant response* is one that alters or reshapes life around some higher and better course. The way we determine and pursue such responses serves to create *transformational narratives* of sufficient power to carry us into a different state of mind and being. Eventually, experiences of this sort can form within us the sense of a *sacred story* worthy of shaping our personal faith and beliefs that follow from it. In this way, the confession of sin creates a confession of faith.

More Definitions

The words *sin* and *faith* appear over and over again in traditional religious language. Some preliminary definitions seem necessary to guide our considerations. I have chosen to approach confession by exploring the depressive triad of guilt, shame, and anxiety that always seems to accompany ideas about sinfulness. This avoids the use of the term itself, which for many is ensnared with emotional and condemnatory connotations. Why include anxiety? The answer takes me back to my graduate school days where I can still hear Reinhold Niebuhr pacing before a packed lecture hall talking about how *anxiety* gives rise to sin. Anxiety comes with our awareness as a human being that we are finite in the face of an infinite universe. Being both free and bound, limited and limitless, makes us anxious. *Anxiety* is an inevitable concomitant of the paradox of freedom and finiteness in which we are all involved.* As I am writing, a continuous hum fills the air outside my cabin. The cicadas are back with their mating song, flying and attaching themselves to trees and whatever else they can find, and, finally, dying by the hundreds under foot, on my patio, and everywhere I go. They have waited to be born in the ground where their parents planted them for 17 years. In 2 weeks, they will all be gone, having reproduced the next generation.

I digress because I cannot help but feel compassion for these little creatures flying about, struggling to crawl or turn over, weakening and dying in droves. I think if I were a cicada, I would sing my song, mate, and keep flying around as long as I could. Until…. This is what Niebuhr was talking about. What a tiny part of the universe even these seemingly infinite numbers of cicadas are. I am not nearly so bound or limited as one of these

---

* Niebuhr, Reinhold. *The Nature and Destiny of Man* (New York: Charles Scribner's Sons, 1953), p. 182.

little creatures I imagined myself to be, yet we both share a fate that is similar. You and I sing our song, and mate, and fly as long as we can, until…. There is considerable difference in our time and our freedom to live; yet in the face of an infinite universe, the difference between their time and ours is not so very much. We cannot avoid anxiety when we consider how to spend the succession of moments making up our lifetime.

Anxiety as such is not sin to Niebuhr, but rather the precondition of sin. It can give rise to either *faith* or *sin*. We are like sailors climbing the mast of a ship, anxious about both the height of the crow's nest above and the abyss of nothingness into which we may fall. Anxiety becomes the soil from which sin may grow, either as *pride* in an effort to replace our Creator with intellect and displays of power and control, or *sensuality* by immersing ourselves in some form of escape (luxury, drunkenness, or sexual passion).

Down the hallway, Paul Tillich echoes a similar theme describing how the *being* we enjoy as humans is lived out under the threat of *nonbeing*, which is the basic cause of all *anxiety.*ˉ None of us can escape witnessing the transitoriness of life, the death of others, and the impression of these events upon the always-latent awareness of our own having to die. Tillich describes this basic anxiety of nonbeing in three types: (a) the anxiety of *fate* and *death,* over which we are powerless; (b) the anxiety *emptiness* and *meaninglessness,* which renders us spiritually bereft; and (c) the anxiety of *guilt* and *condemnation,* in which we feel weighed in the balance of it all and found miserably wanting. We must take this anxiety of nonbeing into ourselves as part of our being, as existential anxiety that goes with being alive. Because anxiety has no object, we need to convert it into concrete fear that can be faced, analyzed, acted upon, and endured. Failure to do so gives rise to the many forms of neurotic anxiety that serve as futile efforts to avoid the threat of nonbeing. The *courage to be* follows upon accepting ourselves despite our unacceptability. Then the possibility of faith is launched.

Tillich's ideas of *sin, forgiveness,* and *faith* may serve as working definitions of these terms as we begin. Hang on to your hats. He is notoriously difficult to follow. Once we take the anxiety of nonbeing into ourselves, the depressive triad that accompanies it introduces us to what Tillich considers as *sin*—estrangement from our essential being. This estrangement is found in the gap between our essence—that full expression of our being for which we are created—and our existence—that partial, finite, limited self in which we struggle to make actual our potential.† Sin embodies the alienation we experience not just from our true nature and from a sense of wholeness deep within ourselves, but also the estrangement we encounter

---

ˉ Tillich, Paul. *The Courage to Be* (New Haven, CT: Yale University Press, 1952), pp. 35–74.

† Tillich, Paul. *Systematic Theology, Vol. I* (Chicago: University of Chicago Press, 1951).

throughout our relationships to others. A relevant response that deals with the consequences of what Tillich calls sin must, by definition, be a step away from estrangement toward our true nature and proper relationships with other creatures and our Creator as well. Tillich's understanding of *forgiveness* as God's acceptance of us in spite of our unacceptability is what enables the courage to affirm our *being.* Accepting relationships, human or divine, have this character of being extended and "given beforehand" in an effort to understand and work with anyone entering the confessional process. Acceptance is offered "in spite of" unacceptability, not because the other person ceases what is unacceptable. Acceptance is not given or withheld in terms of some show of change or standard of accomplishment. For our purposes, *acceptance* is an evolving relationship offered to anyone choosing to reflect in earnest upon some aspect of their private or "secret" story.

Whatever reflects earnestly upon the meaning of life is on the verge of becoming an act of *faith*. Faith, for Tillich, is a condition of being grasped by *ultimate concern*. It leads to engaging and participating in the concerns of that ultimate reality to which he gives the symbolic name of God or *the ground of all being*. To have faith is a universal human need. Human beings must organize life around something of ultimate concern to them, if to no one else. Faith can change and expand across a lifetime. An appearance of the depressive triad of guilt—shame—anxiety serves to underline what has failed us most acutely in the way our lives are organized. Reorganization around something better is quietly, but firmly, demanded. A relevant response may become an act of *faith* and potentially a part of our *sacred story* and our personal beliefs. We are talking about something quite different from traditional Confessions of Faith that systematically organize a set of commonly held beliefs to which one may give cognitive assent. These beliefs have been won in the crucible of hard self-encounter working one's way through painful self-awareness to gain personal understandings of matters to which such formal statements of faith can only point and encourage us to pursue.

The Ancient Mariner

Coleridge understood these dimensions of a full confessional experience when he wrote *The Rhyme of the Ancient Mariner*. Oprah had already whetted my interest in the poem but it was not until a couple of years later when I came across another reference to it by Karen Armstrong, one of my confessors, that I dug it up and read it. She pointed out that Samuel Taylor Coleridge might have been the first English poet to deal with the unconscious. The poem was written in the late 1790s at a time when Coleridge and

---

* Tillich, Paul. *Systematic Theology, Vol. III* (Chicago: University of Chicago Press, 1963), pp. 224–225.

Wordsworth had become close friends and collaborators. The two planned to publish a volume of poems together. Wordsworth was going to show how real poetry lies hidden in commonplace, everyday life. Coleridge was to treat spiritual subjects to illustrate the common emotions of humanity. The idea for the Ancient Mariner was spawned one evening when the two were brainstorming. Coleridge was eager to embody a dream of a friend. Wordsworth suggested the shooting of the albatross from his reading of Shelvocke's *Round the World by the Way of the Great South Sea,* published in 1726.

The poem is written in timeless lyrics and cast as a story told by the Mariner to a wedding guest he stops outside, causing him to miss all the festivities.* It is a long story, 17 pages worth. The Mariner tells of a voyage through storm and icy sea. Then a friendly albatross shows up, bringing a good wind and playful company to join the ship for food and companionship:

> It ate the food it ne'er had eat,
> And round and round it flew.
> The ice did split with a thunder-fit;
> The helmsman steered us through!
>
> And a good south wind sprung up behind;
> The albatross did follow,
> And every day for food or play
> Came to the Mariner's hollo!

Suddenly, without any explanation or reason, the Mariner shoots the albatross with his crossbow. He never really says why, but we do catch some of his deep remorse:

> And the good south wind still blew behind
> But no sweet bird did follow,
> Not in a day for food or play
> Came to the Mariner's hollo!

His shipmates are irate and hang the dead carcass around his neck. The wind dies. And one misfortune follows another, ending in a tragic shipwreck that only he survives. Coleridge depicts a delirium-filled dream state representing the Mariner's suffering. One by one, his shipmates drop and die of thirst, cursing and condemning him. Their spirits depart; he is alone in nightmarish delusions. He is haunted by the horrible "curse in a dead man's eye." Yet in the midst of all his mental chaos, the Ancient Mariner sees the water snakes:

---

* Quotations from wOnKoSITE – *The Rhyme of the Ancient Mariner* (www.wonko.info/default.htm).

Within the shadow of the ship
I watched their rich attire:
Blue, glossy green, and velvet black,
They coiled and swam; and every track
Was a flash of golden fire.

O happy living things! No tongue
Their beauty might declare:
The spring of love gushed from my heart,
And I blessed them unaware:
Sure my kind saint took pity on me,
And I blessed them unaware.

The self same moment I could pray;
And from my neck so free
The albatross fell off, and sank
Like lead into the sea.

In the heightened self-awareness of his shame and guilt, Coleridge's Ancient Mariner discovered the sea snakes, and in them, a symbol of life and a love for living things. The bond between creativity and chaos charts his course afresh. His journey is not over, but beginning to point in another direction. He hears and in his soul discerns "two voices in the air."

"Is it he?" quoth one, "Is this the man?
By him who died on the cross,
Which his cruel blow he laid full low
The harmless albatross."

The spirit who bideth by himself
In the land of the mist and snow,
He loved the bird that loved the man
Who shot him with his bow."

The other was a softer voice,
As soft as a honeydew:
Quoth he, "the man hath penance done,
And penance more will do."

The Mariner struggles to leave behind a certain agony, but it comes upon him from time to time moving him once more to deal with lingering guilt. There is no simple, single act of catharsis. He is moved to tell and retell his story in various and sundry places to whomever he can get to listen.

Since then, at an uncertain hour,
That agony returns:

> And till my ghastly tale is told,
> This heart within me burns.
>
> I pass, like night, from land to land;
> I have strange power of speech;
> That moment that this face I see,
> I know the man that must hear me:
> To him my tale I teach.

The tale resolves itself in a simple but moving confession of the Mariner's newfound faith. The way out of his painful self-awareness has become a new and better way to live. The circle between confession of sin and confession of faith is complete. From chaos comes clarity in the simple affirmation at the center of the old man's heartfelt belief:

> Farewell, farewell! But this I tell
> To thee, thou Wedding-Guest!
> He prayeth well, who loveth well
> Both man and bird and beast.
>
> He prayeth best, who loveth best
> All things both great and small;
> For the dear God who loveth us,
> He made and loveth all.

The *Rhyme of the Ancient Mariner* draws together both aspects of confession—traditionally confession of sin and confession of faith—into one continuous process. What began in painful remorse over killing the albatross leads to an emergent belief in the sacredness of life and the love of God for all creatures great and small. There are other aspects of confession represented in the Mariner's story. It is made in narrative form and can be understood only in that context. There is the theme of estrangement and isolation created by guilt and shame. The Mariner's predicament points beyond itself in the sea snakes and a reverence for life that they came to represent. Such an experience, even if it disturbs the balance of mental health, creating inner turmoil and chaos, can also be creative. He breaks out of his isolation to tell his story to others. And he gives voice to his newfound belief in the sacredness of life and God's love for all creatures, including himself.

A full confessional experience may lead to some form of spiritual encounter, whether or not one realizes it at the time. Spiritual Presence is not contingent upon our awareness — nor on the particular language or metaphor with which we describe it. Faith change follows any sincere effort to reorganize our ultimate concerns. Not all confessions that I identified developed into the full confessional experience I have been describing. A number aborted at one stage or another of the process, but for many, like

Martha Key and Anton Boisen, honest confession did prove good for the soul. And it can prove good for yours and mine as well.

Getting Started

I invite you to experiment with the experience of confession. It begins in the awareness of something painful that gains our attention. We may find ourselves ruminating over it. There may be feelings of guilt or shame, or both. Or we may simply find ourselves in a prolonged state of anxiety, the hallmark of which is not knowing what it is all about. More often than not, we will engage in some habitual attempt to override the experience that beckons. We will get busy, try harder, run away from, find some work to do or some activity to capture our attention, eat or self-soothe in some other habitual way, or self-medicate the experience away with alcohol, prescription drugs, or something even more addictive.

We start by paying attention to what disturbs us emotionally. Instead of denying it, we address it and permit it to become the focus of our complete attention. We guard against the many ways we habitually distract ourselves from the kind of self-awareness we are after in confession. Martha Key had the right idea. Stop denying the painful feelings. Once you give them your full attention, handing over the reins of your self-awareness to where they lead, you are free to explore whatever comes to consciousness. The task of confession begins in full acceptance of the experience at hand: what it is, what it is about, what is disturbing to you, how it came to be, what you did or did not do, and any consequences that seemed to follow.

When you have done this, you will have constructed a narrative. You have a story to tell, like that of the Ancient Mariner, although rarely so dramatic. Perhaps you share with him the urge to tell in order to cope with what has happened. How many times have you gone through a painful experience by retelling it to some trusted friend, lessening its emotional charge, slowly wearing it out of your system, and probably fudging a bit here and there to make yourself look better and give others the brunt of any blame to be shared? This is normal and healthy. Congratulate yourself for having the wisdom to do it.

You are probably also becoming aware that you have a cutoff point somewhere between narratives that are easy to tell and those that are not. Usually the ones we do not talk about are more painful and involve stronger internal dialog that is self-critical and sometimes self-condemning. There are things we just do not want others to know about us. That is also OK, normal, and healthy, provided they do not torment us unduly and interfere with our well-being or our ability to enjoy life. As we proceed, we will pay some attention to confessional issues of this magnitude and ways that you may address them. For the present, select something current and ordinary. If there is a biggie that is bothersome, put it off for a while and practice on something less formidable or complicated.

Self-Awareness and Internal Dialogue

1. Select some area in your current self-awareness about which you ruminate, are anxious, or experience some measure of guilt or shame. Give it your full attention as described above, being careful to note measures of self-distraction that take you away from constructing a narrative about it. You may choose to find the time to "talk it out to yourself" during a period of relaxation or meditation. In privacy, you can talk out loud, even into a tape recorder if you choose. Or you can write out your confession together with any subsequent thoughts you have about it. If you like, you may choose to start a journaling process as you go through the book—a private record of your experiences and thoughts.

2. Remain open to whatever ideas, insights, intuitions, inner promptings, or other new awareness that may come. Your mind is deep and rich with experiences, connections, and resources far exceeding your everyday consciousness. Give it free rein and remain open. The Mariner suddenly saw the beauty of the sea snakes, and subsequently all living things, in the midst of his confession. Don't miss anything within your own vision.

3. When you are finished, take time to reflect on the process as a whole, perhaps at a later time. Be mindful of what went well for you, where you had difficulty, and anything else in your life you may want to address in the same way. Also make note of anything so far that you have come to think, feel, or believe about the process of confession. And as you continue, you will get better at establishing a constructive self-awareness.

Confessional Partnership

1. If you are thinking about forming a Confessional Partnership, give some thought to what kinds of conversation you imagine would benefit you. Be mindful of things you would like to share, are reluctant to share, or reserve to your own personal privacy. Decide whether you would like to start with someone relatively distant, a close friend, or a family member. There is no rush, and you can consult with anyone else you know reading the book. You could try a partnership once or twice to see if you have a good fit.

2. At your first meeting, discuss your covenant or contract of confidentiality and any other pertinent agreements. These may include

the time and frequency of meetings, boundary issues, the right to privacy, what kinds of responses you would like to make to each other, and what thoughts you may choose to share from your reading and general experience.

3. Your initial confessional conversation could be constructed along the lines indicated in the first section on "Self-Awareness and Internal Dialogue," or you could experiment with a spontaneous conversation about something that has become more relevant in the interim. Of course, the two of you may start as a mini-discussion group talking over issues outlined below.

Discussion Group

1. Members of a Discussion Group are encouraged to complete the exercises for Self-Awareness/Internal Dialogue privately. Some may wish to pair off and form a Confessional Partnership that meets beyond the group time. It is recommended that someone from the group act as discussion leader and focus the group's attention on pertinent ideas from the reading to kick things off.

2. Discussion Groups can have a regular leader, rotate leadership among various members, or come at it as a free-for-all, whatever best suits the group. Frequently, groups do better when someone takes responsibility to organize questions and stimulate reaction and discussion. Find the best way for your group to do it. You can also experiment with different approaches.

3. Some ideas for things you can discuss after reading this chapter are listed below. They are purely suggestive to stimulate your own ideas and reactions.

   a. Share various impressions and experiences with confession that members of the group have developed in the past.

   b. Discuss some of the reactions to different types of confession; such as general prayers of confession in public worship, confessions of faith, confessional rituals in various world religions, the confessional booth, impromptu and unintended confessions, and "true confessions" in magazines and on the Internet.

   c. What different attitudes toward confession do you encounter among friends and acquaintances?

   d. Using the Mariner as a metaphorical model, react to the confessional narrative in the poem. You could even dig up a copy on your bookshelf, from the library, or on the Internet, and read portions aloud in the group. Compare it with other confessional narratives that occur to you in biblical stories, movies, books, and any shareable real-life experience in the group. Have you ever shot an albatross?

e. Kick around Paul Tillich's notion of sin as "estrangement," forgiveness as "acceptance," and faith as "ultimate concern." What other ideas about these terms are present in the group?

Confessional Group

1. The purpose of a Confessional Group is to encourage and assist one another in developing a self-chosen pattern of personal growth through confession. It is not to "tell all" or invade the privacy of each other's psyches. It provides the opportunity to express to others and receive from others mutual understanding and support. You will want to start slowly to allow an appropriate level of trust for each other to develop.

2. Members of the group may ready themselves for participation through any or all of the first three levels of experience described above. The first two sessions could be spent as a Discussion Group. Many Confessional Groups devote an early portion of later sessions to discussions that serve as a prelude to the mutual sharing that follows.

3. As you start, the group will want to establish what covenants or contracts you will make about your conversations. Several agreements are important in succeeding. Confidentiality involves an understanding not to discuss anything that anyone else says outside the group. It is necessary that you come to trust in one another's intentions to protect your welfare. There is no invasion of anyone's privacy. There is an understanding that anyone may call a halt to what is being said at any point until enough confidence and comfort are restored to continue.

4. The group will want to experiment with different ways of sharing confessional conversations as it proceeds. Often, a designated leader for an evening or a period of time can assist the group in staying on task, managing time appropriately, distributing conversation and reactions among members, and making sure no one gets left out. Confessional Groups are small. They range from four or five to eight in number. Discussion Groups can go up to as many as 12 to 20 members and still function well, but not Confessional Groups, where the aim is to afford each person the experience of being accurately perceived, understood, and responded to in a timely and supportive manner. The emphasis is on mutual acceptance. More follows at the end of the next chapter on how each member can contribute effectively.

CHAPTER 2

The Full Confessional Experience

You never know what is going to change your life. I am fairly certain the big changes develop across time for most of us. Often we become aware of them only in retrospect. Sometimes when we look back, some event marks a turning point. Such was the case when I returned to visit a small rural parish in the knobs of central Kentucky where I was a student pastor while in seminary. I had lived among these people for 3 years. Now, 5 years later, I had begun teaching at Louisville Presbyterian Seminary. I was shocked by what had happened in the interim.

There were ten principal families in the parish. What unsettled me was learning that since I had left, seven of these families had suffered severe emotional distress in one form or another. There was one suicide. There were two hospitalizations for depression, two divorces, and two cases of chronic alcoholism, one of which I had known about but was unable to help. One of the divorces involved a shooting. And I had missed it all. Where had I been? Asleep, I decided, and in dire need of waking up to some of the realities of everyday life. My job at the seminary was to teach Pastoral Theology, which, when I was a student there, included no courses in Pastoral Care and Counseling. I decided then and there that whatever else Pastoral Care involved, it had to do with responding to tragedies like these in the making. So I made what I now understand to be a relevant response. Since that time, I have worked hard learning to practice, teach, and write in search of ways the church can contribute to better mental health among its members. I trained in individual and group psychother-apy at the old Louisville Area Mental Health Center in the 1960s under the supervision of Warren Cox, M.D. At the seminary we developed strong programs in Clinical Pastoral Education and graduate degrees in Pastoral

Counseling. In the late 1980s, we designed our own master's degree in Marriage and Family Therapy and were accredited by The Commission on Accreditation for Marriage and Family Therapy Education. During this time, I maintained a small but substantial private practice for purposes of research and training. It grew to five weekly treatment groups and around 8 hours of individual, couple, and family therapy. I always felt the bane of all education lay in the old adage "those who can do, and those who can't teach."

From the beginning, the more involved I became in counseling and psychotherapy, the more interested I was in integrating what went on there with my training in theology. Obviously, both set out to deal with the same realities with which we human beings struggle, but with different language and from different perspectives. Points where the two intersect were immediately evident everywhere. An obvious one for our purpose is in the concept of forgiveness. For theologian Paul Tillich, "God's acceptance of us in spite of our unacceptability" could be freely given and received by us and extended to one another. For virtually all psychotherapists, the course of treatment is based upon a similar acceptance of their clients where they are, without rejection or condemnation. All confessions are made in anticipation of an accepting relationship with someone who hears them, whether in a religious setting or in psychological treatment. In either case, both persons making and receiving confessions accept the *reality* of one's human predicament without denial, accept a *relationship* committed to working out a relevant response to it, and accept the *responsibility* to choose their own course through what follows. From neither perspective does forgiveness become some tacit tolerance that condones everything and demands nothing. Instead, it offers the promise and presence of an accepting relationship that makes honest confession possible, whatever the setting.

Ten Characteristics

Before I set about the task of reading some of the classic confessions, I decided to put down what appeared to be the characteristics of a full confessional experience among people I had seen. I believe most people working in the field would produce a similar list if they were alert to confessional themes. These present-day confessions would bear a remarkable similarity to confessional patterns from the past. I would probably write some of this differently now as I'm putting the manuscript together, but I chose to leave it as it first appeared so you can come on this journey with me in the same order in which I took it.

The following ten characteristics took shape in what I came to consider a *full confessional experience*. Some may be present to varying degrees in many conversations. However, if you follow the confessional experience to its logical and natural conclusion, all of these will probably be involved at some point. That is the hypothesis with which we begin.

1. Self-Encounter

Confession begins with a significant heightening of self-awareness stimulated by mounting discomfort with our own painful personal experience. The "depressive triad" of guilt, shame, and anxiety is normally present in sufficient measure to command our attention. The guilt and the shame tend to isolate us, as Anton Boisen suggested, rendering us reluctant to share these experiences, fearing disfavor or rejection by others. But something propels us toward breaking our silence. For Martha Key, it was her anxiety accompanied by chronic physical pain, penetrating and disarming her defenses of denial and feigned contentment. Finally, she decided to break her silence, fueled by finding herself unable to cope with the frustrating circumstances of her life. It was, as she put it, time to stop lying to herself and those around her. With others it could be any number of things: guilt over betraying a friend, shame at being rejected by a lover, guilt over failures in parenting, grief over divorce or death, guilt over an affair, or harm to someone physically or emotionally, anxious avoidance of challenges or social situations or responsibilities, growing estrangement from family members or friends, uncontrollable anger or frustration or suspicion, loss of a job, self-confidence, or self-respect, to mention some common ones.

What these confessors shared was the kind of self-encounter that corners all of us when we fail to live the way we really want to live. Always there is another side of the confessor at work, a higher self that opposes what is happening, that operates from a position of self-worth and self-respect. It is different from conscience, which at times can prove spectacularly untrustworthy. It is a realistic self-acceptance that refuses to surrender the positive aspects of oneself while facing the negative or darker side with which we struggle. This is a precondition to honest confession. Without it, we lack the courage and resources that Martha Key brought to bear in facing her denial and deceit. It is this duel aspect of self-acceptance that drives a full confessional experience, and I have learned to look for its positive influence beneath the surface of anyone's genuine despair about his or her present predicament.

2. Choice and Inevitability

Self-disclosure in most confessions usually presents some mixture of choice and inevitability. Martha Key's was by choice. There was little external pressure to surrender her denial and face her unhappiness. The pain in her shoulder did provide some internal sense of urgency and added an aspect of what we may call "involuntary confession" to the process. Often, some similar physical symptom or signal of stress appears at an unconscious level if we stay in denial too long. Martha's served to unseat her capacity to go on pretending that everything was "fine."

Just the opposite was the case with Alfred Pugh, a clergyman in his early 40s. He sat, fighting back tears, as he confessed an affair with a woman in his congregation. Someone had written the chairman of the church board disclosing their relationship after intercepting an errant note he sent her. This external pressure made Alfred's confession inevitable. Who knows how long he could have continued their relationship had he not been exposed. His whistleblower's disclosure suddenly brought everything in Alfred's life to a head. Yet there is probably an element of unconscious choice in the errant note. Across the years, I have witnessed an endless series of diaries, credit-card accounts, answering-machine messages, letters, bills, text messages, articles of clothing or personal effects "carelessly" left in conspicuous and revealing places. There are genuine accidents, but they are few and far between.

Whatever the case, whether a confession is made more from internal pain or external pressure, there is obvious relief in the socialization of this otherwise isolating experience. What has been concealed, worrisome, inescapable, unmentionable, demoralizing, unspeakable, or unbearable is now disclosed to another human being. The response is crucial. For the process to continue, it must be acceptance. Both the confessor and the person who hears must experience a sufficient measure of acceptance to welcome such a disclosure to the light of day where it can be addressed without fear of condemnation. Once it has become speakable, there is the possibility of dealing not only with the disclosure, but also with its consequences. Only what Paul Tillich termed "acceptance in spite of our unacceptability" can sustain the confessional relationship.*

3. Guilt and Shame

The content of confession encompasses whatever in our life has produced feelings of guilt or shame. These two words have both distinct and overlapping connotations. *Guilt* is the more legal term, designating the state of having committed an offense, crime, or wrong, particularly against moral or penal law. It carries with it feelings of remorse and fear of punishment, whether the offense is real or imagined. A relevant response often requires one to distinguish between guilt that is considered real and neutoric guilt, which is rooted in childhood training that is no longer appropriate.

---

* Tillich, Paul. *Systematic Theology, Vol. III* (Chicago: University of Chicago Press, 1963), pp. 224–225.

Shame is a much broader and more elusive term. It describes the painful feelings arising from some notion that we are unacceptable to others for any number of reasons. It can evoke a range of reactions from embarrassment to outright humiliation. Social disapproval or contempt looms larger in the picture. Developmentally, we may learn to feel shame much earlier than guilt. If guilt centers on wrongdoing as unacceptable, shame surrounds confessions of a quite different character. We may feel shame at being too skinny or too fat, for soiling our underwear, for having a penis or breasts that are "too small," for being unable to do something others can (whether physical or mental), for being afraid, or feeling weak, dirty, ugly, inferior, sexual, or just plain helpless. We don't have to do anything people consider wrong to feel ashamed. Shame comes from being something we sense is unacceptable to others, and it is much more difficult with which to deal. Some researchers identify shame in the earliest experiences of an infant's bid for Mother's attention and not receiving it. The visceral experience of not "being" what she desires at the moment provides a vivid introduction to our primal experience of helplessness.

So we cannot define the purpose of confession in the purely religious terms of seeking forgiveness for our sins. Confessions, whether ancient or modern, have always involved a mixture of all that marks our estrangement from ourselves, from others, and from our Creator. Confession has always been accompanied by the distinct but overlapping experiences of both guilt and shame, usually so intermingled as to be difficult to separate. Perhaps it is here that organized religion has stubbed its toe in the confessional task. It has never seemed to deal in a satisfactory way with the patterns of shame governing our everyday life, not since Adam and Eve became aware that they were naked and were ashamed.

Martha and Alfred experienced both guilt and shame in varying degrees. Martha's shame centered on her history of trying to be perfect. Growing up in an alcoholic home with an abusive father, she became a second parent, helping Mother out with the smaller kids. She was driven by an intense desire to create a better life for herself and her siblings, which involved maintaining the fiction that everything was "fine." It was extremely painful to admit all the friction and conflict she lived with daily, either as a child or in the present. Given her tendency to deny the unacceptable, she had little sense of guilt, having tried so hard to please everybody else.

Alfred, on the other hand, was overwhelmed with guilt. He felt he had betrayed everybody: his wife, his children, the other party, the church, as well as God. At the same time, shame surrounding his own sexual desires drove his pursuit of their satisfaction underground, adding fuel to the fire. His confidence was shattered, not only in his ability to function professionally, but even to hold his job. Shame is such a relative thing. Only a week before, I heard a man who held a prominent position in a small community discuss his fear of coming out of the closet as a homosexual to face the shame of exposure to his family and the people in his town. "I could survive having an affair with someone's wife," he added wryly, "but not being caught in a gay relationship."

4. Acceptance

We crave acceptance from one another. Someone once described us as living in a hotel universe, each in our own separate room, tapping out messages on the wall to each other. We assume other people's rooms look something like ours; but we can come to trust this is so only through understanding and being understood. In isolation we become progressively detached, disoriented, and delusional. Only when we get something into words clearly enough for someone else to understand, do we really understand ourselves. Acceptance forms the ground from which mutual understandings can grow.

So many thoughts follow. I think of Daniel Siegel's study of integrating brain functions so essential to personal growth and mental health. The accepting force of a *contingent relationship* with another person who accurately perceives, understands, and offers a timely response is essential to the developing brain. I think of Senator McCain's experience as a POW in the Hanoi Hilton. He and fellow prisoners survived isolation and maintained their sanity by tapping out messages to one another on the walls of their cells.

Acceptance is the opposite of condoning. By acceptance, we are not talking about treating what has gone on in Martha or Alfred's lives as insignificant, tolerable, or of little consequence. That would be rejection. Honest confession is a two-way street that demands straightforwardness from both parties. To fail to respond to Alfred's complete sense of moral failure is to refuse to accept him where he is and to join him as he faces the consequences. He has broken one of his most cherished moral standards. His career and family life are in jeopardy, but this is just the beginning. We have a lot more to do and say about what has happened. Acceptance means we can clear the air, continue our relationship, and start to deal with the situation at hand. Despite what he has done, Alfred will not be abandoned. And we are free to proceed from here to address what he needs to do next. This commitment to stand with another governs any full confessional experience. The same is true for Martha as she stops denying the things about which she is ashamed to talk. Honest confession addresses, step-by-step, her despair at failing to deal with so many conflicts in her relationships at home and at work.

5. A Continuing Process

A full confessional experience takes place in the context of a relation-ship committed to dealing with what is disclosed. Here may be the dif-ficulty with ritual confessions in organized religion. Whether made in the confessional booth to a priest or embedded in the weekly liturgy acknowledging our sins in corporate prayers, ritual confessions end in some kind of absolution or declaration of pardon. A priest, minister, or rabbi pronounces that our sins are forgiven. And it's over. That's that. Symbolically, ritual confession can come to suggest a two-step process where the confessor declares a moral failure and the clergy declares it forgiven. End of story. If we stop there, we ignore the possibilities sur-rounding a relevant response. Confession can never be a one-night stand. For the kind of confessional experience we are considering, we are only at the beginning.

A full confessional experience requires time to unfold. What is declared always points beyond itself to things worthy of our best consideration. The human problem in Martha's confession of lying is to be found in the con-text of her *private story*, which her falsehoods only served to conceal. Time is required to explore the layers of truth that unfold beneath her deceptions that can now come to light. She may start with lying, but very soon she is dealing with the painful consequences of a perfectionistic pride she devel-oped as a small child. Her position as oldest involved assuming grown-up responsibilities in her family. Her efforts to keep others content were made at the price of denying her unmet needs. Her lying was a noble failure to convince everybody, including herself, that all was well—when it never was. In listening to honest confessions, one learns to expect a series of self-confrontations unfolding like layers of an onion. When you are faithful over a little, you will be trusted with much.

6. Responsive Context

Honest confessions, then, tend to be made in a context that promises an accepting response, coupled with some prospect of resolving or coping with the predicament they present. A chance to dispel guilt or shame and the anxiety that comes with them is not enough. We must also address implications or consequences of the events that occasioned them. Both Alfred and Martha sought something substantially beyond mere exonera-tion. Neither had any desire to return to the status quo in a life that had become unmanageable. Martha would not have found any satisfaction in some single event of confessing her self-deceit and frustration. Neither would Alfred. Both carefully selected the venue of psychotherapy, which could respond to their self-disclosure with ongoing conversation. Both had to reach the breaking point before they did.

So how can religious institutions offer and maintain the accepting relationships necessary to encourage honest confession? This continues to be a problem where both laypersons and their clergy labor in settings that remain unresponsive to the perils of one another's private stories. It certainly was in the rural parish of my seminary days. Both Martha and Alfred were also in religious settings where confessional conversations had fallen into virtual disuse. The average church or synagogue requires a high-level of inventiveness to bring a full confessional experience into being beyond its ritual expressions. Those who seek to establish it often find themselves working against a climate of "fellowship," "propriety," and "public persona" that seems prohibitive. Martha chose the venue of psychotherapy over her church, her colleagues in education, her family, and her friends. Her shame led to the assumption that there would be little acceptance within the circle of her daily relationships.

How many others choose to leave the fragile fellowship of congregational life to seek help through psychotherapy where conversations with the troubled are sanctioned? A precondition to honest confession is the availability of some anticipated relationship to deal with what is revealed. This can be developed in a religious setting. I have seen sensitive pastors, priests, and rabbis provide this function in congregational life. I have seen small groups form for sharing, mutual support, and accountability, and caring friends offer genuine acceptance to one another. Where this happens, people like Martha and Alfred can find meaningful confessional conversations long before they reach the breaking point. Once this is established, others learn about it and it spreads. Not that both Alfred and Martha didn't require psychotherapy by the time I met them. What haunts me is the thought that all they went through might have been avoided if those on watch in their religious relationships had met them much earlier with a responsive context of confession, instead of being asleep as I was in my seminary parish. Where acceptance is missing, no amount of ritual celebration of confession and forgiveness can establish the practice of hearing and responding required.

7. Narrative Form

Confession always presents itself in narrative form. No one gains acceptance by simply declaring some unacceptable act to another without any effort on the part of the teller or hearer to understand what led up to it. There is always a story behind what one confesses that begs to be told and heard. No disclosure of shame or guilt stands alone, apart from its own unique history of unfolding events in that person's *private story*. We can only understand the present situation through the context in which it occurred. A sense of forgiveness always turns upon the narratives surrounding particular events. Without them, the meaning of any act remains unclear.

The accumulation of stress in Martha Key's life and her tendency to deny it all is easily understood when we know something about her *private story*. As noted, she grew up the "hero child" or "parentified sibling" in an abusive family system where Father drank heavily and often struck Mother and the children. When Martha was a teenager, she and her sister spent hours trying to convince Mother that she should leave. Mother didn't, and the outcome for Martha was a miserable high-school experience in which she was ashamed to bring her friends home. She vowed never again to live with such secrets. Now here she was stuck repeating a similar drama with her own husband, but it was easier to deny his gambling addiction, which threatened the family's economic stability. It was easier to cover his absences from work and the growth of indebtedness with falsehoods and pretense. It was all to preserve the family. At her school she began to compromise her standards the same way, failing to enforce policies and tolerating incompetence among others in her responsibilities as a principal. Slowly and despairingly, she felt her integrity slipping away. She was "living a lie."

Martha's confession became a series of narratives coalescing around the grasp her private story held upon her present life. Honest confession exposed her desperation. One by one the stories surfaced, unearthing increased self-understanding, new levels of her complicity in her failures, and a growing sense of personal responsibility. Her own story proved to be interlocked with her husband's precisely at the point of his need to impress everyone with his own ability and success. He had grown up the son of a struggling grocer whose store never made enough to support the family. Like his father, he never felt "good enough." All his efforts were directed toward winning Martha's affection and providing the "good life" for the family she craved. Eventually she acknowledged how she played into his weakness with her righteous indignation and critical yearning for things they didn't have. "I am not to blame for what he's done," she said quietly, "but I certainly had my part in it which didn't help a bit."

The narrative character of honest confession lays the groundwork for a relevant response to what troubles us. Our story continues. We cannot not respond. Understanding where we have been and where we are heading invariably creates choices. In this way our human predicament always points beyond itself. It can empower us to become responsible ("response-able"), to choose among the growing number of scenarios and possibilities that present themselves. Our own unique resolution of every confessional issue awaits our attention to a relevant response.

8. *Transforming Narratives*

Of central importance to this narrative character of confession is the opportunity to create new and transformational narratives in place of present ones. Telling lays the groundwork to continue the story with new possibilities and different outcomes. The same old story over and over again has begun to forfeit its power. The more honest the confession, the greater the empowerment for change. New narratives that emerge in crisis may have a frantic and hopeless character about them at first. In Alfred's case, his first fantasies about the future were catastrophic. How could he go on? He must leave the church as soon as possible. How could he face anyone? What if everyone found out? What would he tell his wife? Should he tell her immediately before she heard it elsewhere? One devastating consequence after another filled his conversation with projections of losing his family, his career, and his livelihood. He even thought of ending at all. He now possessed a small handgun, freshly purchased. Care must be taken here to get a covenant or contract not to commit suicide. No, he wouldn't kill himself. Yes, he would get rid of the gun. Yes, he would give himself at least 6 months to work things out. Yes, he did have some support among a group of friends. Yes, the chairman of the board and the other people he had met with desire to protect his confidentiality, and would work with him to get through the crisis. He had already seen to it that the woman involved was receiving appropriate professional help.

When I asked Alfred what he believed about forgiveness, he said it was for others—not him, not for this. He was different from his parishioners. They expected much better from their pastor. No one could accept this, least of all his wife. Then some of the history of their marriage followed. They had not had a sexual relationship since the birth of their youngest child. Five years ago, they stopped discussing it. Whenever he suggested marriage counseling, she refused to go. Now they sleep in separate bedrooms. What was this like for him? He felt hurt and hopeless, but without anger, feeling he had forfeited all rights to that. "But if we get through this," he said quietly, "we're going to have to deal with our relationship. We're just coexisting."

Already a number of possible narratives are beginning to emerge, even in a first conversation. Beyond the initial rash of catastrophic scenarios, other narratives begin to occur to Alfred, presenting fresh choices for the future. He does not have to run or resign. Sometimes when a person doesn't know what to do, nothing is a pretty cool choice, particularly until some better response takes shape. There was a potential narrative of support and understanding from others, particularly from several leaders in the congregation with whom he had spoken. Even more significant was the possibility of a new and different relationship with his wife. Could the two of them work out their differences, and actually establish a closer relationship? All these narratives have some transforming qualities, in marked contrast to the initial catastrophic ones. They carry hope that with the introduction of remedial measures, better solutions to the past may appear.

There are many ways to shoot an albatross, and just as many, if not more, narratives that may follow, presenting more promising pathways in the future. In Alfred's case, telling his wife proved a turning point in their relationship. They entered marital therapy and set about rebuilding the bonds of trust. They chose to leave their congregation and move to a small community where Alfred retooled his career and became a schoolteacher in the local high school.

There is something uncanny, almost mystical, in the way any human predicament points beyond itself to some relevant response. I have seen it follow upon hours of rumination and brooding. I have seen it emerge in the middle of the night through some dream or clarity that comes in the twilight of altered consciousness while we fall asleep or lie in bed half-awake in the morning. I have seen it won in the protracted energy of earnest conversation. I have seen it burst suddenly upon therapist and client like some bright flare on the horizon when things seemed so dark that no one could possibly see ahead.

Harold was a minister whose story paralleled Alfred's in many ways, but with a different ending. He, too, had an affair, which his wife discovered and took to the governing board of the church. His marriage was deeply estranged. Convinced that his life as a minister was over, he discussed plans to leave the church for another career. After several hours of conversation, I found myself saying to him, "How about staying there for a while and exploring the meaning of forgiveness with these people?" We had both wrestled with the seeming impossibility that he could both receive it and vividly demonstrate its acceptance. He decided to give it a try. It was not easy. He confessed to his executive superior in the denomination, and found support and encouragement. He stood with the same honesty before the official board, and then the members of his congregation. The church proved itself a fellowship of the forgiven and he stayed on for 7 years. He had developed a deep love for the other party and later married her. He has since moved on to a lifetime of service as a leader in his denomination.

9. Constructive Meaning

By openly confronting estrangement from ourselves and from others, we move into a position where we may learn and grow. A relevant response brings more than release from pain. It creates the possibility of learning firsthand what will prove worthy of our best purposes and efforts. A sense of higher selfhood that stands the test of time can be won in the struggle with our guilt or shame. We may reach the ground from which fresher and deeper commitments to our faith can emerge. Matters of ultimate concern shift and rearrange themselves in challenges to our well-being, even to our very survival. Life has demanded a new and higher integration of what sustained us in the past, one capable of coping with the realities of the present.

Other confessions emerge in a much different context. Martha Key's did not begin under circumstances nearly so threatening. It arose from her own inner frustration and mounting discontent. This did not lessen the opportunity for a similar reorganization of her beliefs and commitments. The absence of urgency cast her confession more as an experience of general awakening and a progressive realization that she wanted her life to be different. She yearned for a better way of relating to others than "pleasing" them. She wanted to feel closer to her husband. She searched for an inner sense of integrity in making decisions, confronting others, and standing up for what she thought was right. No external demand pressed her to break away from the feeling that she was "living a lie." Martha chose to take the plunge into the flowing waters of change, while others are swept off the bank through no choice of their own. Either way, their resulting self-confrontation can carry both into fresh waters of new and different scenery, provided they don't quickly scramble back onto the bank of their familiar discontent or denial.

10. Self-Formation

A full confessional experience involves not only self-confrontation, but also self-formation, which bears the potential for spiritual encounter. It draws together into one continuous process the ancient task of confessing our sins and confessing our faith. One leads to the other naturally and will happen differently for each person, as elements in our private story emerge to disestablish our well-being. Often, our public story is severely threatened and its weaknesses exposed. Alfred could preach sermons about forgiveness for a lifetime without recognizing and accepting its relevance for himself. Suddenly all the meanings of his faith were deeply and personally challenged. Harold helped me understand some of the courage required to battle shame and guilt. "I never realized," he later put it, "how hard it is to receive forgiveness from other people and make it your own."

Our struggles with the darker side of our secret story can lead us to affirm the stronger parts of our personal faith that emerge to offset them. Whatever our human predicament, it drives us to search for a new and better way. In the process, we may discover precisely what will prove worthy of our deepest loyalty. Suddenly we stand on fertile ground for spiritual encounter, regardless of whether or not we are consciously aware of a higher Spiritual Presence. Sometimes these experiences come with physical as well as emotional healing, as was the case with the chronic pain in Martha's shoulder. Sometimes they contribute to the reconstruction of beliefs long held in partial realization of their true meaning, as with Harold. Often it is the weaving together of transformational stories that leads us to describe in our own words and symbols what we have come to hold sacred in our own life. Whatever the case, this kind of spiritual encounter contributes to the pool of evolving human consciousness that may shape the beliefs of the future. It marks the recurrent task of reformulating our faith that each new generation must address. What has occasioned anxiety, guilt, or shame can lead us to embrace what is authentic and worthy of our belief, our trust, and our devotion. Our hope for the life we share together on this planet can continue to take its shape.

Practice

These ten characteristics came from reflecting on experiences with confessions while doing psychotherapy, but psychotherapists or pastoral counselors have no franchise or monopoly on them. In fact, they are more the property of ordinary people everywhere, whether or not in church. It is time for the full confessional experience to be restored to its rightful ownership. Martha Key and Alfred Pugh are real people, but don't let the drama in their circumstances make you think that confession is reserved for big deals or dire straits. It's for any aspect of daily life that proves troublesome or problematic.

All of us can practice confession any time we choose, any way we choose. We don't have to make ours in anyone else's language or follow somebody else's ideas of what it should be. The practices I describe here are purely suggestive. Don't feel bound to them in any way. Pick and choose what fits your own experience. I have written in language as neutral as possible. You notice that I have "steered" clear of "God-language" and ideas of prayer (little play on words there). That's to encourage you to give the confessional process free rein regardless of your current beliefs. Consciousness of a higher Presence is neither required nor necessary. You are free to remain open to any kind of spiritual encounter that might occur.

Self-Awareness and Internal Dialogue

1. Make your confession in your own language to yourself, the deeper part of yourself. Consider any painful experience that is troublesome. Rather than trying to get it out of your mind, get it fully in mind. The more recent the event, the more relevant it may be. Remain mindful of what you experience. Be aware of ways you distract yourself. Sit comfortably, relaxed, eyes open or closed, as you want them. When your attention wanders, bring it back until you have finished to your satisfaction. Construct a full narrative of the troublesome event you have brought to mind. Think it through, talk it through, or write it through in quiet.
2. Concentrate on self-acceptance. Be alert to any ways that you fuss at yourself—both now and in the past. We will work on silencing them later; but for now, substitute genuine self-accepting messages

to yourself in their place. You may recall a time in the past when you have felt completely accepted by someone important to you. Build on that experience. Accept the care and concern present then and rekindle it now for yourself.

3. Privacy enhances the possibility for some deeper level of self-encounter. Should you experience awareness of a larger Presence, feel free to address it in silence or out loud. I stay with neutral language to create room for readers of any number of persuasions to pursue the confessional process in their own preferred terms. Non-theological images of a Guide, a Figure of Wisdom, or a Spiritual Companion will do; and, of course, you can use the term "God" if you prefer. In any case, you have struck an important vein deep in yourself by remaining open to a different message among your inner promptings from the old, judgmental voices of critics from your past.

4. Be mindful of any new narratives that emerge. They may come in the form of different possibilities, other endings, or opportunities to change something about the confessional narrative. Be willing to be surprised, and to entertain different feelings from those you brought into your confession.

Confessional Partnership

1. Confessional partners will always have the option of sharing their experience in the Self-Awareness/Internal Dialogue exercises, or there may be something fresh that begs for attention. Part of your conversation may be devoted to following previous events you have discussed, sharing how they have turned out. As you proceed, your agenda will grow naturally and you will develop your own style.

2. Some discussion of the meaning of acceptance may benefit your conversations. Sharing past experiences of having been accepted, difficulties in giving and receiving it, and instances in which you failed to receive it, may increase its availability for both of you. You are creating a responsive context of ongoing conversation. Remember Daniel Siegel's idea of contingent relationships in which each person accurately perceives, understands, and responds in a timely, receptive manner.

3. Part of a responsive context is the creation of transforming narratives. Once the confessional narrative is complete and understood, you may begin to develop a mutual way of exploring the range of new narratives that suggest themselves to each partner. It is not necessary for each person to confess each time you meet.

You can move at your own pace. You can take turns. The right style for both of you will become clear as you go.

Discussion Group

1. The ten characteristics of a full confessional experience can receive discussion one by one. The leader might pose the main points in each of them for reaction.
2. Are there any dangers in self-encounter? Can it be carried too far? What checks and safeguards could be put in place?
3. Certainly the concepts of acceptance, self-acceptance, and contingent communication are important parts of the study. Members of the group may choose to talk about some of their experiences with acceptance or its absence in the past.
4. Another important concept for confession is a responsive context as opposed to "one-shot" conversations. Ways to create this could receive consideration.
5. The narrative character of confession is a topic worth exploring together. How do transforming narratives grow from constructing a confessional narrative? Is this a natural outgrowth of the process? Also, there may be some parallels and some differences between confessional groups and therapy groups worth discussing. (See below.)

Confessional Group

1. You may be spending the first few sessions as a Discussion Group in order to get to know one another and ease into the process gradually. Any of the above suggestions for the Discussion Group can work for you.
2. Some consideration of the differences between a Confessional Group and a Psychotherapy Group can be beneficial. The following can serve to start discussion:
   a. Therapy Groups are organized to offer effective treatment for a number of psychiatric problems and relational dysfunctions. Confessional Groups gather to share and support one another in conversation, addressing troublesome personal experiences dealing with our general human condition.
   b. Leadership in Therapy Groups is provided by trained professionals who use their expertise to enable curative experiences among members. There are many approaches based on different theoretical perspectives. Confessional Groups are organized and led by peers who share a mutual commitment to engage in the traditional experience of confessing together. They may or may not have a professionally trained leader.

c. Psychotherapy in all its forms begins with a diagnosis of the patient's presenting problem. Its course is determined by the particular form of psychopathology at hand. Professional expertise determines the composition of the treatment group. Confessional Groups are self-referred, presenting problems are self-diagnosed, and members provide self-help and care to one another.

d. Psychotherapy Groups vary widely in the particular methods employed in professional treatment. For example, those who follow the Group Analytic approach give a great deal of attention to how "the group as a whole" transfers various feelings toward the therapist from significant figures in their past. Client-Centered Groups concentrate on mutual acceptance and the cultivation of unconditional positive regard among members. Encounter Groups encourage mutual confrontation. Gestalt Groups concentrate on "here-and-now" experiences, while one member takes the "hot seat" and the rest are like a Greek chorus. And so on. Confessional Groups develop their own unique pattern of perceiving, understanding, and responding to one another. The contract or covenant is to share one another's troublesome experiences in search of ways to cope with or resolve them. Each person's right to privacy and choice of self-disclosure is respected.

e. The goal in a Therapy Group is to cure various forms of psychopathology and to alleviate existing symptoms. There are also concerns for personal growth and general well-being. In a confessional group, the goal is to establish forgiveness and overcome our preoccupation with the guilt, shame, and anxiety that surrounds painful personal experiences. There is also the goal of helping each other complete a full confessional experience of discovering a relevant response, exploring transformational narratives, and opening possibilities for spiritual encounter.

CHAPTER 3

Some Classical Confessions
Augustine and Patrick

With ten characteristics of a full confessional experience in mind, I read some of the historic confessions of the past for comparison. I was interested in their structure rather than their specific content. Did their organization correspond to the ten criteria we just considered? How were they conceived and put together? Were there similar declarations of estrangement from a *private story,* leading to *transformational stories* of faith and belief? Was there a similar, discernible movement from one to the other through some relevant response? I was more interested in how these confessions handled core issues of shame and guilt than in particular ideas about what occasioned them. For instance, when I read *The Confessions* by Augustine, I did not expect to agree with his notions of sexuality as a constant source of shame and sinfulness. My attention was on how the confessional experience developed from self-awareness to faith, rather than upon particular theological understandings or practices.

As you might expect, I started by picking up St. Augustine's famous work, which I had not read since my seminary days. What difficult reading, yet what a clear expression it provided of a full confessional experience. Then I came across a similar *Confession* written by St. Patrick, heretofore unknown to me. It appeared, in large part, more legend than entirely from the pen of its author. It reflected Augustine's style but lacked its depth, sort of like *Son of Godzilla* or *Jaws II.*

Augustine's *The Confessions*

Augustine's father was an official of the Roman administration in the North African village of Tagaste. His mother Monica was a devout Roman Catholic who enrolled her son as a catechumen in the Catholic Church. Both conspired to delay Augustine's baptism, believing it wise to withhold its cleansing power until he had sowed his wild oats. And with this license, sow them he did. Even today, some theologians wonder how different the course of Western Christianity might have been if Augustine hadn't felt so guilty about his sexual exploits. His father wanted Augustine to be a lawyer and, with the help of a patron, sent him off to Carthage in 370 to study rhetoric.

Narrative Form

Augustine wrote *The Confessions* around 397. The book was written as an autobiographical self-disclosure, delivered in narrative form. Each confession acquires its meaning in a specific life situation. His encounters with guilt or shame are deeply embedded in his personal history. His offenses never arise from some preconceived list of specific sinful acts, legalistically perceived or unrelated to his life course. None could be said to occur without reference to motivation, occasion, growth, or stage of life.

At the start, Augustine confesses some of his boyhood sins. He was troubled by the conflict of wills in the "stormy intercourse" of life with grown-ups. Disobeying the commands of parents and schoolmasters was sinful. It was a sin to write, read, or study less than was exacted but the scope of what was sinful soon grew to much more. For Augustine, every inordinate affection carried its own punishment, and there were opportunities for many such offenses. An ever-present propensity to sin appeared throughout each stage of life, marked by an undefined mixture of shame and guilt that surrounded his confessions from the start. These two terms remain undistinguishable from each other, lacking the vivid descriptions that normally accompany Augustine's penmanship. He simply assumed that the meaning of both terms was clear to everybody. For example, he confessed stealing pears as a boy from a neighbor's orchard but the pleasure was not so much in the pears as it was in the offense itself and the excitement he shared with his fellow accomplices in sin. Augustine wryly acknowledged there was so much peer pressure from his buddies that everyone was "ashamed not to be shameless."

Fornication with the World

For Augustine, the essence of sin lay in "that deadly pleasure" that lures us away from God. Any friendship with this world could become fornication against God. But at the heart of deadly pleasures was sex. "In that sixteenth year of the age of my flesh," he wrote, "the madness of lust (to which human shamelessness giveth free license, though unlicensed by Thy laws) took rule over me, and I resigned myself wholly to it."*

So began Augustine's lifelong struggle with his sexual desire. He described "the briers of unclean desires" that grew rank over his head. It was as though he had no hands to root them out. He described having walked the streets of Babylon, wallowing in the mire as if "in a bed of spices and precious ointments." When his friends boasted of their conquests, he joined in seeking their praise and regard. He even made himself out to be worse than he was, claiming to have done forbidden acts he had not, still ashamed to be less shameless than his companions. All the while, his mother stood in the background, learning of this behavior from Father who saw him at the baths. Mother constantly advised chastity, or at least sufficient restraint to wait until he was married if he couldn't pare his desires to the quick. In her devotion to God, she had long since given up such distractions. Later, when Augustine went to Carthage to begin studies in law, he lived with a woman for a decade without benefit of marriage. His partner bore him a son named Adeodatus out of wedlock. She disappeared conspicuously from his confessions; but when the two broke up, Adeodatus remained with his father until he died, failing to outlive his famous parent.

Augustine's struggles with his sexual desire continued until he was baptized. Before that, he frequently prayed for "chastity and continency, only not yet." He confessed fear that God would hear his prayers and cure him of this "disease of concupiscence," which he "wished to have satisfied, rather than extinguished."† Even after he abandoned all sexual activity in celibacy, his old lust reappeared to haunt his dreams, for then all reason was gone, lulled asleep with the senses of the body. In sleep, old images from his memory arose to give pleasure and even attain assent from his repressed lust. Only with the restoration of reason upon awakening could he return to "peace of conscience," discovering that "we did not what yet we be sorry that in some way was done in us."‡

Anything that distracts us from God became sin for Augustine. It was just that sex was so powerful a distraction, perhaps the most powerful for him. But anything could become another means of "fornicating with the world." Friendship was dangerous because it could displace spiritual presence from our awareness. Augustine was disturbed when a close friend died, and his grief became so acute that he lost awareness of God. He confessed his arrogance in rhetoric school, where his pride in his position subverted his attention from God's presence. He confessed his seduction

---

* *The Confessions.* (Great Books, Encyclopedia Britannica, Inc., 1987), p. 9.
† *Ibid.* p.57.
‡ *Ibid.* p.81.

by Greek philosophy, constantly seeking to embrace wisdom. He wrestled with what he considered his inordinate love of art, music, the praise of others, and even the beauty of the earth. Still, each encounter with such lowered attention thrust him back into awareness of the constant presence of God, the Creator of it all.

From Shame and Guilt to Faith

Every struggle with shame and guilt became for Augustine an occasion that could lead beyond itself to spiritual encounter. Each confession led to some new affirmation of truth, surprise, or joy in the beauty and plea-sure of God. "For what is nearer to thine ears," he wrote, "than a con-fessing heart and a life of faith?"* A constant rhythm: confession of sin, followed by confession of faith, marks *The Confessions* from start to fin-ish, a pattern similar to the honest confessions I was hearing. Grappling with the negative in life need never be lost to futility when we follow in the direction it points, toward our higher purpose as human beings.

This movement from the negative to the positive marked all of Augustine's confessions. It was this "medicine of mercy" that finally cured his desire for "enfoldment in female arms." The same sense of Presence delivered him from the teachings of the Manichees, who believed we were engaged in an eternal struggle between good and evil. His teacher, Faustus, unwittingly began to loosen his grip on Manichean philosophy. Poor Faustus did not know the answers to many of Augustine's searching questions, but he was "not ashamed to confess it." Augustine observed he "had a heart" and "was not altogether ignorant of his own ignorance."† These events moved Augustine to confess "the wondrous ways" God was present to lead him beyond heresy to the truth.

A similar sense of spiritual guidance appeared when Augustine reflected on his own teaching. Once when he gave a lecture attended by his good friend Alypius, an analogy of the races at the circus occurred to him to illustrate a point. He chose to season it with a "biting mockery of those whom that madness had enthralled." He had no thought of "curing Alypius of that infection" and was amazed when his lifelong friend "took it wholly to himself, and thought I said it simply for his sake." There followed a characteristic doxology of positive confession by Augustine: "Let him be silent in thy praises, who considers not Thy mercies, which I confess unto Thee out of my inmost soul."‡

Anyone could become such a participant in God's intentions, quite unaware. Augustine tells of his mother's maidservant who, during a trip to

---

* *Ibid.* p. 10.
† *Ibid.* p.27.
‡ *Ibid.* p. 38.

the wine cellar, was making light of her mistress' love of fine wines, calling the good woman a "wine bibber." With this taunt, his Mother was "stung to the quick, saw the foulness of her fault, and instantly condemned and forsook it." Nor did the outcome depend upon anything but God's purposes, Augustine observed, noting that this spiritual presence "didst by the very unhealthiness of one soul heal another."*

A Mother's Influence

Paramount among the influences shaping Augustine's faith was that of his mother. He reflected many times upon her steady concern, her tears, and her prayers for his well-being while he "wallowed in the mire" of concupiscence and falsehood. Augustine's sexual life came to serve as the supreme symbol of his sinfulness—his turning away from God in fornication with the world. His sexual desires became the core of his human predicament, always pointing beyond to chastity. Only through relinquishing the hold of his sexual behavior could he make his peace with God. And with Mother.

Mother was a devout Catholic, seeing that her son was thoroughly grounded in his religious heritage long before his studies carried him far afield. Her grief over the way he was living was obvious and continual. Then she had a dream that interrupted her daily mourning. In this dream, a "shining youth" appeared and inquired about the cause of her tears. When she told him, the youth told her to look and observe "That where she was, there was I also." When she looked, she saw her son standing there beside her. Later when she told Augustine, he had his own interpretation: she should not despair of being some day where he was. Instead, his mother aimed her own interpretation of the dream straight at him, saying, "No; for it was not told me that, 'where he, there thou also' but where thou, there he also."† An overwhelmed Augustine confessed that the impact of her faith impressed him more than the dream itself.

Mother's tears and prayers, however influential, did not deter Augustine from escaping her loving clutches and pursuing his studies in Rome. He was also certain that God took him there as clearly as she would have detained him. Even as he did "evil things" there, she continued in "spiritual labor" for his soul. Years later, this same vision of his mother's vigil returned at the time of his conversion. Augustine was in the midst of "a deep consideration" at the secret bottom of his soul that had heaped up all his misery in full sight of his heart. A "mighty storm" arose in him, bringing with it a torrent of tears. He retired to himself, confessing his uncleanliness, crying out, "O Lord, how long?"

---

* *Ibid.* pp. 66, 67.
† *Ibid.*, p. 18.

Suddenly, he heard from a neighboring house the voice of a boy or a girl, he does not know which, chanting and repeating, "Take up and read; take up and read." He picked up his Bible and in silence read the first thing on which his eyes fell: "Not in rioting and drunkenness, not in chambering and wantonness, not in strife and envying; but put ye on the Lord Jesus Christ, and make not provision for the flesh."* To this, Augustine added, "In concupiscence." He dashed in to his old friend Alypius, who asked to see what he had read. Alypius read one line further: "Him that is weak in faith, receive," and applied that verse to himself. The two of them immediately ran to tell Augustine's mother, who was overjoyed at the news. Her son's conversion involved his decision to seek "neither a wife, nor any hope of this world," and he had elected to stand in the same "rule of faith" shown her in her vision so many years before. For both Augustine and his mother, this was "a much more precious and purer way than the one she erst required, by having grandchildren of my body."

I must confess the lack of appeal that this confession of Augustine holds for me. My interest is in the pattern of confession that dominates Augustine's thinking, whether or not I agree with his choices. Hardly a day passes that I fail to enjoy having four grandchildren, and I count them among the stronger influences in my own spiritual experience. But for Augustine, celibacy became the purer, higher way to express his own deepest spiritual commitment. Sexual activity was "fornication with the world," and all such pleasurable pursuits interrupted our relationship to God. They were distractions to be overcome and surrendered. It stood to reason that his conversion involved attacking the most formidable "fornication" of all. Augustine acknowledged the importance of his mother's influence by taking his stand "beside her" in her vision.

Confession of Sin/Confession of Faith

We are concerned chiefly with the structure of confession in Augustine's writings. The movement is decisively from negative to positive. His confessions attack the central problem at hand, in this case acknowledging the grip that sexual preoccupations held over his life. Through wrestling with what dominated his attention with shame and guilt, the most positive aspects of his faith took shape. By embracing his mother's celibacy and the Christian faith, he found viable positive beliefs and practices, and was nurtured by their energy. Shortly thereafter, he, Alypius, and his illegitimate son Adeodatus were all baptized together. We are left to wonder what the course of Western Christianity might have been had Augustine located some other aspect of our predicament as human beings at the center of his estrangement. Instead of associating our original sin with the sexual act

---

* *Ibid.*, p. 61.

of conception, it could well have been attached to some other troublesome passion such as violence, warfare, greed, or oppression of the poor.

Structurally, Augustine's confessions followed the pattern of grappling with the dominant issue of his human predicament with heightened self-awareness. He acknowledged it, explored it, and owned its power over his life. In the process, he discovered positive experiences and beliefs that enabled him to overcome it. For Augustine, confession of sin pointed to and culminated in confession of faith. This is not to suggest that a full confessional experience would follow a similar course or conclusion for everyone. As we shall see, other confessors in other times and places pursued the same pattern of confession in very diverse directions. And other matters troubled Augustine as well, with a different outcome.

Death and Grief

The grief Augustine felt when someone close to him died posed a continuing struggle, which, of course, came to a head with his mother's death. Grieving the loss of a friend brought disturbing distractions to his commitment to love God above all else in his world. It was as if the love of another creature eclipsed and diminished his love for God. The problem of death itself demanded faith. Never would God have wrought so many great things in us "if with the death of the body the life of the soul came to an end." Wavering in the face of loss from one's attention to God's faithful presence made for shame, even in momentary onslaughts of overwhelming sadness at someone's death. It was as if, for a short while, he loved them more than God.

So when Mother died, you can imagine what Augustine went through. At the moment she took her last breath, his son, Adeodatus, burst into a loud lament. Everyone around him immediately restrained his outburst, and "he held his peace." Neither Augustine nor those close to him thought it fitting to solemnize Mother's funeral with "tearful lament and groanings." Augustine confessed to silencing the "childish feeling" in himself, which through his "heart's youthful voice," wanted to find its vent in weeping. But deep inside, the flood of grief he considered as weakness came again as with the tide. Although others could see no change in his countenance, he knew full well what he was keeping down in his heart. This only doubled his sorrow, adding a new grief in which he grieved for his grief itself.

Still Augustine repressed his feelings, ashamed to permit anyone to see his emotions. Little by little, as he recovered memories of his mother's "holy tenderness," he decided he could weep alone in God's presence. Finally he gave way to the tears he had restrained, permitting them "to overflow as much as they desired," and his heart "found rest in them." Yet Augustine still feared others would be scornful of his weeping. He continued to struggle with shame in his confessions, making clear to his readers that they could think what they want, but for anyone who finds sin in his tears for his mother, he wrote, "If he be one of large charity, let him weep for my sins unto Thee."* Thus, Augustine managed to establish some measure of acceptance in his grief. Confessing his tears to others reduced his shame, a lesson some of us still require in completing the "grief work" necessary to recover from our own personal losses.

The pattern repeated itself throughout Augustine's confessions. By openly struggling with his most bitter negative experiences, he found his way to their resolution and to some positive expression of faith and belief. This was true in matters both large and small. When he had an annoying pain in his teeth that hurt so badly he could scarcely speak, he confessed it was the healing power of God that soothed it. Sometimes he confessed his faith through witnessing some similar experience of healing in others, as with several persons "vexed with unclean spirits," or a blind man whose sight was restored by touching his handkerchief to the bier of one of the saints. Positive aspects of faith became matters of confession wherever Augustine encountered them.

Joy and Love

Augustine's anxious avoidance of fornication with the world did not keep him from a profound sense of joy in, and love for, all that God created. This sense of constant Presence permeated all his perceptions. As far as he could see, everything around answered, "We are not God, but He made us." As Augustine continued his self-searching, he decided that "I will confess what I know of myself, I will confess also what I know not of myself."† He came to believe the process he had begun would be completed by this Presence, and his "darkness be made as noon day." He confessed a growing love for his own "inner man" where there "shineth unto my soul what space cannot contain."

Like other confessors we shall consider, Augustine had little confidence in the theologians of his day and their statements of doctrine. He gained what he came to believe through the process of intensely personal confession that we have described. When I had finished reading *The Confessions*, I jotted down my own reaction: "Seek the truth through your own immediate experience of spiritual Presence and not through the accumulated opinions of others."

How ironic, I thought, that Augustine went on to produce what became the standard doctrinal statement for the Western Church. Perhaps it followed from his sense of duty when he was named Bishop of Hippo in North Africa around 395. He spoke of carrying "the burden of the episcopate" for

---

* *Ibid.* p. 70.
† *Ibid.* p. 73.

35 years. In 397, he wrote *On Christian Doctrine*, then one of his greatest doctrinal treatises, *On the Trinity*. Following the sack of Rome in 410, he wrote *The City of God*, which appeared in installments over a period of 13 years. Finally, in 426, when a successor took over as Bishop, he read through all his writings, and in his *Retractions* noted all the revisions he would make in their doctrine. His work became formative, not only throughout Catholic Christendom, but also for Protestants who took as their banner for the Reformation: "Back to the Bible by way of Augustine." Perhaps, somewhere between *The Confessions* and all these books, the full and intimate connections between the human narrative, the confession of sin, and the confession of faith got lost in the politics of a worldwide church and its dogma.

The Confession of St. Patrick

By coincidence, perhaps serendipity, or, as some might term it, synchronicity, I began to write about St. Patrick on the seventeenth day of March, traditionally St. Patrick's Day. I wear no green, but I am strangely grasped by a sense of propriety and a touch of merriment. Patrick, the patron saint of Ireland, was not Irish but a British Celt. The exact date of his birth or death is unknown, although he is believed to have been born around 389 and to have died in 461, making him a contemporary of Augustine. His *Confession* is the only document that survived, save one letter to Coroticus, the British king of Strathclyde, protesting the slaughter and enslavement of newly baptized Christians. He was considered a "saint" long before the Roman Catholic Church created such a status. As I have noted, much of his *Confession* appears legendary or perhaps the product of community editing of some sort. Incidentally, there were never any snakes or other reptiles in Ireland for Patrick to chase out.

Confessional Narratives

We know Patrick's father, Calpornius, was a deacon in the church and the son of a priest in the English village of Bannavem Taburniae. It was from there that Patrick was carried in captivity to Ireland at the age of 16. He began his confession by describing himself as "a sinner, most unlearned, the least of all of the faithful, and utterly despised by many."* Patrick attributed his capture by enemies to his turning away from God and failing to obey his priests. The experience opened his eyes to his unbelief and forced him to remember his sins. Yet Patrick developed the sense of being

---

* All quotations are from *The Confession of St. Patrick*, Translated by Ludwig Bieler available on the Internet, OrthodoxyToday.org, unpaginated.

watched over by a larger Presence long before he could distinguish good from evil. He felt comforted by it as a father would comfort his son.

For years Patrick hesitated to write, afraid of exposing himself "to the talk of men." He was unable to speak out as a boy and used to blush in fear of revealing his lack of education. Before he was taken captive, he was "like a stone, lying in the deep mire"; but when he was captured, he felt as though "He that is mighty came and in His mercy lifted me up, and raised me aloft, and placed me on the top of the wall." Now he must choose, regardless of the danger, to make his faith known to others without fear.

While captive in Ireland, Patrick tended sheep to earn enough money for his passage back to England. Six years later, he ran away to the coast in search of a ship to take him home. Something, perhaps Patrick's growing Christian zeal, caused the pagan captain of the ship to turn him away. Patrick began to pray desperately, and, quite miraculously, he heard someone from the ship shouting for him to come on board. His shipmates agreed to take him on good faith, and permit him to make friends with them "in whatever way" he liked.

The ship reached land in deserted country. Everyone disembarked and wandered for 28 days without food. Overcome with hunger, the captain taunted Patrick by suggesting that if he were such a great Christian and his God so powerful, why not pray for food to relieve their hunger? Patrick countered his challenge with an invitation to believe and be converted and, in all confidence, promised that God would send food that very day. Suddenly a herd of pigs appeared on the road before their very eyes, and the band stopped for 2 days to eat their fill and restore their strength.

I have never known how to deal with such stories. Similar ones appeared in Augustine's confessions—a child's voice chants, "Take up and read," and suddenly he opens the Bible to the verse that pertains to him. I remember trying this exercise as a teenager, and failed miserably. There was an old joke around our neighborhood about a fellow who tried the same process and came up with, "Judas went out and hung himself." So he tried again: "Go thou and do likewise." Miraculous stories like these from Augustine and Patrick represent a supernatural view of spiritual Presence that breaks into ordinary life from above and beyond the commonplace, interrupting the natural course of events. I find myself wanting to measure these tales against the steady sense of spiritual Presence Augustine experienced throughout his life, or the feeling of being watched over that Patrick related long before his captivity in Ireland. More about this later.

Troubles

Like Augustine, Patrick cast his confessions in narrative form around the struggles he encountered with opponents or decisions he felt forced to make. Back in England, he sensed a strong call to return to Ireland as a missionary, which, of course, he eventually did. In the meantime, he was attacked by a number of unnamed authorities who brought up his past sins. There was some kind of proceeding against him concerning an undisclosed sin he confessed to a childhood friend when he was 15 years old. In his own defense, Patrick pointed out at the time he was not yet a deacon or even a believer. Unlike Augustine, he was hesitant to say what the sin was. It happened one day in his boyhood and took place "in one hour." Your guess is as good as mine.

During these trials, Patrick had a vision in which God voiced displeasure at his persecutor, Deisignatus. The experience gave Patrick the strength to prevail, even to express sorrow for his "dearest friend" to whom he had confided his secret sin, knowing his friend would realize that "he'd let me down before all." As Augustine, Patrick gave praise to God, who not only freed him from slavery, but also delivered him from "twelve dangers" in which his life was at stake, not to mention numerous other plots that defied expression in words. Again, we are left to our imagination as to what went on. These struggles with his superiors back home helped persuade Patrick to return to Ireland. His human predicament in England served to reinforce his sense of calling. His return to missionary work in Ireland became the relevant response to many of his troubles.

Patrick shared Augustine's view of sexuality and the virtues of continence. Among his converts he mentioned a "blessed Irish woman" of noble birth who became "a virgin of Christ." The fathers of women following her course didn't always agree with such decisions. Although these good women often suffered persecution and reproach, Patrick was pleased at their growth among his followers. Patrick had his own struggles with "the hostile flesh" that was forever dragging him down "towards the forbidden satisfaction of one's desires." He confessed he had not lived a perfect life as had some of the faithful, but acknowledging his sins, he offered praise to God for the grace to keep the faith he had acquired.

Other matters troubled Patrick. Once back in Ireland, he longed to return to Britain to see his parents and friends, but he also feared losing the labors he had begun and gradually realized his mission was to stay in Ireland the rest of his life. Patrick confessed his "folly and carelessness" and his "rusticity," which I had to look up in the dictionary to discover meant his "country ways." He often felt backward, uneducated, and ashamed of his background, like some "country bumpkin." He was very sensitive to criticism, and, at times, his confessions went on the defensive. At one point, he insisted that, having baptized thousands of people, he never expected as much as "half-a-scruple" in return. He ordained priests everywhere for free, and if he had asked anyone for as much as the price of his shoes, he challenged them to speak up, and he would return the money.

Death and Martyrdom

Toward the end of his confession, Patrick appeared increasingly to antici-pate martyrdom at the hands of his opponents. His fears in no way affected his overarching sense of being "watched over" by a powerful spiritual Presence. His missionary work brought him into inevitable conflict with the High-king Loigaire and his Druid subjects. Legend has it that he once defied royal authority by lighting a Paschal fire on the hill of Slane at Easter, challenging the pagan festival of Tara, during which no fire might be kindled until the royal fire was lit.

Patrick wrote, "Daily I expect murder, fraud, or captivity, or whatever it may be; but I fear none of these things because of the promises of heaven. I have cast myself into the hands of God Almighty who rules everywhere." He even begged to shed his blood with the exiles and captives, even though he be "denied a grave," or his body "woefully torn to pieces limb by limb" or "the fowls of the air devour it" because upon that day "we shall rise in the brightness of the sun…as sons of the living God and joint heirs with Christ, to be made conformable to his image."

The Confession of St. Patrick parallels St. Augustine's *Confessions* in many ways. Both were in narrative form. Their faith took shape in the con-text of struggles with their human impulses. Issues of guilt and shame always led beyond themselves, moving from a confession of sin to a confes-sion of faith. This repeated encounter with the vicissitudes of life yielded a sense of spiritual Presence, constantly pointing to a higher way. Patrick concluded by once again confessing that he wrote as a sinner, unlearned, and ignorant. As far as whatever in his life was worthwhile, "let this be your conclusion and let it so be thought, that—as is the perfect truth—it was in the gift of God."

Practice

These classical confessions evidence striking similarity to the honest con-fessions discussed in the previous chapter. They are in narrative form. They originate in prolonged self-encounter, striving for self-acceptance and for acceptance by others as well. Guilt and shame are confessed with little effort to distinguish between the two. Confession is made in a responsive context to friends and companions. Transforming narratives emerge; fresh meanings are constructed, leading to the positive formation of new belief and faith.

I want to note Augustine's efforts to explore what he called the "inner-man." He openly confessed not only what he "knew about himself," but also "what he knew not about himself." He paid attention to his dreams and to his mother's dreams about him. He had a profound sense of how people in relationships could "participate in the purposes of God," often without even realizing it. His respect for Faustus' honesty as a teacher persuaded him to discard alien philosophies. He had no idea of his own influence in teaching his friend Alypius until Alypius quit going to the Circus. These experiences wove themselves into a growing knowledge of a spiritual Presence deep within himself. I mention them here because we will encounter a similar approach to self-knowledge among other confessors, particularly the women.

Both Augustine and Patrick had a sense of "being watched over" by a Caring Presence. I have known many people who expressed a similar feeling. Some of my own experiences with this phenomenon come to mind, creating a confessional mood. During my senior year in college, I began running a high fever with the flu. The timing was disastrous for one so young. It happened to be homecoming week, which concluded with our final football game. My old roommate, Jim Brown, who later became my brother-in-law, moved out to avoid exposure. I missed the entire week of practice; and at midnight before our last game together, I lay in our room with a temperature of 103, thinking the world had come to an end. Feverishly, I prayed for a miracle recovery. To my astonishment and everyone else's, I awakened in the morning, thrust a thermometer in my mouth, and it read sub-normal. Soon I was in the office of the team physician. Armed with three pills to take just before we went onto the field, I dressed and played the entire game, most of it 3 feet off the ground, I might add, with more energy and speed than I can ever recall.

Whatever Dr. Dick gave me only fueled my belief in some form of spiritual Presence working on my behalf. I must confess that it still lingers, along with a mild sense of shame that others may consider me naive or simplistic. Not long before, I had prayed just as fervently for Mr. Pryor, my friend who lived nearby, who was desperately ill. He died. Why answer my paltry needs and ignore his? I soon surrendered any clarity of belief or faith based on the outcome of such events. My girlfriend of long-standing did not help matters that homecoming night when I blurted out my positive confession taking her home from the dance. I told her I thought God somehow wanted me to play in that game. She unequivocally told me that was stupid, and, to this day, I'm somewhat ashamed that I cannot decide whether she was right or wrong.

Now that I've gotten started, I must relate another, more serious situation about which I have similar feelings. Years later, my wife and I were driving home through Virginia from the beach, our three children playing in the back of our station wagon. We were on one of those old two-lane highways that had been recently expanded to four lanes by adding two new lanes, nice and flat, going the other way separated by a tree-filled median. Our side was now two lanes on a somewhat hilly old road. As I set out in the left lane to pass another car, I had an eerie sense that we were about to meet an oncoming vehicle just over the rise ahead. Suddenly, a pickup truck going the wrong way burst into full view, coming head-on toward us. Somehow, our two cars met this truck all abreast on those two lanes with narrow shoulders and ditches on either side. To this day, I am uncertain how I managed to steer safely between the two. My companion driver in the car beside me pulled alongside, wiped his brow, rolled down his window, and shouted, "That was some driving you did back there!"

I confess I felt delivered by a power greater than I. And I still do, although the years have dulled my memory with doubt and uncertainty. And before I stop, I also have a sense of what Patrick meant by feeling "watched over" during the latter years of his life, when he thought he might be martyred. Nothing so noble comes to mind in my case, more than the need to confess some of the stupidity and danger involved in my own capacity to deny what I don't want to face. Shortly after I retired from the seminary, I had bypass surgery—six bypasses, the most I have ever heard of. I did not know we grew arteries other than the three big ones we all studied in high-school biology. For several years prior to that time, when I exercised I would frequently feel a burning sensation in my chest, nothing I ever determined to be chest pain. Usually, if I kept going, it would subside and I could breathe easier again. I continued playing tennis vigorously, although I found myself tiring more easily. Finally, Dr. Kemper, my primary-care physician, sent me for an echocardiogram, which measures the output of the heart over the volume of input. Normal is 50 to 55 percent. Mine was 25 percent. The next stop was Jewish Hospital for a cardiac catheterization. I was determined to "cram" for my heart exam and continued exercising, swimming a half-mile the day before I went in.

Dr. Raburn injected dye into my arteries, enabling both of us to watch it flow through my heart on a screen above. He stood there calling out numbers that the nurse wrote down. I spent the time trying to figure out what they meant. Finally, I heard Dr. Raburn exclaim, "Holy moly!" I knew I was in trouble then. "That wasn't very professional," I quipped, an anxious effort at humor. He pointed to two arteries that were blocked 100 percent and suggested we handle the problem with "one admission," which meant they would not let me out before the surgery.

Why do we all have a story about our surgery? Because it's an encounter with the prospect of death, always. I recall sitting with three fellow candidates, getting X-rays the night before. One of them gave me a toothy smile and observed, "I ain't scared. Are you?"

To which I replied with not nearly so much tooth and grin, "You bet I am."

We all have our denial. Mine was a much more dangerous one: discounting the existence of coronary symptoms as long as I could. They say there are no atheists in a foxhole, going into surgery, or taking off in an airplane. We so want to stay in control of our lives, and we can't. And some of us, from time to time, do get a sense of being "watched over."

I am also aware that Patrick's sense of being watched over did not mean he thought he would be protected or spared from trial, hardship, or enemies. As he grew older, he fully anticipated death by martyrdom, even his body's being torn apart by wild animals, being deprived of a proper grave. This sense of being watched over never seems to carry with it any assurance against failure, disaster, or death. It is more a sense of being accompanied, sustained, or supported, come what may.

Self-Awareness and Internal Dialogue

1. Have you had experiences of being "watched over?" You may have chalked these times up to your imagination, even refused to acknowledge them to anyone else. Have you had intuitions, premonitions, inner promptings, close calls, coincidences, and the like? Make a list of the ones worth pondering. How do you deal with them? Are they convincing, or do their meaning and significance erode with time? What is certainty anyway?

2. Can you recall instances when someone else was profoundly influential, reassuring, comforting, helpful, or otherwise significant to you, as though a participant in some kind of caring Presence?

3. Give consideration to contrasting experiences, ones that bring discouragement, doubt, or despair. Are there times you do not feel watched over? How do you deal with them? Can you find a way to accept both experiences into your belief system? A journal sometimes helps us think, so don't hesitate to write out your ideas, even when they are incomplete or contradictory.

Confessional Partnership

1. Share whatever you choose from the first set of exercises. It's OK to think out loud with someone else when you're having trouble getting your thoughts into words.

2. Here is a chance to open up a bit about negative aspects of your experiences that countermand easy belief in or simple acceptance of some constancy of supernatural Presence.

3. Continue conversation about building your confessional relationship. What would help you to speak more freely? Do you want to set some limits or boundaries with time, content of conversations, advice giving, suggestion making, or responding?

Discussion Group

1. Begin by sharing general reactions to what you have read. A leader's summary of salient points is not necessary each time and can engender laziness on the part of group members.
2. Augustine and Patrick's attitudes toward human sexuality could command considerable attention. An interesting array of beliefs may emerge, considering the place of sexual relations in our lives.
3. Some other topics for discussion are:
   a. The influence of Augustine's mother throughout his life
   b. Augustine's notion of sin as fornication with the world
   c. Augustine's ideas about becoming a participant in God's intentions
   d. Supernatural Presence for Augustine and Patrick
4. Members of the group may become increasingly comfortable sharing their own ideas and experiences, especially when one or two people jump in and demonstrate how. No one should feel coerced to say or do anything. Some groups set time aside at the end to do a post-mortem, make suggestions, and consider plans for the following week.

Confessional Group

1. Your transition from a Discussion Group into a Confessional Group can begin at any point. Sharing ideas paves the way to sharing our own personal experiences. Talking about positive confessional events is an excellent way to start, as I chose to do. That can free you to share the doubts and uncertainties that normally follow.
2. You might open up time for personal sharing toward the end of the session, if it has not occurred spontaneously. Once the time is right, someone often feels ready and jumps in, setting the standard for self-disclosure.
3. At the end, groups often benefit from the practice of discussing how a meeting went, permitting members to evaluate the session, suggest changes, and plan for next week.

CHAPTER 4

More Confessions

Tolstoy and Vonnegut

My search continued for other confessions. The Internet was replete with "true confessions" of all kinds about one secret life or another. Of course, there were the formal, doctrinal Confessions of Faith made by various church councils across the years, but confessions in the tradition of Augustine and Patrick were difficult to find. Then, to my surprise, I came across a confession by Leo Tolstoy of which I had never heard. It makes an excellent bridge between the classical and the contemporary. I was even harder put to find a twentieth-century confessor to add to the group. Finally, I decided to include Kurt Vonnegut's *Palm Sunday* as a worthy representative. Here's what I found.

Leo Tolstoy

Leo Tolstoy wrote *A Confession* in 1884. He was 51 years old at the time. Born into a life of privilege, he had amassed considerable wealth and had gained world renown as the author of *War and Peace* and *Anna Karenina*. But now, he was profoundly depressed. His life had come to a standstill. He could only go about the motions of living with no enthusiasm or desire. Truth be told, to him life had become meaningless.

Disillusionment

Although he was baptized and brought up in the Orthodox Christian Church, Tolstoy had lost his faith. This lapse, he insisted, occurred in a rather usual way for a person of his educational level. Most people lived on the basis of principles that had little to do with religious doctrine, which played virtually no part in the normal course of human relationships. Religious beliefs were encountered only as external phenomena disconnected from life. Tolstoy found it quite impossible to judge by someone's life and conduct if that person was a believer. In fact, most of those who professed to believe, he found to be dull, cruel, and arrogant.

As far as his own life was concerned, Tolstoy was overwhelmed with a sense of guilt and failure. He summed up his young adulthood as years he could not recall without "horror, loathing, and heart-rending pain."[*] He confessed to killing people in war, challenging others to duels with the same intent, losing at cards, and squandering the fruits of peasants' toil, only to have them executed. He called himself "a fornicator and a cheat." He was guilty of lying, stealing, promiscuity of every kind, drunkenness, violence, and murder. There was not a crime he had not committed.

Tolstoy went through the mother of mid-life crises. His accomplishments meant nothing to him. He felt his contribution to the world of literature and art was simply a fraud. He wrote only to seek success and praise from others, but now he had become preoccupied with his own mortality. Life had become meaningless before the reality of death. He was like a man wandering in the woods, horrified at having lost his way, rushing about searching for a road, only to find each step he took more and more confusing, yet still unable to stop rushing about this way and that. He wrote of his mental condition, "My life is a stupid and spiteful joke someone has played on me."[†]

Death and Despair

The idea of death for Augustine and Patrick served to arouse hope and faith that, whatever else, their Creator would not permit all the soul achieved in a lifetime to perish into nothingness. For them, the reality of death commanded belief in resurrection and new life beyond, but not so with Tolstoy. For him, the truth was that life had no meaning. It was as though he had lived and walked until he came to a precipice and saw nothing ahead but destruction. It was impossible to stop, impossible to go back, and impossible to close his eyes or avoid seeing that nothing was ahead but suffering, death, and complete annihilation.

So Tolstoy lost his will to live. He became preoccupied with suicide. He hid a cord, afraid he would hang himself from the crosspiece of the partition in his bedroom. He stopped going out shooting with his gun, fearful of the temptation to end his life so easily with one blast. He confessed a fear of life itself, not knowing whether he wanted to escape from it or pursue

---

[*] Tolstoy, Leo. *A Confession*. Tolstoy Library Online, I. p.1.
[†] *Ibid.*, IV, p. 1.

his fading hope to make something of it. Such was the depth of despair in his confessions.

All this befell him, Tolstoy noted, at a time when everyone around considered him to have complete good fortune. He was not yet 50 years old. He had a good wife who loved him, good children, and a large estate that prospered with little effort on his part. He was respected by his relations and acquaintances, well praised by others, and without self-deception could consider his name famous.

The master of metaphor, Tolstoy couched his confession in an old Eastern fable about a traveler who was overtaken on a plain by an enraged beast. The traveler escaped by climbing into a dry well, only to discover he was confronted by a dragon at the bottom, opening its jaws to swallow him. In desperation, the traveler seized a twig growing in a crack and clung to it, unable to move. His hands grew weaker, and he knew he would soon be forced to resign himself to the destruction that awaited above and below. Then two mice appeared, one black, one white, and began to gnaw around the base of the stem of the twig to which he clung. When it snapped, he would fall. As the traveler looked around, he saw some drops of honey on the leaves of the twig, reached out his tongue, and licked them.

"I tried to lick the honey which formerly consoled me," said Tolstoy, "But the honey no longer gave me pleasure."[*] The black and white mice of night and day gnawed at his branch. He saw the dragon clearly, and the honey no longer tasted sweet. He could not tear his gaze from the inescapable dragon and the mice. This was no fable. It was the real, unanswerable truth, intelligible to all.

A Search for Faith

Tolstoy's predicament pointed clearly beyond itself. Somehow, in the midst of all this despair, he found the energy to reach for some kind of faith. It became his "ultimate concern," an essential if he were to continue to live. Such a faith would have to provide meaning to life sufficiently strong to persuade a man not to destroy himself. This faith must be based upon a sense of union with God, strong enough to provide a higher purpose or reason for living. Where could he discover someone with such faith? He would look for which man did not destroy himself. Who had the strength to live and live well? So Tolstoy set out in search of a way to reconstruct a conception of an infinite God connected to human affairs. He was mindful that all such conceptions were hidden in the frailties of human thought. However, without some connection between finite humanity and infinite Presence, neither life nor he should exist. Only such a faith would permit reason to prevail.

---

[*] *Ibid.*, IV, p. 2.

In Tolstoy's confession, we see clearly the precondition of all honest confessions. Underneath or alongside the despair of the human predicament, there exists an awareness of something more to which the predicament points. For Tolstoy, it was reasonable to believe that his life could become meaningful and purposive when linked to a Presence greater than himself. His despair demanded he search for it. The possibility of the positive, its worth and value to him, was indicated in the very force of the negativity he confronted. So he began to look for a way to reconstruct his concept of relating to an infinite God. It must contain both the connection of this being with human affairs, together with some unity and "divinity" of the soul, hidden though they may be in the infirmity of human thought.

Tolstoy followed this quest into the mainstream of life about him among the people of the land. Not the theologians and philosophers, not the wealthy and privileged, not the proud and the learned, but the ordinary people of the land who lived and worked and died in the strength of a faith that granted them courage, energy, caring, and some measure of joy. Somehow the very beliefs that had repelled him and seemed meaningless, when professed by people whose lives conflicted with them, began to seem attractive and reasonable. Now he accepted them and found them full of meaning. Now he understood his error. It was "not so much because I thought incorrectly as because I lived badly." And he adds, "I came to love good people, hated myself, and confessed the truth."[*]

The Truth

The faith Tolstoy found, he discovered among the common people of the countryside whose courage to live out their lives disclosed the meaning for which he searched. A workable faith lay in the uncertain possession of truth mingled with falsehood. What did it matter that there were gaps in their reasoning or incompleteness in their understanding? They lived and lived well. In their simple faith, he found the basis for a relevant response. Clearly not everything was true in the religion he had been taught as a child; but whereas he once would have said it was all false, he could no longer say that. Most of these people possessed some knowledge of the truth, or they could not have lived as they did. The people of the land had made this knowledge accessible to him. He had felt their faith. He had begun to live by it. He knew there was also falsehood in their beliefs, but he saw among these peasants a smaller admixture of lies than those that had repelled him among representatives of the church. Still, everyone was dealing with falsehood mingled with the truth.

This journey formed Tolstoy's rediscovery of religion. Now his consciousness could contain beliefs that were inseparably connected to

---

[*] *Ibid.*, XI, p. 1.

everyday human affairs. Fallible as we all may be, the shifting and uncertain possession of truth, preserved beneath whatever veneer of partial falsehood and error encases it, was sufficient truth by which to live. He went on to formulate his own, unique "Christian philosophy," which reached far beyond the stagnant orthodoxy of his time. Chief among Tolstoy's revolutionary ideas was his espoused nonresistance to evil as the proper response to aggression. He put great emphasis upon the fair treatment of the poor and working class. He made strong pleas for Christians to reject the state when seeking answers to questions of morality. Instead, they should look within themselves and to God for their responses. Tolstoy's *Confession* in 1884 was followed by *What Then Shall We Do?* in 1886 and *The Kingdom of God Is Within You* in 1894, outlining his radical and well-reasoned revision of traditional Christian thinking. The latter book is said to have won Gandhi over to the idea of nonresistance to evil. Tolstoy gave up seeking a completely rational understanding of life. "I know that the explanation of everything," he wrote, "like the commencement of everything, must be concealed in infinity. But I wish to understand in a way which will bring me to what is inevitably inexplicable."* He recognized the limits of his intellect. He simply wanted whatever cannot be explained to be presented to him as necessarily so, not as something he was under some arbitrary obligation to accept.

Kurt Vonnegut

A more contemporary expression of classical confession proved difficult to find. I mentioned the many forms of "true confessions" on the Internet. There are Web sites for anyone to confess anything at any time to everyone. They take on a rather jagged uniformity that consistently amplifies our imagination about the sinful, negative, and shameful capabilities of human nature. No one, I thought, appeared on the scene like an Augustine, a Patrick, or a Tolstoy. Until, quite by chance, I picked up Kurt Vonnegut's *Palm Sunday*. I was reading it in the airport while waiting to catch my plane, not realizing I was chuckling so hard at his wit and the porously muted sarcasm with which he destroyed his conservative, right-wing critics that I disturbed a woman across the aisle, who simply had to come over and inquire what I was reading that was so profoundly amusing.

Letters

Vonnegut assembled an assortment of letters, speeches, and articles he had written during the 1970s in Indianapolis and published under its unlikely title in 1981. The occasion was a book burning in Drake, North Dakota, in

---

* *Ibid.*, XVI, p. 1.

which the school board sent his *Slaughterhouse Five* up in flames. This was after the book had been banned and removed from high-school reading lists by numbers of zealous citizens, protecting young minds from what Vonnegut was convinced they had never read in the first place. He opens with a series of furious rejoinders.

To the good people at Drake, he undertakes to explain the outcry their action brought across the country. He reminds them that they are part of American civilization and their fellow Americans have trouble tolerating such uncivilized behavior. Books are sacred to free people. Wars have been fought against nations that burn books. Good Americans allow all ideas to circulate freely in their communities, not merely their own. Later, in New York where *Slaughterhouse Five* was also banned, he proposed that school-board members be given a lie-detector test to determine if they had read a book from start to finish since high school, or even read a book in high school. Should the truthful answer prove "No," they cannot get on the school committee to blow off their "big bazoo about how books make children crazy."* He continued by not so gently proposing someone—the American Civil Liberties Union or somebody like that—should read them the First Amendment to the Constitution out loud, explain to them what it means, and to whom it applies.

So what was all the fuss about *Slaughterhouse Five*? Vonnegut's antagonists disliked some of the language with which he chose to represent scenes from his experiences in World War II. For example, Vonnegut recounts an army sergeant shouting at a misplaced chaplain blocking traffic in the middle of a road, "Get the fuck out of the way." So how else could one accurately represent such an event?

More important are some confessions about his military experience. First, Vonnegut admits he was not a very good soldier, no doubt a reflection of his constitutional disrespect for arbitrary authority of any kind, public, military, and especially religious. As we shall see, he came by this rightfully through three generations of independent, stubborn, liberal-leaning wisdom in his family tree that grew around Indianapolis.

Second, *Slaughterhouse Five* was the building, literally a slaughterhouse, where Vonnegut and several companion prisoners of war huddled together to survive the devastating carpet bombing of the German city of Dresden at the end of the war. This he never forgot. Dresden was an ancient city of no known military or industrial significance. Its chief claim to fame was the delicate numbers of finely crafted Dresden dolls produced there, noted worldwide for their beauty and craftsmanship. The needless destruction of innocent people and products haunted Vonnegut. The book confesses his involvement in such acts of war and his lifelong commitment to

---

* Vonnegut, Kurt. *Palm Sunday.* (New York: Dell Publishing Co., 1981), p.8.

nonviolence and peace, following the corporate guilt he felt. Again we note movement from the negative to positive belief in full narrative confession.

Divine and Human Law

Still a third confession concludes Vonnegut's discussion of the banning and burning of *Slaughterhouse Five*. It appeared in 1976 as a comment for the Op-Ed page in the Long Island edition of the *New York Times*. This time he confessed a rather spectacular disregard for his memory of Thomas Aquinas' hierarchy of laws governing our planet, which, he noted, was flat at the time. St. Thomas believed the highest law was divine law, God's law. Next came natural law, and, finally, human law, the lowest of all. In terms of cards, divine law was an ace, natural law a king, and the Bill of Rights a lousy queen.

Now everybody knows there are laws governing life much grander than the human laws printed in our statute books, no quarrel there so far as Vonnegut is concerned. The difficulty lies in our ability to agree what they are or how to word them. Theologians struggle to give us a "hint." Only dictators can lay them down exactly for everybody. Vonnegut had just come through a war against "a mere corporal in the army" who did that for Germany, and then for Europe. Hitler knew everything about divine and natural law, playing fistfuls of aces and kings.

For Vonnegut, we are not playing with the full deck. The U.S. Constitution insures that the highest card anyone can play is a lousy queen. That incompleteness is obviously good for us, and he celebrated it. Why? Because no one can really be trusted to understand nature or God that well. Children are seldom taught that their freedom will vanish if someone grows up to insist that our courts, policemen, and prisons be guided by divine or natural law. The American Civil Liberties Union insists our government authorities can be guided by nothing grander than human law. This organization often defends people who lay the groundwork for this lesson. In fact, Vonnegut insists, it is his willingness to lay such a groundwork that got his book in so much trouble in the first place.

Family Influence

Having thus dealt with his critics, Vonnegut launches into a discussion of his family's genealogy over the past century. As one might suspect, he found "no war lovers of any kind." The family tree was literate, well educated, and moneyed. His parents, Kurt and Edith, presided over a dwindling estate in the Depression. Mother dreamed of the day their lot would be restored to its proper stance in Indianapolis society. She also vigorously wrote unsuccessful short stories, in an effort to stave off the inevitable depletion of their resources. Kurt came by his literary skills quite naturally, no thanks to his father's unbridled ambition that he become a chemist. Mother died of an accidental (?) overdose of sleeping pills, barely 7 months before her son Kurt was captured by the Germans in the Battle of the Bulge and imprisoned at Dresden until the end of the war.

Kurt described his own childhood as reasonably content. He enjoyed public school and would have, by his own account, lost all his friends if his mother's "half-cracked" ideas of wearing expensive clothes, riding on ocean liners, and visiting German relatives in real castles had been realized and reinstated. He made passing note of becoming what his mother attempted to be—a professional writer. This he ascribed to the American rule that a middle-class son can be expected to try hard with his own life to make some of his disappointed mother's dreams come true.

When it came to religion, Vonnegut focused on the "technological cures" he came to know on the shelves of the largest hardware store in Indianapolis, which his family owned. A hammer was his "Jesus," the Virgin Mary a cross-cut saw, religion enough to satisfy his inherited skepticism. He described his loss of innocence when the atomic bomb was dropped on Hiroshima, compelling him to abandon any trust in technology, which, like all other great religions, had to do with the human soul. It marked for him the startling discovery of how diseased the human soul can be, not just the American soul. The sickness of every soul in every highly industrialized nation had led to the creation of "a new physics" based upon nightmares. Now we would place in the hands of mere politicians a world so "destabilized" (a term he borrowed from the CIA) that "the briefest fit of stupidity" could guarantee its end.

Vonnegut's confessions, more than those of the others, intertwined his personal narrative with the turbulent events surrounding his life. His story melds into history, sealed by a sense of involvement in and responsibility for the disastrous possibilities of his time—and ours as well, I might add. His response was to become a tireless advocate for peace, the environment, and the First Amendment, not necessarily in that order.

Organized Religion

Organized religion was another matter. Toward the end of his marriage to Jane, Vonnegut observed, the two of them fought mainly about religion. Her increased devotion to "making alliances with the supernatural" became painful for him. She had no sense of his family's studied skepticism for all authoritative certitude, or even that her religious practices were any of his business at all. His reaction illustrated both the negative deconstruction and the positive reconstruction of honest confessions. A quotation from his free-thinking great-grandfather, Clemens Vonnegut, serves to explain some of the offense to the family tree her religious devotion inflicted: "Whoever entertains liberal views and chooses a consort that is captured by superstition risks his liberty and his happiness."* Vonnegut went on to present Clemens' comments on life and death, which the old gentleman insisted upon having read at his own funeral:

> Friends or Opponents: To all of you who stand here to deliver my body to the earth:
>
> To you, my next of kin:
>
> Do not mourn! I have now arrived at the end of the course of life, as you will eventually arrive at yours. I am at rest and nothing will ever disturb my deep slumber.
>
> I am disturbed by no worries, no grief, no fears, no wishes, no passions, no pains no reproaches from others. All is infinitely well with me.
>
> I departed from life with loving, affectionate feelings for all mankind; and I admonish you: Be aware of this truth that the people on this earth could be joyous, if only they would live rationally and if they would contribute mutually to each others' welfare.
>
> This world is not a vale of sorrows if you will recognize discriminatingly what is truly excellent in it...that we base our faith on firm foundations, on Truth for putting into action our ideas which do not depend on fables and ideas which Science has long ago proven to be false.
>
> We also wish Knowledge, Goodness, Sympathy, Mercy, Wisdom, Justice, and Truthfulness. We also strive for and venerate all of those attributes from which the fantasy of man has created a God. We also strive for the virtues of Temperance, Industriousness, Friendship, and Peace. We believe in pure ideas based on Truth and Justice.
>
> Therefore, however, we do not believe, cannot believe, that a Thinking Being existed for millions and millions of years, and eventually and finally out of nothing—through a Word—created this world, or rather this earth with its Firmament, its Sun and Moon and the Stars.
>
> We cannot believe that this Being formed a human being from clay and breathed into it an Immortal Soul, and then allowed this human being to procreate millions, and then delivered them all into unspeakable misery, wretchedness and pain for all eternity. Nor can we believe that the descendants of one or two human beings will inevitably become sinners; nor do we believe that through the criminal execution of an Innocent One may we be redeemed.†

---

* *Ibid.*, p. 193.
† *Ibid.*, pp. 193, 194.

Faith and Belief

Such was Vonnegut's ancestral religion, to which he laid a rather oblique claim. He declared it was a mystery how it was passed on to him. My irresistible guess is that somehow old Clemens' virile and bold self-assertiveness served to offset the rather weak modeling provided by his failing father. Such a legacy of disregard for traditional Christian solutions to life's problems laid the negative framework from which the positive aspects of Vonnegut's own beliefs could emerge. One has to sneak up and catch him developing these hard-earned articles of faith.

In 1974, Vonnegut addressed the graduating classes of Hobart and Smith Colleges, heaping shame upon the current scene for its failure to use our knowledge to develop what human beings need in the way of bodily and spiritual nourishment. He challenged the seniors to go out and create stable communities in which the terrible disease of loneliness could be cured. This confession of profound and pervasive loneliness ran through many of his speeches and writings. What was needed was a new religion, an effective religion, one that allows people to imagine from moment to moment what is going on and how they should respond. Christianity used to perform this job. The trouble was that the old-time religions were too superstitious, too full of magic, too ignorant about biology and physics. Our new task was to go out, identify, and expound theories about life in which sane human beings everywhere could believe.

From his disillusionment, Vonnegut quietly reconstructed his own "new religion," without calling it that. His efforts began with a heartfelt moral code, acquired in the midst of everyday living. He steadfastly refused to volunteer his positive confessions up front, often disguising them with humor. Here and there we catch glimpses of him "flashing" what he holds sacred. When Sargent Shriver wrote him for ideas in his campaign for vice president, Vonnegut noted there was plenty of money around, but so far as ideas went, both parties were in a state of destitution. He wrote back that Shriver hadn't been paying attention. The number-one killer in America was not cardiovascular disease—it was loneliness. If he and McGovern would promise to cure that disease, they would swamp the Republicans. The slogan could be on buttons and bumpers: "Lonesome no more!"

Many concerns proved worthy of political attention. Vonnegut remained appalled at how quickly we are wrecking our topsoil, our drinking water, and our atmosphere. We know now that any wound we inflict on the life-support systems of this planet is likely to be permanent. Ideas about good and evil follow quite naturally. Evil disgusts us; good fills us with joy. This might fit into a simple moral code: whatever wounds the planet is evil; whatever preserves it or heals it is good.

Family Values

Another article of faith took shape out of the profound loneliness Vonnegut observed around him, and I am certain experienced firsthand himself. He watched the Biafrans fight on to the bitter end during the Nigerian civil war. Their rifles were outdated. They were blockaded so only the barest rations of food got in to them. They had no recruiting program or government-controlled distribution of food or social programs to care for the aging or the sick. What they did have was families.

Every Biafran was a member of an extended family. Their families took care of their wounded, their lunatics, and their refugees. Their families divided the food fairly without government control and even decided who went into their army when new soldiers were needed. This social system has worked for most human beings from the beginning of time. "We should return to extended families as quickly as we can," wrote Vonnegut, "and be lonesome no more, lonesome no more."*

The virtues of extended families were many for Vonnegut. In our nuclear families, children and their parents can be locked into "hellish close combat" for 21 years. In extended families, there are scores of homes to which a child can repair for safe haven and attention. In our marriages, two persons are supposed to fulfill the need most human beings have for a hundred like-minded, affectionate companions. In extended families, anyone can "bug out of his own house" for a time and still be among relatives. Nobody has to search the streets for friendly strangers, a hopeless quest in most American bars, massage parlors, and the like.

Vonnegut sparred with organized religion, sometimes flirting with its energy and potential to combat loneliness, while maintaining the long tradition of religious skepticism in his family heritage. The fact that his daughter deserted the fold to become an Episcopalian priest represents something in his DNA that he never quite got out of his system. There is a respect for human dignity and the grandeur of things spiritual.

The last piece in Vonnegut's book is a sermon he preached on Palm Sunday at St. Clement's Episcopal Church in 1981. He started by declaring his enchantment with the Sermon on the Mount and his belief that being merciful is the only good idea we have received so far. The rest was vintage Vonnegut, masterfully playing with the text where the *Gospel of John* has Jesus responding mercifully to Judas at dinner the night before they entered Jerusalem. In the scene, Mary massages Jesus' feet with a costly ointment. Judas embarrasses everybody by objecting to the extravagance and insisting the ointment should have been sold and the money given to the poor. Jesus gracefully responds with humor, "Judas,

---

* *Ibid.*, p. 206.

don't worry about it. There will still be plenty of poor people left, long after I'm gone." This, Vonnegut insisted, does no violence to the text, and harmonizes it with Jesus' saying, "Blessed are the merciful..." in the Sermon on the Mount, demonstrating that such mercy can never waver or fade.

At other times, Vonnegut could train the full force of his humor on the religious establishment. At one point, he mused that the acceptance of a creed, any creed, entitles one to membership "in the sort of artificial extended family we call a congregation." To him, religion was one way to fight loneliness: "Anytime I see a person fleeing from reason and into religion, I think to myself, there goes a person who simply can't stand being so goddamned lonely anymore."[*]

And sometimes the same Kurt Vonnegut could quite gracefully acknowledge a sense of the sacred in a growing faith that he can't shake despite himself. At the conclusion of his commencement address at Smith College, he could speak of a new willingness he sensed among people to do what is necessary to sustain life on our planet. This willingness had to be "a religious enthusiasm" because it celebrated life and called for meaningful sacrifices.

"And thank God," he went on, "we have solid information in the place of superstition! Thank God we are beginning to dream of human communities which are designed to harmonize with what human beings really need and are.

"And now you have just heard an atheist thank God not once, but twice. And listen this: 'God bless the class of 1974.'"[†]

Some Conclusions

With minor differences, Augustine, Patrick, Tolstoy, and Vonnegut reveal the same characteristics of confession discussed in Chapter 2. Our interest is primarily with structure, not specific content, which we would expect to differ broadly from person-to-person and age-to-age. The confessions of all four originated in some significant self-encounter, produced by events that affected them deeply. With Augustine it was the shame surrounding his sexual exploits and a growing sense of guilt over his prideful pursuits that carried him far astray from his early Christian roots. For Patrick it was a similar mixture of guilt and shame over behavior he believed led to being carried away into slavery. In Tolstoy's case, depression and disillusionment set him searching for a way to restore his will to go on living. With Vonnegut it was more a sense of corporate guilt and shame in which he shared, witnessing the Allies carpet bombing Dresden back into

---

[*] *Ibid.*, p. 215.
[†] *Ibid.* p. 210.

the Stone Age. Crouching with his comrades in *Slaughterhouse Five*, he became fully aware of the evil that the human soul is capable of doing to others and to the planet as well.

Each confessor had his own reason for self-disclosure. Augustine and Patrick made their confessions out of a need to cope with personal vicissitudes, and a profound sense of gratitude for God's help. Tolstoy was driven by an inner compulsion to make sense of his life and discover a purpose for which to go on living. Vonnegut's defense against his critics led him to confess a well-placed mistrust of religious bigotry in particular, and arbitrary authority in general. None bothered to distinguish between guilt and shame, simply assuming everyone understood the role they play in the human predicament.

We must guess at how each received enough acceptance from others to develop the measure of self-acceptance represented in their confessions. All shared with their contemporaries a common disillusionment in organized religion and launched a search for truth that fit an inner sense of integrity. Each drew energy from their struggle with growing despair over intensely personal matters of guilt and shame, except for Vonnegut, who represents the sense of social sin and corporate responsibility more characteristic of our age and its spiritual homelessness. Even Vonnegut confessed his own failure in marriage, his loneliness, and his struggle to find a new and more satisfying spirituality. He went so far as to show sketches of his own anal aperture—I assume to represent his writings as "showing his ass."

All of our confessions were in narrative form. None involved isolated acts. All were made within the context of specific and ongoing events. Family and the influences of childhood were prominent. Augustine and Patrick were raised in Christian homes. Augustine confessed the strong influence of his mother's faith, particularly in his conversion to celibacy. Tolstoy grew up an Orthodox Christian among the wealthy and privileged in Russia. Each found his own way of returning to the faith of his childhood, renewed and enriched by his personal quest. Vonnegut explored his family tree over three generations to convey indebtedness to his genealogy. Not only did he acknowledge that his mother's efforts at writing influenced his career; but he also laid claim to old Clemens Vonnegut's scathing funeral dissertation against Christian orthodoxy as characteristic of his family's skepticism. Like Augustine, Patrick, and Tolstoy, he was deeply influenced by the family tree from which none of the apples fell too far.

In each case, the circumstances surrounding their confessions created the possibility for new and transformational narratives. A sense of personal failure, guilt, or shame drove them to examine their human predicament in search of a relevant response to carry them beyond its clutches. Coping with these events brought the discovery of meanings and beliefs heretofore unclear or unknown, to which each gave voice. Some sense of what is sacred emerged in their stories. In short, confession of sin led to confession of faith.

The full confessional experience involves both self-confrontation and self-formation. It remains incomplete with mere forgiveness and self-acceptance. It presses beyond the events at hand to a renewed awareness of what gives life meaning. This has nothing to do with any notion of moral perfection, absolute truth, psychic flawlessness, or final state of being, to which any or all should aspire. It is simply their own story, told their own way, about what really matters to them.

Practice

Tolstoy and the Vonnegut focus our attention in two very different directions. Tolstoy points ahead to death, the inevitable outcome of life. In doing so, he anticipates the existentialism of the twentieth century. Death's stark stare back at us in the passing of each day reminds us of how tenuous and fleeting our existence is before that dark wall beyond which no one can see. How do we gain and keep hold of the meaning of our days? Vonnegut directs our attention back through the roots of our family tree to those who came before us. He is clear that our ancestors shape our life, even in the womb. Whether in our DNA or in transgenerational processes of human communication, we are the product of our genealogy. How do we lay claim to it and avoid being determined by it? Both questions are worthy of our best attention.

Self-Awareness and Internal Dialogue
1. How does death cast its shadow over your life? In this quiet time alone, give your awareness free rein: see, feel, listen, and remember. Mindfully entertain the range of experiences you have had with death. Preoccupation with thoughts of death often means we are avoiding living in some important respect. Preoccupation with ways to avoid thinking about death often means we are discounting our purpose in some way. Draw your own conclusions, particularly ones that are fitting and beneficial to you.
2. If you wish, you may take a Fantasy Trip. You may imagine yourself dying. How old are you? Of what are you dying? Where are you? Who is there with you—physically or in your mind's eye? Who has been notified? Hear what people important to you may say, think, or feel. What have you left undone? And then come back to the present. Today is the first day of the rest of your life— want to do anything different?
3. Figure 4.1 provides the form for a genogram. There are spaces for your immediate family, your family of origin, your

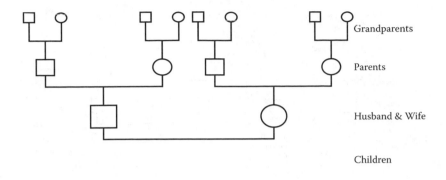

Figure 4.1 Genogram.

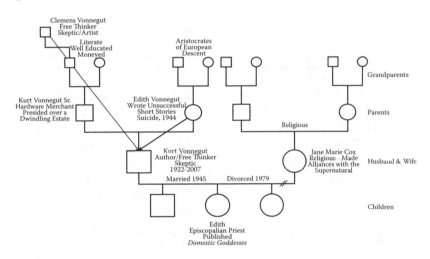

Figure 4.2 Kurt Vonnegut's genogram.

grandparents, and even your great-grandparents. You can be inventive, finding places for children, siblings, second marriages, and divorces, noting what comes to mind as you go. You may show life spans, vocational choices, themes, parallels, successes, failures, closeness, distance, religious interests, spiritual pursuits, and anything else that comes to mind. To help you start, Figure 4.2 depicts the principal influences Kurt Vonnegut shared about his family tree in what you have just read, particularly old Clemens Vonnegut's religious skepticism and his mother's penchant for writing unsuccessful short stories. Figure 4.3 adds information gleaned from Vonnegut's Web site and his Wikipedia biography, showing his younger brother Bernard (an atmospheric scientist), his sister Alice

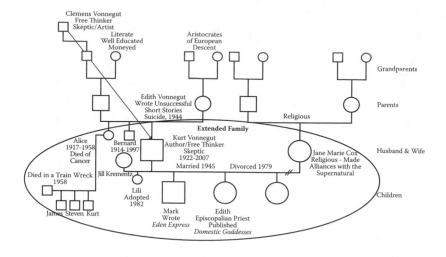

Figure 4.3 Kurt Vonnegut's genogram expanded.

(whose three children he adopted when she died of cancer after their father was killed in a train wreck 2 days before), and his second marriage to Jill Krementz (with whom he adopted Lili, a seventh child). Some of his beliefs in the extended family may take shape for you, as well as the way the contagion of his mother's urge to write spread beyond his own fame as an author to other family members, his son Mark writing *The Eden Express,* and his daughter Edith publishing *Domestic Goddesses.* Now you can do your own genogram in the same way.

Confessional Partnership

1. Any of the three experiences in Self-Awareness above could take a full session, perhaps more. Take your time; it is OK to linger with anything that becomes important in your sharing.

2. If you are part of a study group, you do not have to keep pace with your readings. You can also return to unfinished exercises at any time.

3. Your reactions to each other's genograms can play an important part in gaining a working sense of their influence. Brainstorming together usually adds meaning to the exercise after show-and-tell.

Discussion Group

1. Tolstoy's encounter with the reality of death is worthy of some time. We have Augustine's assurance that God would not permit everything achieved within the human soul to slip into oblivion. We have Tolstoy's despair at sensing death's relentless approach,

bearing us into nothingness beyond. Then there is old Clemens Vonnegut's notion of resting in peace where nothing can ever disturb one's deep slumber: no worries, grief, fears, passions, pains, or reproaches. Participants can be invited to share their own ideas and reactions.

2. Tolstoy believed in religion where we are always dealing with truth mingled with falsehood, never the Truth with a capital "T." How would you put it?

3. Vonnegut poses some interesting ideas to pursue. What about the notion that loneliness is at the heart of our human predicament? How important is the extended family? Is it growing stronger or weakening in contemporary society?

4. What part is played by the family tree in shaping our destiny? The influence of parents, grandparents, great-grandparents, siblings, and others is part of every life. How much of our life course do they determine?

5. In searching for a moral imperative, Vonnegut suggests that whatever wounds the planet is evil; whatever preserves or heals it is good. Do you buy it? What are some other moral imperatives to which we may look in measuring the outcome of our actions?

Confessional Group

1. Members of the group may resonate to Tolstoy's encounter with death by sharing their own experiences and ideas.

2. The fantasy trip into your own death scene, outlined in the "Self-Awareness/Internal Dialogue" section, often produces strong feelings or surfaces troublesome aspects of our present life. Members of the group may wish to disclose some of their reactions.

3. The genogram assignment can lead to mutual sharing and feedback. By this time, the group has developed its own style of working together. You may choose to spend several weeks dealing with these materials. Careful, unhurried conversation with each person will go a long way toward team building and cohesiveness.

4. More often than not, a study group or confessional group will not "keep up with" a schedule that calls for reading a chapter each week. It is OK to regulate reading assignments, discussion time, and confessional conversations to the pace most productive for your purposes.

CHAPTER 5

The Trouble with Adam

None of our confessors devoted much attention to defining sin. Augustine did later in his life, but not as part of his confession. He and the others simply assumed its existence disturbing our feelings about ourselves, infecting our relationships with each other, and separating us from the purposes of our Creator. The task of formulating its definition and place in the church's body of belief fell to theologians and officials in the religious hierarchy, whose company Augustine later joined. Thus far, we have discussed the confession of sin without discussing any of its varied meanings. Virtually all its definitions arise from some human effort, scriptural or otherwise, to make sense of what has gone wrong in our world and what needs to be done about it.

The Human Predicament

A story made the rounds at the height of the Cold War when people built bomb shelters and stocked them with food and water for survival: the wrong blips appeared spontaneously on everybody's radar screens. Rockets were launched; New York and Moscow went up in flames almost simultaneously, followed by rest of the civilized world. All except one tiny monkey, that is, who stuck his head up from an underground sewer near the Bronx Zoo, looking for signs of life. Finding none, he headed south past Washington, the Carolinas, over through Alabama, Texas, Mexico, and down into Central America. Exhausted and half-starved, he stumbled into the jungles of Guatemala. There he finally saw another monkey in a clearing ahead, a female monkey whose eyes brightened as he approached.

"Have you anything to eat?" he asked. The little female monkey reached into a sack behind her and pulled out a bright, shiny, red apple, offering it to him. But instead of taking it, the little male monkey stepped back and exclaimed, "Look, whatever we do, let's don't start that again!"

Adam and Eve

The ancient creation myth of Adam and Eve and their fall from innocence is shared by all of Abraham's descendants—Christian, Jew, and Muslim alike. Incidentally, there is no mention of an apple in Genesis 3, just the tree in the midst of the Garden of Eden that bears the fruit of the knowledge of good and evil, which the serpent persuades Eve to eat and give to Adam. It was the first "Mussentouchit." They could have anything else they wanted but not that. It was a "No! No!"—right there in the middle of creation. That's where it all started.

Once there was disobedience, there was no more innocence. There was a knowledge of good and evil. And death. Adam and Eve had their eyes opened in all sorts of ways. They knew they were naked, and they were ashamed. They ran and hid from God. The curses followed. There was something for everybody. The serpent must go on his belly eating dust all his life. For the woman came pain in childbirth, and her husband would rule over her all her life. The man was cursed with the toil of tilling the ground by the sweat of his brow all his days until he returned to dust. Enmity between the woman and the serpent was thrown in to boot.

I refer to this story as a myth because it is obviously not a historical event witnessed and recorded by anybody. Actually, it is a story about everybody—not just for Jews, Christians, and Muslims, but the whole human race. Some similar myth about what's gone wrong accompanies most descriptions of the human predicament. With Freud it was the story of the primal hoard of apes.[*] The father possessed all the women. His jealous sons banded together and killed him, taking the females for themselves. Then, filled with fear and guilt, they deified the father, making a god of him, and created a moral code around his worship to protect their society from repeating what they had done. A ceremonial meal feasting on the father's flesh became a ritual commemorating their pact. For Eric Berne, the myth was simpler: every little boy and girl is born a prince or a princess, and their parents turn them into frogs.[†] So they wander around looking for someone to kiss them and turn them back into their rightful state, until they realize what has happened and decide they can stop and be OK by themselves. And so on.

---

[*] Freud, Sigmund. *Totem and Taboo* in *The Basic Writings of Sigmund Freud*. Translated by A.A. Brill (New York: The Modern Library, 1938), pp. 807–930.

[†] Berne, Eric, M.D. *What Do You Say After You Say Hello?* (New York: Bantam Books, 1972).

The Genesis story conveys in poetry and symbol a cluster of ideas larger than any one religion. First, we are created not just innocent but essentially good. Then there is the notion that we all experience some inevitable disobedience in the process of growing up. When that happens, a knowledge of good and evil begins to develop, without which we would not be human at all. Not only does this knowledge distinguish us from the animals, but it also becomes the source of all our grandeur and our misery. The curses may be particularly descriptive of the debilitating and demoralizing effects of gender roles we learn that somehow originate in this primal drama of human development. Women have been cursed with pain in childbirth and male dominance. Men have been cursed with meaningless toil and senseless conflict. I don't know about the enmity between the serpent and the woman, but the symbolism can suggest some kind of sexual estrangement between men and women, if you want to be Freudian about it. At any rate, the "Fall," as we call it, represents an awareness of the depth of our estrangement from what we actually are created to be. It is, as theologian Paul Tillich suggests, a fall into humanity, not out of it. However, there is still no mention of sin, only shame.

Sin

Sin enters the picture when organized religion addresses the inevitable task of describing the way this estrangement plays itself out in our human predicament. Theologian Ed Farley observes that in ancient Israelite religion and its modern heirs (Judaism, Christianity, and Islam), sin follows from an inclination in human beings to disobey, ignore, or replace God's intentions with lesser purposes that lead to moral corruption, both individual and societal.[*] The term comes to represent both a state of being in which our lives are not as they should be, as well as particular acts that follow from it. There is widespread agreement that something has gone wrong, at times terribly wrong, with the way we are and the way we live with one another. You don't have to be religious to agree with that. Just watch the news. Read the morning paper.

My dictionary proved spectacularly unhelpful in defining sin simply as "any transgression of the law of God." But then again, that may attest to the wisdom of its authors to avoid entanglement in the many meanings the word has taken on. It reminded me of the Shorter Catechism in the *Westminster Confession of Faith* where sin is "any want of conformity unto or transgression of the law of God," which I learned as a child. This meant there were sins of both "omission" and "commission," and so on. But we all knew sin

---

[*] Hunter, R.J. (Ed.), "Sin/Sins," in *Dictionary of Pastoral Care and Counseling* (Nashville, TN: Abingdon Press, 1990), pp. 1173–1176.

was drinking, smoking, gambling, lying, stealing, cheating, being selfish, hurting other people, cursing, and having sex before you're married.

Sin has many different meanings, depending upon who's talking about it. There are complicated theological notions about the nature of sin that scholars and professors can discuss at length. But the practical, day-to-day meanings that the word takes on among us ordinary people often have little to do with these discussions. I remember as a youth vowing weekly in church not to get angry and curse playing tennis that afternoon. Somehow the same vows didn't apply to football or basketball. I also learned that what was sin for some folks wasn't sin for others. For example, the Baptists couldn't dance, but I could. There was an old joke about why Baptists were against having sex. If they did, they might want to dance.

Years later, when I got to seminary, I quickly learned that these two levels of conversation surrounding the word sin—its formal theological meanings and its common everyday meanings within the culture—have persisted throughout history. Nor has any one understanding of the term ever prevailed. Among the spiritual disciplines, sin has always stood for whatever separates us from God. More recently, Cornelius Plantinga defined sin as any "culpable disturbance" of the peace (shalom) God intended for creation in *Not the Way It's Supposed to Be: A Breviary of Sin.* Of course, there are a lot of ways to disturb the peace, depending on what you believe God actually intended for creation in the most varied of circumstances, but such notions can get us started thinking about what has gone wrong and what needs to be done about it.

Many Meanings

Formal theology offers a broad range of meanings we can bring to the word *sin.* There is the idea of rebellion against God or disobedience of God's will or law. There is the biblical notion of "missing the mark," "falling short," or "failing to realize what we may become as creatures." Sin has been commonly defined as breaking one or more of the Ten Commandments. Long lists of specific acts in defiance of God have been constructed from each commandment, casting disobedience into a catalog of forbidden behaviors, together with equally long lists of duties required to avoid them. The presence of sin has been ascribed to all kinds human motives or qualities, such as self-centeredness, pride, sensuality, estrangement from God and from our true selves, absence of love, or lack of faith. Lists like "The Seven Deadly Sins" have been constructed, containing such things as pride, avarice, envy, anger, sloth, gluttony, and lust. These even found their way into

---

* Plantinga, Cornelius. *Not the Way It's Supposed to Be: A Breviary of Sin* (Grand Rapids, MI: William B. Eerdmans, 1995), p. 18.

the Enneagram, which has been used for centuries as a confessional tool in Judaism, Christianity, and Islam. More about this later.

Whether we look at sin as a single act, a series of acts, or an ongoing state of being into which we have "fallen," in every tradition sin serves to separate us from our Creator and from meaningful relationships in the human community. Sin is often described as a "bondage" from which we must be set free. This freedom never involves some state of moral perfection or purity but, rather, release from the radical claim of sin upon our lives. We may become free to pursue a proper relationship with God and with our fellow human beings. This last idea parallels the way many clinicians consider what constitutes a "cure" in psychotherapy. It's not that we never feel it again, think it again, or do it again. Most "cures" involve a similar process of breaking free from the radical claim our symptoms had upon our lives.

In any case, traditional theology has always gone back to the Genesis myth of the "fall" to preserve something very important about its understanding of sin. On the one hand, theologians have never been willing to say that we were created as naturally sinful human beings. The Genesis myth preserves some notion of a historical "fall from innocence," the result of an act of free will by the first people (Adam and Eve). The fall myth locates the origin of sinfulness in our human freedom, not our human nature, which has always been regarded as part of "good creation," or "made for relationship with God," or "created in the image of God."

On the other hand, this same theological tradition has never been willing to say we can avoid the disastrous effects of sin upon the first parents or its accumulated effects among our predecessors from one generation to another. Companion doctrines of "original sin" proposed a biological transmission of its effects through procreation, rendering its presence inevitable. Augustine believed this, and so did Patrick. In this way, theologians could preserve the idea that we were neither naturally prone to sin nor able to avoid its presence in our lives.

These doctrines enabled theologians to foster some sense of balance between optimism and pessimism. People could sustain hope in their natural possibilities for positive change and right relationships, while, at the same time, grappling with the reality of all the tragic and discouraging failures that make up life as we know it. Theologians have never been willing to make shame and guilt a natural part of life, although they recognized that we all must struggle inescapably with both, and require some measure of belief that we can cope with them.

Failure to Communicate

The problem is that these classical formulations of our human predicament as "sin" fail to communicate with the spiritually homeless or even practicing members of the religious community with any precision or meaning that fits their contemporary experience. Farley points to the progressive erosion of sin doctrines since the Enlightenment.* From then on, mainstream theology joined in rejecting its biological transmission from one generation to the next, together with any literal belief in a "primordial fall" as an event in time. Further erosion followed upon what Philip Reiff called "the triumph of the therapeutic," in which classical doctrines of sin were seen as operating largely among cultural forces for repression and renunciation. In return, the therapeutic world responded by encouraging freer and fuller self-expression. Psychiatry gave human problems a compelling, nonreligious description in the range of emotional disorders requiring treatment. Psychotherapy began to fill the void left by the failure of theological language to generate any comparable means of assessing and intervening in the dilemmas of everyday life.

Part of the problem was the judgmental use taken on by the term "sin," reflecting blame or culpability apart from any attempt at understanding or acceptance. For instance, drunkenness is no longer sin. It is a sickness. Alcoholism is listed in the *Diagnostic and Statistical Manual of Mental Disorders IV* as an illness requiring treatment. This is due, in large part, to the blame and condemnation associated with the religious term. In Alcoholics Anonymous, however, we treat alcoholism in very much the way the church used to treat sin. The first step in recovery is confession: "We admitted we were powerless over alcohol—that our lives had become unmanageable." In the second step, we "came to believe that a Power greater than ourselves could restore us to sanity."†

So severe were problems with the word "sin" that in 1970 the noted psychiatrist Karl Menninger wrote a short but significant book entitled *Whatever Became of Sin?*‡ His strong appeal for a renewed sense of moral and social responsibility was occasioned by a widespread recognition of what the title suggested. Something had happened to relegate sin to the periphery of our attention, particularly when we searched for viable ways to address the range of problems that make up the human predicament.

Clinical judgments assessing addictions and other forms of psychopathology could be made supportively under a "sickness" metaphor, shielding the caring relationship from condemnatory language and attitudes. The difficulty was not with the ideas many doctrines of sin conveyed, but with common tendencies in everyday practice to make shallow use of them. Describing people as sinners, apart from efforts to understand

---

* *Op. cit.*
† Alcoholics Anonymous. *Twelve Steps and Twelve Traditions* (New York: Alanon Family Group Headquarters, 1989), p. 3.
‡ Menninger, Karl. *Whatever Became of Sin?* (New York: Hawthorne Books, 1973).

their behavior, is seldom if ever helpful, particularly when circumstances surrounding their actions are ignored or divorced from the context of the narratives surrounding them. The result was a one-sided analysis of most social situations, concentrating on individual wrongdoing to the neglect of the all-pervasive, corporate dimensions of those of very doctrines themselves. Any sense of mutual participation in and shared responsibility for events labeled as "sinful" was forfeited, as the religious establishment increasingly focused its attention upon the purely individualistic concerns of personal salvation. At the popular level of everyday practice, confession of sin became the means of ridding oneself of accumulated guilt and obtaining forgiveness through channels available in organized religion to assure salvation in an afterlife.

Two Metaphors Governing Confession

In Western Christianity, two metaphors came to dominate the common practice of confession. Together they proved so influential that they shape many of our present-day conceptions of its place in the spiritual life. Both originated in this concern for personal salvation of the individual. Both assumed that some final judgment would determine the destiny of each soul in an afterlife. Some means of gaining forgiveness through confessing one's sins became a paramount concern in organized religion.

The Medicinal Metaphor

In the Catholic tradition, a medicinal metaphor prevailed. The sacrament of confession became the principal means for "the cure of souls." Slowly it grew into the prime measure necessary to counteract the day-to-day accumulation of particular sinful acts. Confession followed by appropriate penance and absolution provided healing to the "sin-sick soul." The confessional booth offered an ongoing remedy for the mounting weight of guilt incurred by every sinful act. By Shakespeare's time, Hamlet could envision revenge for his father's murder by catching the culprit in some despicable act of sin, plunging a knife into his heart, and sending his soul to eternal hell before he could confess and seek absolution.

With the medicinal metaphor, three practices evolved to undermine and diminish the relevance of confession. First came the gradual separation of confessions of faith from confessions of sin. The antidote of absolution was offered for confessing particular sinful acts, which were increasingly treated without reference to their context in one's unfolding life narrative. Companion confessions of faith, like those of our confessors, growing out of vital encounters with guilt and shame, dropped out of the picture. One began to submit to a regular means of cure in a process that led to little beyond its own repetition.

Second, regulating this "cure of souls" demanded an ever-increasing legalistic catalog of "sins" requiring confession. Our Catholic forefathers followed the pattern of ancient Judaism that started with the Ten Commandments; produced the *Midrash* in commentary clarifying some point of law or moral principle; then collected oral laws into the *Mishnah*, followed by the *Gemara,* which served as a commentary on the *Mishnah*; and, finally, produced the *Talmud* in the year 500, which contained everything. That was only the beginning. The Canons of Catholicism stretch back through the Middle Ages, from earliest times to the present. Christians and Jews scarcely outdo Muslims here. Recently, I read a list of 100 sins cataloged from Islam, while I was gathering on the Internet similar commentaries on the law of God by Catholics, Lutherans, Presbyterians and others. As Kurt Vonnegut observed, the law of God can receive a most varied and conflicting array of interpretations at human hands.

For instance, the Larger Catechism of our own *Westminster Confession of Faith* set out to define sin for Presbyterians by creating a list of specifics required and forbidden by each of the Ten Commandments. The sixth commandment—"Thou shalt not kill"—required everything from "resisting all thoughts and subduing all passions which tend toward the unjust taking away of life" to "the sober use of meat, drink, sleep, labor, and recreation." It forbade all "sinful anger, hatred, envy, or desire for revenge," "provoking words," "quarreling," and so forth. The seventh commandment—"Thou shalt not commit adultery"—required everything from "chastity of body, mind, affections, word, and behavior" to "watchfulness over the eyes and all the senses" and "modesty in apparel." It prohibited "all unclean imaginations, thoughts, purposes, and affections," "wanton looks," "impudent or light behavior," and "long engagements." Such was the religious and moral culture that the Westminster Divines sought to create in the lives of common folk in the seventeenth century.

A third casualty of the medicinal metaphor was the exclusion of shame as a viable part of the confessional conversation. Legalistic concerns with judging the individual's culpability focused entirely upon guilt. Adam and Eve knew shame. In the Genesis myth, shame belongs at the heart of their developing knowledge of good and evil. For Erik Erickson, shame is present in the second stage of human growth, in which the infant begins to experience autonomy or draws back in shame and self-doubt. Guilt comes from some conscious act of wrongdoing or disobedience. Shame comes when we feel a sense of being unacceptable in the first place. Guilt is for doing; shame is for being. Augustine confessed both freely. None of his confessions were limited to some codified list of offenses dictating what was to be regarded as sin. The medicinal model with its increasing demands for legalistic precision served to bypass shame as a vital part of the confessional conversation, despite Augustine's broad influence and liberal use of the term throughout his confessions.

The Judicial Metaphor

With the Protestant reformation came the second metaphor. It was a judicial one as the times required. Western civilization was poised on the brink of the dawning of a modern legal system. The scene was an eternal courtroom in which justice must be done. Here all humankind stood guilty as sinners before God's judgment. No one was innocent. All were condemned equally before the Creator. The issue now became how can the individual soul be justified (treated as just) and receive salvation?

Here a German monk named Martin Luther led the way by scribbling in the margin of his Bible at Romans 3:28 "The just shall live by faith" the word "Alone." People were justified by faith alone, not by their records, their sacramental acts, or their good deeds. Justification by faith meant throwing oneself at the mercy of the court, accepting the forgiveness for one's sins offered through Jesus Christ to those who believe. This justification by faith, not "works," became the means for salvation in the judicial metaphor. Individual sinners escaped condemnation through accepting their forgiveness as a saving grace.

Both the medicinal and the judicial metaphors served a vital purpose in their time. The seal of sanctuary surrounding the confessional booth provided a safe haven to the deeply troubled for hundreds of years. Private confession in many forms offered a regular and effective means of dealing with guilt and renewing the soul well into the past century. Neither Luther nor other reformers sought to eliminate its practice. Luther himself considered it a source without peer for healing guilt. He and his followers simply refused to accept the sacrament of confession as a means of assuring salvation in an afterlife. The reformers all believed salvation was a gift of God's grace, and an individual's confession could be heard by any believer. This permitted confession to take on many new forms, which I discuss in Chapter 6.

In popular use, however, both the medicinal and the judicial metaphors fostered a static function for confession in contrast to the dynamic character of the confessions we have been considering. The pain of self-encounter moved Augustine, Patrick, Tolstoy, and Vonnegut toward some form of recognizable resolve or direction in life that yielded understanding, belief, and faith. These metaphors centered more attention upon the status of the sinner before God. Increasingly, confession served to prepare one for an anticipated final judgment that determined the soul's eternal destiny. This contributed to a more static view of its practice as an act that had little to do with a relevant response of any kind. In the medicinal model, regular confession erased the accumulation of sin, offsetting the necessity for punishment in the afterlife. In the judicial model, individual confession slipped farther into disuse through its focus on conversion among evangelical Christians and its increasing restriction to liturgical repetition in mainline Protestant churches.

I grew up as a teenager in the 1940s with little grasp of the meaning of confession. There were the evangelical Christians who wanted you to come down front, confess your sins, and be saved. I often went to the Baptist Church to date an attractive blonde Baptist girl who always had to go (to church, that is). I sat through many services where the emphasis was upon "converting sinners to Christ." These were on Sunday nights when we Presbyterians didn't have church. Always there was a "call" for people to come forward and "accept Jesus Christ as your Lord and Personal Savior." Sometimes there would be a revival, and everyone would go to the high-school football field to hear Angel Martinez appeal to sinners in the stands to "come down front and be saved." I always felt I should go, but I never did. It was clear that I was a sinner and needed to confess. Some did many times. Old Sam Hoskins did every summer. It was never clear what you did afterward, but you were saved. Unless, I used to guess, you became a real bad sinner again. But if you didn't smoke, drink, or dance…?

As Presbyterians, we confessed our sins every week in Prayers of General Confession followed by the Assurance of Pardon. Sometimes the minister would read them from the *Book of Common Worship*. Sometimes the prayers were printed in the bulletin for everyone to read in unison. Occasionally, they were silent and everybody confessed on their own, only you had to hurry because Presbyterians can't stand much silence. Phrases from these old liturgical confessions still stick in my mind. I remember confessing "our sinful nature prone to evil and slothful in good," "following too much the devices and desires of our own hearts," "all our failures and shortcomings toward Thee and toward our fellow man," and the especially onerous confession that covered everything: "we have left undone those things which we ought to have done, and we have done those things which we ought not to have done, and there is no health in us." These confessions were always followed by the Assurance of Pardon, which normally, with the help of Scripture, declared God's faithfulness to forgive us week in and week out for these same sins. I don't know why I can't remember much about the way these assurances were worded.

We (I, my family, and everybody else I knew) prayed these General Confessions each Sunday. We never mentioned them—or any of the things they suggested we had done or not done—to anyone at church, at home, or anywhere else. Later in the service each week, normally after the sermon, the minister would say, "Let us confess our faith," or "Let us stand and say what we believe," and we would all get up and recite the Apostles' Creed in unison and sit down. At the level of popular religious practice for ordinary folks like us, the Confession of Sin and the Confession of Faith were completely separated from each other, both in their liturgical expression and in our understanding.

Battling Irrelevance

I have since come to realize that such carefully crafted irrelevance was completely unintentional. But metaphors from the Middle Ages, once teeming with relevance for angst about the afterlife, faded in their significance before the shifting spiritual concerns of a different time. Take Tolstoy, for example. His struggle was to find a reason to go on living. What could lend sufficient meaning and purpose to his days to keep him from committing suicide? Or consider Kurt Vonnegut, whose attention centered more around the survival of the planet than the salvation of individual souls in an afterlife. Both are representative of the collapse in modern times of the system of beliefs surrounding a final judgment and an eternal hell. The view of our lifetime as the soul's proving ground gave way to more evolutionary understandings of growth and fulfillment of our purpose on earth here and now.

Our current scene is not without serious efforts to recover a meaningful practice of confession. Among progressive Catholics, it has become "reconciliation" with a free exchange of conversation between confessor and priest, face-to-face. My friend Bill, with whom I play tennis, tells me it's "OK." You just talk about your life and anything that bothers you. Bill said his priest complemented him on his honesty and candor. My client Anna, who was molested by her priest as a child, remembers talking to another priest years later about her troubles at school. She trusted this man and could talk freely about her doubts and her dishonesty. Near the end of their conversation, he asked her if she wanted to make it into a confession and conclude it as a sacrament. Even at that, it was years later before she told anyone about her abuse. When she did, she chose to confess the shame she felt to a psychotherapist. In many respects, contemporary confessional practices have somehow failed their most sacred purposes, only to be taken over elsewhere.

Reestablishing Full Confession

A number of obstacles confront anyone seeking to restore the practice of confession in our time. There are difficulties with the word "sin" in its common meaning that render it virtually unusable. No abiding agreement within organized religion has ever existed about what we should confess. In the theological seminary where I taught for 35 years, there was a requirement that each graduating senior complete a Statement of Faith. It was a telling exercise, calling upon ministers-to-be to organize what they believe into a coherent whole. It was telling for professors as well, in that it often revealed more than we wished to know about the impact of what we thought we had taught. Each spring, the faculty divided into teams for oral examinations of our seniors on their written statements.

As director of the Marriage and Family Therapy Program, I was always interested in how our students described the human predicament—mainly what has gone wrong with us human beings and what do we need to do about it? To my amazement, fully a third of our graduates-to-be ignored "sin" doctrines altogether. The majority of the remainder mentioned sin in passing but made little effort to relate it to the system of beliefs they had assembled to address the significant issues of our lives. Clearly the word "sin" had lost its relevance for most of them.

Three suggestions to recover the practice of confession take shape. First, we need to open the process to address whatever troubles us most. This can encompass any experience that creates guilt, shame, or anxiety. In the Eden myth of the Fall, it is shame that causes Adam and Eve to run and hide from God. Let's start there. Let's pay attention to the inevitable guilt that accompanies the fruit of a knowledge of good and evil, endemic to every person who grows up a member of the human race. Let's embrace the struggle all of us have with obedience and disobedience, from "no-nos" and "Mussentouchits" to the loftiest moral standards with which we have been raised. Whatever troubles us most about whatever we are experiencing at whatever stage of our lives is a proper matter for confessional conversation. This is how Augustine confessed, as did Patrick, Tolstoy, and Vonnegut.

Second, each of our four confessors wrote in his own words, in terms of his own concrete life experience, and in the idiom of his own time. We do ourselves a great disservice if we attempt to make our confessions in archaic words with ideas of other persons in other times and places. Our most honest confessions arise within the context of our own life narrative and our own unique experience. As we participate, rituals, liturgical prayers, and unison prayers of confession may point the way but we are the only ones who can give our confessions authenticity. We need to encourage and pursue the practice of self-awareness.

We can use all the help we can get to restore confession in our time, which suggests a third measure. We need to make a concerted effort to create confessional relationships with one another. We have considered ten characteristics of honest confession, several of which had to do with providing a context for acceptance and ongoing conversations. Understanding the range of confessional relationships that are possible may be helpful. Chapter 6 provides a brief overview of four types of confession that have risen to prominence in its history.

Practice

Chapter 6 introduces some ways to explore the sources of self-criticism and judgment that emerge in our internal dialogue. Most we have acquired from influential people who remain important to us. Meanwhile, feel free to open up the range of painful personal experiences that claim your attention and interrupt your well-being. Reflect on instances that carry emotional twinges of regret, shame, guilt, anxiety, and even fear. Perhaps Cornelius Plantiga's idea of whatever "disturbs the peace (shalom)" given by our Creator can serve as a good starting point. Whether or not you choose to use the term "sin" is secondary to our purposes. Feel free to use it, if you are comfortable and it fits. You need not avoid it unless it distracts or limits your attention. We are interested in developing sound personal judgment, and we need never use the word "sin" with ourselves or anyone else when it bears judgmental connotations of condemnation or serves to alienate us from one another.

Self-Awareness and Internal Dialogue

1. Take an inventory of what troubles you most. Privacy will entitle you to make your own list free from anyone looking over your shoulder. As you go, you may choose to label the feelings that accompany each item. You can set these aside in a safe place, either written or in your memory, to work through during the weeks ahead.
2. Explore the way you have come to think about "sin" in your life. Remember early teachings about it. Often, these can lurk just beneath the surface and surprise us with guilt or shame, "disturbing the peace." How many of these ideas have changed? How many do you want to change?
3. Return to the inventory of what troubles you most. Check the ways you were taught to think about sin in the past and examine these ideas for any relevance they have to this inventory.
4. If you journal, record what you believe concerning sin. Do you need a new word? Do you need to revise any archaic understandings? Is there some definite value for you in preserving the term? Should you replace it with something else, or should you simply discard it? Even if you don't keep a journal, writing your own thoughts often proves helpful.

Confessional Partnership

1. Share your reactions to the exercise above.
2. Consider any agreements or understandings you wish to establish

about "sin-talk," preferred alternatives to the term, and shared ideas or reactions to its use.

3. Work on any chosen item from the inventory of what troubles you most.

Discussion Group

1. The group may benefit from a discussion of memories surrounding the meaning of the word "sin." This could come either before or after the leader's summary of the reading.

2. Various meanings of the word could be evaluated in terms of their helpfulness in describing the human predicament or what we are up against in life: disobedience, missing the mark or falling short, breaking the Ten Commandments, self-centeredness, pride, sensuality, estrangement, bondage, absence of love, etc.

3. Genesis 2:15–3:24 could be read. Encourage the group to discuss their reactions as if hearing it for the first time.

4. Is there some consensus among members of the group about what should be done with the term "sin?" How may it become relevant again? Do we need an entirely new term? Can we modify its present usage in a way that recovers its meaning without judgmental and condemnatory baggage?

Confessional Group

1. You may wish to return to the discussion format to consider meanings the word "sin" has for members of the group.

2. Can the word be used constructively in your work together? If so, you must shed any non-accepting or condemnatory connotations, as well as some of the perfectionistic expectations that can come with it.

3. Is there any consensus among members as to some common meaning for this term or for the phenomena it describes?

CHAPTER **6**

The Confessional Relationship

Nineteen sixty eight was a banner year. I began my first sabbatic leave from the seminary in September. Sam Keen and I went to California with grants from the American Association of Theological Schools to study the human potential movement. We spent time at Esalen and Kairos, the two leading growth centers on the West Coast. I met people such as Michael Murphy, Fritz Perls, Virginia Satir, Alexander Lowan, Al Pesso, Stan Kellerman, Jim Simkin, Bob Goulding, Mary Goulding, and Eric Berne. Dr. Warren Cox had made Berne's *Games People Play* required reading for those of us working at the Louisville Area Mental Health Center. He suggested, half jokingly, that I look up its author when I got there. Just before leaving, I wrote to Eric Berne, asking where I could learn something about transactional analysis (TA). To my surprise, when I arrived, the author had gone out of his way to arrange for me to meet Chaplain Hedges Capers at the Naval Hospital in San Diego and psychiatrist Ted Olivier with whom I trained for the year.

Later it was my privilege to meet Berne himself. The International Transactional Analysis Association at that time was a small, intimate group for such an immodest name. When I became a Clinical Member, there were 38 of us and only 20 Teaching Members. The story was that Grove Press refused to publish *Games People Play,* saying it wouldn't sell. Members of his San Francisco seminar got together sufficient funds to pay for its initial publication. Within months it was a bestseller. Berne's precision, wit, extraordinary intuition, and passionate belief that everyone was a card-carrying member of the human race laid bare the most intricate psychological patterns of interaction so clearly that everyone could understand them. Interestingly enough, after two-plus decades of flourishing in

85

the United States, TA spread abroad through Europe, Asia, and the Orient, becoming truly the International Transactional Analysis Association. Here in the United States, it never quite established itself in academia, where many regarded it, rather unfairly I would add, as "pop psychology" without substance.

In this chapter, I give a brief history of confession, which reveals different types of confessional conversations evolving across the years. I can characterize them best by describing their different transactional patterns and ensuing relationships. Berne's simplicity can serve us well, once we grasp his understanding of ego states.

Ego States

Berne used to say that you understand TA if you understand five words: Parent, Adult, Child, Games, and Scripts. Transactional analysis focused attention on specific "transactions" or exchanges between people. The first three words constitute the three ego states you can observe in each individual. Our Parent ego state is acquired from significant parental figures. As we grow up, we incorporate their postures, mannerisms, gestures, together with their ideas about right and wrong, clean and dirty, proper and improper, and so forth. When we are in our Parent, we have the voice, expressions, and vocabulary of a parent addressing a child. We can be a Nurturing Parent, comforting and caring for others, or a Critical Parent, criticizing and controlling others. When we are in our Child ego state, we are responding in ways of thinking, feeling, and acting we developed growing up. There are Adapted Child ego states of compliance or rebellion honed in response to various authority figures. There are Natural or Free Child ego states, responding spontaneously, creatively, and intuitively, especially when nurtured rather than encumbered by critical restraint. There are Adult ego states with age-appropriate thinking intact, given to reason, awareness, and objectivity about what's going on in the other two.

The practice of confession has always involved the creation of relationships with others. Something about authentic self-encounter compels us to seek out someone to listen and respond. Many different kinds of confessional relationships have been formed across the years. A very brief history of their evolution in Western Christianity can best be summarized in the simple and direct terms that Berne suggests.

Child-to-Parent Confession

We are most familiar with confessional relationships that develop a pattern of Child-to-Parent transactions. Someone in a Child ego state, troubled by guilt, shame, or remorse, confesses to a parent figure, Divine or human, from whom acceptance and forgiveness are sought. The aim is amelioration of guilt and restoration of a relationship that is somehow threatened or broken. The transaction may be perceived as taking place between a human being as Child and a heavenly Father or a representative parental figure, such as a priest, often called "Father," or a minister, a pastor, or other clergy, sometimes addressed as "Reverend." Whatever the human instrumentality, there is usually some sense of being forgiven directly by God.

The practice of private confession, as we have come to know it, probably originated in the monastic community sometime during the first three centuries.* In the fourth century, Cassian described how a monk in training was required to confess all his thoughts to some senior member of the community. By the time the rule of St. Benedict was established, all monastic life was shaped around obedience to the abbot, who assumed the role of a Father to his sons. Members of the community regularly confessed their sinful behavior to him. Being an abbot was no easy job. One lived under constant danger of allowing his own will to supplant the Divine will, which he determined through much study of scripture and monastic tradition. His job placed him under even greater danger of hell than those he counseled should he falter in his own dedication and obedience to the rule.

Gradually this practice of private confession was extended to the entire church. In medieval times, the village priest became the corrector and physician to members of his flock. His task was to counteract the presence of sin throughout his congregation by hearing its confessions regularly. By the twelfth century, the entire Western church was penitent. The prayers of absolution administered by a priest evolved from "May God absolve thee…" to "I absolve thee…." Lists of specific sins and penalties for each transgression were meticulously constructed. These were the clear product of a primitive society mixed with the particular judgments and predispositions of its correctors. The thirteenth century brought the *Celtic Penitential Disciplines* with practical manuals designed to equip priests to deal with persons in all sorts of moral and spiritual predicaments. Different types of penance were to be undertaken for different types of sin, requiring specific acts, prayers, pilgrimages, or monetary gifts.

The Sacrament of Confession became the means of assuring one's spiritual status in the afterlife. The Child/Parent relationship it engendered tended to arrest the confessional process at a level of dependency and repetition. Its restorative function was made normative. Its capacity to develop

---

* See McNeill, John T. *History of the Cure of Souls* (New York: Harper and Brothers, 1951) for an overview of the development of confessional practices. See also Clebsch, William A., and Jaekle, Charles R. *Pastoral Care in Historical Perspective*, (Englewood Cliffs, NJ: Prentice Hall, 1964).

spiritual maturity, as found in the lives of people such as Augustine, Tolstoy, or Vonnegut, was cut short. On the one hand, ongoing confessional conversation tended to adapt itself to the level of scrupulosity. Obsessive concern with confessing an ever-growing list of sinful acts could well increase shame and guilt, even unwittingly serve to exacerbate someone's propensities toward the forbidden. Interestingly enough, Burchard, Bishop of Worms in 1025, warned against priests questioning a man about all sins, "lest perchance when he is gone away from him at the devil's persuasion he fall into some of those offenses of which he previously did not know."*

On the other hand, the Reformation with its judicial understandings of justification by faith dealt confession an increasingly diminished role. In the face of forgiving grace, scrupulosity could give way to indifference about the need for private confession or regular self-reflection. Increasingly, Protestant confession became centered in its liturgical repetition through Prayers of General Confession in public worship, easily reduced among ordinary folk to perfunctory repetition and irrelevance to their way of life.

An unfortunate result of the dependency created by Child/Parent confession was its tendency to delete the profound sense of developing faith we encountered in the confessions of an Augustine, a Patrick, a Tolstoy, or a Vonnegut. Increasingly, one became dependent upon the representative Parent figure, not simply for forgiveness, but also for knowledge and instruction about what to believe. No longer did one's own unique struggles with the vicissitudes of life become the occasion for personal growth and renewed faith. There was nothing new to be learned from exploring one's darker side—no new understandings to be acquired through moving beyond a personal impasse with guilt. Self-confrontation ceased to serve as a reference point to new and better means of self-expression. Organized religion quietly took over the task of presenting well-constructed creeds and formal statements of appropriate doctrine, making them available for all believers in this context of a Child/Parent relationship. Formal Confessions of Faith grew to be required of all "believers" as a measure of membership and heresy as well, which, if great enough, could merit exclusion or excommunication from the religious community, and, on occasion, even death. Under such a structure, Child/Parent confession presided over an ever-increasing separation of an individual's personal confession of sin and commonly shared confessions of faith.

This is not to suggest that Child/Parent confession should be abandoned as entirely detrimental or irrelevant. Historically, as well as clinically, it remains an essential step in many of the honest confessions we have been considering. It is a necessity for someone so overwhelmed with guilt or estrangement that self-esteem and self-direction are lost. It is a saving

---

* McNeill. *Op. cit.*, p. 130.

grace for the outcast soul who at this point in a crisis needs to depend for a while upon someone who can be trusted. But to make the Child/Parent relationship normative for all confession is to surrender its rich purposes in the development and growth of the human spirit throughout life.

Adult-to-Adult Confession

A second level of confession can be characterized as Adult-to-Adult. It moves beyond the restorative and dependent dimensions of the Child/ Parent relationship. The confessor is concerned with how to cope with what occasioned guilt and shame, and how to go about setting relationships right in a climate of mutual acceptance and responsibility. This kind of full-grown self-reflection is motivated not so much by a sense of estrangement as by a growing commitment to discover and make a relevant response. Adult/Adult confession seeks to establish what Jewish theologian Martin Buber described as an "I–Thou" relationship.* There is mutuality, openness, and directness—a true dialogue. Buber saw this as our authentic relationship to the world, to other human beings, and ultimately to the Eternal Source of all that is. To him, the essence of religious life is not the affirmation of religious beliefs but the way one meets the challenges of existence. In Adult/Adult confession, we come to measure our striving in response to a like-minded Presence so great that we are moved to shape ourselves after the image of our Creator.

In this level of confession, a "faith come of age" is often born in the doubt and upheaval of adolescence, and won at the price of inquisitiveness and rebellion. This faith is not composed of beliefs formulated by others to which one gives arbitrary acceptance. It is rooted in the maturity of self-acquired certainty that follows from working our way through our own personal predicament as a human being, whatever that may be. We reach it by a process of journey and return, of leaving, growing up, and reestablishing a relationship similar to the one a son or daughter may eventually enjoy with a parent as two grown-up adults.

The history of spiritual direction in Western Christianity is filled with efforts to extend the confessional process into such an experience. Here, an ongoing conversation was established between a maturing, growing believer and a spiritual consultant who, by mutual agreement, served as guide, confidant, and companion. The spiritual director could be a symbolic or official representative of organized religion or some experienced layperson committed to helping others overcome whatever impeded their spiritual growth or alienated them from their community of faith.

---

* Buber, Martin. *I and Thou*. Translated by Walter Kaufmann (New York: Charles Scribner's Sons, 1970).

In the Catholic tradition, laymen's handbooks on spiritual improvement began to appear in the 1500s. The Jesuits paid great attention to the confessional, and many became spiritual directors to persons of importance. Among seventeenth-century French Catholics, the art of spiritual direction reached new heights. By 1787, Alfonso de Liguori wrote that such direction had to do with the pursuit of higher spiritual attainment rather than with the sacramental pardon of sins. Among the great spirits that emerged were Francis de Sales, Pierre de Berulle, Jacques-Bénigne Bossuet, and Francois Fenelon, and with them a wealth of literature and letters. Some elements of a Child/Parent relationship between confessor and director still remained. Many spiritual directors insisted upon strict obedience. Francis de Sales, for one, felt women must be led; but interestingly enough, Madame Guyon, who promised to obey Fenelon, actually began to direct her director, leading him to assert doctrines that proved unacceptable to the authorities, eventually bringing him papal condemnation. Other relationships evolved more happily into one of mutual respect and equality.

In the Protestant Reformation, confession shifted decisively in the Adult/Adult direction. John Calvin urged against private confession, encouraging confessional practices that stressed mutual admonition, advice, and consolation among the faithful. A similar stance was evident in Martin Luther's letters of spiritual direction.[*] Luther favored forfeiting any distinction between clergy and laity. Not only Luther's theological treatises, but his whole life seemed immersed in Scripture. He spoke in biblical language; he thought in biblical thought forms, and he wrote letters of spiritual counsel in predominantly biblical terms. It was the Devil who spoiled the wine at Wittenberg. The plague was the work of God as a judgment upon sin and a test of faith.

Luther spoke as a sinful man standing as fully in need of grace as anyone else. All of us are sinners, and sin is not so much a matter of wrong acts as it is a matter of wrong orientation to life. The only correct orientation lies in God's grace and here alone resides all our hope. Whatever confessing one does after the faithful acceptance of this grace is on an entirely different basis from a guilty Child addressing a forgiving Parent. Now every matter of life becomes a spiritual matter. Any experience can involve God, sin, the Devil, temptation, grace, forgiveness, and salvation. Whatever concerns one's physical health, one's mental well-being, or one's relationships to others is a proper matter for confessional conversation.

For example, Luther viewed some sickness as the will of God. He wrote his aging mother to accept her illness as part of God's "gracious fatherly chastisement," trusting in his promises of life beyond death. To others, he

---

[*] See Luther, Martin. *Letters of Spiritual Counsel.* Translated and edited by Theodore G. Tappert (London: SCM Press, Ltd., 1955).

wrote that our physical health depends in large measure on the thoughts in our minds. He quoted the scripture: "A merry heart doeth good like medicine, but a broken spirit dries the bones." He once suggested to Nicolas Hausman that the fear of disease is often as disastrous as the disease itself. He described to Hausman how he and his friends had aroused a number of persons who had taken to their beds with sweating in the midst of a local epidemic. Now they laughed at themselves, saying they would have remained ill without such measures. Luther didn't think we should ignore disease, just that we need to distinguish carefully people who contracted their sickness from imagination rather than from actual contagion.

Luther attacked the mental problems of his day with the same aggression. Solitude was a great enemy, breeding melancholy and despair, feelings he knew all too well himself. "More and graver sins are committed in solitude," he wrote, "than in the society of one's fellow man."* He urged a depressed Jerome Weller to drink more, joke, jest, and engage in some form of merriment. He urged Prince Joachim of Anhalt to hunt, make merry, and go gaming to overcome his anxiety, insisting that such pleasures are good for people and pleasing to God, even if one may, at times, carry playfulness a little too far. Music was a great enemy of the devil to Luther, "a good antidote against temptation and evil thoughts."

Then there was Jonas von Stockhausen, who was afflicted with melancholy and hypochondria. Luther wrote him not to struggle against his thoughts but to ignore them and act as if he were not aware of them. He urged old Jonas to take the Devil on, forthrightly addressing him, "Well, Devil, do not trouble me. I have no time for your thoughts. I must eat, drink, ride, go and do this or that thing." If necessary, Luther told Jonas to speak coarsely and disrespectfully like this: "Dear Devil, if you can't do any better than that, kiss my toe. I have no time for you now."† The original German places the anatomy in question a bit higher on the body.

Confessional conversation like this took place between Luther and a maturing believer, no longer a guilty and estranged Child. It was conducted Adult-to-Adult between two individuals on common footing, seeking to bring life into an ongoing relationship of trust, self-assessment, growing health, and well-being. The major battle for spiritual orientation had been won. The search was on for whatever relevant responses can be made to any remaining encumbrance to a full life of the spirit.

We witness Adult/Adult confession throughout the history of spiritual direction. In the eighteenth century, William Law wrote pithy and searching letters with spiritual advice for all occasions. His *Spiritual Call to a Devout and Holy Life* encouraged daily self-examination and confession

---

* *Ibid.*, p. 85.
† *Ibid.*, p. 90.

by the individual believer without benefit of priest or spiritual advisor. The Oxford Movement of the nineteenth century sought to restore the confessional, claiming *The Anglican Prayer Book* authorized "entire absolution" for the penitent. It developed practices of group confession with widespread influence that we shall consider presently. Quakers also practiced mutual admonition and correction, commissioning overseers to visit those in trouble and give spiritual support. This was akin to similar measures of "fraternal correction" found in Calvinism.

Two things characterized Adult/Adult confessional practice. First, there was an open examination of lifestyle and the full range of human experience in search of mental and physical well-being that pressed far beyond mere forgiveness of sins. One sought to bring all of life into some kind of harmonious relationship with God and with fellow human beings. Second, despite the tendency of some forms of spiritual direction to elevate human counsel to a superior position, the spiritual director was no longer an official or necessary representative of God with more power and influence by virtue of some holy office. Increasingly, he or she was seen as another human being, no different from the person receiving guidance, extending the task of confessional self-reflection firmly throughout the entire body of believers.

Parent-to-Child Confession

With the emergence of spiritual direction came a third level of confessional relationships best characterized as Parent-to-Child. These were positive confessions of faith earned through the process of a full confessional experience. Their own relevant responses in personal confessions took shape as affirmations of what they had come to believe. They had acquired their expertise by having been through what they now guided others to undertake. The early church was accustomed to such a confessional stance among its "Fathers." Both Peter and Paul described themselves as "Chief among sinners"—Peter because he denied his Lord, Paul because he persecuted the Christians. Their authority lay in their own personal experience of judgment and forgiveness, enabling them to show others the way.

This progression from confession of sins to an emergent confession of faith grew among spiritual directors who began to advocate certain practices that had helped them. Their own faith began to take shape as personal formulations of what enabled them to cope with their own particular human predicament: "This is what I have found to be true. I have faith in it because it has helped me and because I know how to follow its process, and I believe it can help you too." The Recovery movement in our time follows this ancient formula. Expertise in overcoming addictions is established by having been there, done that. The role of parent, counselor, or guide in most spiritual direction has been regarded as a temporary one, assisting a beginner to move through a process one had completed for oneself.

Most spiritual directors developed beliefs of their own through their personal experience with the confessional process. This was true of Augustine, whose personal struggles against "fornication with the world" led him to the faith statement "Love God and do what you want." William Law warned against running after spiritual advice on every occasion. He concluded that "a state of absolute resignation, naked faith, and pure love of God" was the highest form of perfection. Luther's earthy encouragement to battle temptations, sickness, depression, and anxiety grew out of his own bouts with melancholy. By attributing sinfulness to the work of the devil, he provided a vivid means of fighting against its grip over one's life. Contemporary narrative therapists who develop interventions that externalize one's symptoms or problems as "outside" the self can only admire his ability to muster the resources of his "clients" that way.

Of course these affirmations of faith among spiritual directors remained open to perversion and abuse. There were spiritual directors who insisted their followers commit their "soul and will" to them as disciples, demanding complete submission. Any form of spiritual direction or counsel that fetters one person's conscience to another's will and refuses to move toward Adult/Adult parity is open to an escalating abuse of power and control.

When incorporated into the body of organized religion, this mentality is capable of large-scale atrocities. Its perspective was present in the Inquisition, the Crusades, the forced conversions, the bitter excommunications, the burnings of heretics at the stake, and the holy wars and holocausts that blight Christian history. On a smaller scale, the doors are opened to an abuse of power whenever authority figures deny their personal limitations, underestimate their capacity to make distorted perceptions or judgments, and blind themselves to any tendencies to exploit others. It is all too easy to shrink from confronting the unacceptable in our own lives and project it onto others. Such "defense mechanisms" are well known to practicing psychotherapists. They are unwitting confessions, Parent-to-Child, made by persons who unconsciously choose to deal with their unresolved sense of "sinfulness" by coming to hate, fear, and persecute others who remind them of their own internal struggle. The good fathers of Salem, Massachusetts, made such a confession when they tried two local barmaids, Bridget Bishop and Susanna Martin, for witchcraft because they "left their bodies" and hovered as "shapes" over the beds of several prominent male elders, disturbing their sleep.* James Michener wrote of similar unwitting confessions among missionaries in Hawaii

---

* See Starkey, Marion Lena. *The Devil in Massachusetts* (New York: A.A. Knopf, 1949) for a study of this period in New England history.

battling the mores of a peaceful society to impose Western culture, even dress codes, blindly wedding spirituality to colonial exploitation.* Most clinicians have seen the preoccupation of parents who married hurriedly to cover the early advent of their first child make a comparable confession through bombarding a daughter with admonitions, surveillance, and overcautious suspicion when she begins to date. Such obsessions with the unacceptable often provide the framework for struggles that are repeated from one generation to another. Our blind spots often convey an elegant and unconscious confession of what we would deny.

The Salem witch trials in sixteenth-century Massachusetts etched into history the tragedy of such failures in self-awareness to confront unconscious Parent/Child confession. The city fathers not only had to deal with troublesome barmaids, but there was a whole world of lizards, red cats, spectral murder, rape, and other forbidden contaminations of the soul that came from permitting any such "league with the devil" to go unconfessed. The city court was forced to uncover spiritual excesses of the fabled "Witch's Sabbath" with maypoles and dancing, and bright colors that stood out in resplendent protest against the stark gray sky of New England theocracy. Witches came to represent release from virtually all the rigidities of stern Puritan life. One "warlock" was hung because he believed that "all men were created equal" and should be permitted to vote whether or not they belonged to the church.

Sometimes, under such circumstances, it is difficult to tell the difference between God and the Devil. These excesses of an age past are not simply isolated perversions of Parent/Child confession. The urge to eliminate in others what we cannot forgive in ourselves can become a part of any life, religious or otherwise. We simply have trouble accepting in another person what we fear in ourselves. Perhaps this is why John Calvin could consent to the city council of Geneva deciding to burn Servetus at the stake for heresy, or Luther turned his back on the peasants who rebelled against the oppression of their German princes.

Child-to-Child Confession

A fourth level of confession is based upon the bond of mutual self-disclosure. It becomes possible only in a nurturing, accepting climate that makes it safe to share. The relationship is best characterized as Child/Child because its qualities of intimacy, spontaneity, and creativity are so characteristic of what Eric Berne described as the Natural or Free Child ego state, present in persons of all ages. Beneath Adult/Adult exchange that has reached full parity, there can come a growing energy of mutual

---

* Michener, James. *Hawaii* (New York: Fawcett Crest Books, 1973).

transparency and self-disclosure. Conversation takes place in an expanded space of open and shared trust. The estrangement of guilt or shame has been overcome, making it permissible to speak of whatever troubles us most and whatever matters most. Mutual acceptance is assured, whatever is shared. At this level of confession, we can come to love our wounds and to integrate the darker side of our personal story as a vital source of what makes us who we are.

These four levels of confession are not mutually exclusive, separate, or distinct. A natural progression exists from the restorative process of Child/Parent confession, where the concern is overcoming guilt and estrangement, toward an Adult/Adult stance of growing relational parity, where the issue is more personal growth and spiritual fulfillment than belonging, already secured. A sense of camaraderie lays the groundwork for Child/Child confession as one moves through the first two levels. The struggles of self-encounter give way to the satisfactions of mutual self-disclosure and openness. Child/Child confession can sustain communal life on an ongoing basis in the way more private and individualistic levels cannot.

Some practice of group confession formed a vital part of common life in the New Testament community. The Reformers insisted upon "the priesthood of all believers," which envisioned a congregation of people engaged in hearing one another's confessions, reassuring one another of forgiveness, and creating an ongoing relationship of mutual care. These ideas persisted in the Pietism that sprang up in the midst of the German Lutheran Church. There, Jacob Spener led a protest against prevailing practices of private confession. He insisted that every earnest Christian could join in confidential friendship with other understanding, enlightened believers, rendering account to each other.

Such a vision of mutual care has never been easily realized in the life of organized religion. There have been a number of significant movements with this purpose in mind. Among the Moravians, Count von Zinzendorf organized their community into small groups known as "choirs." Their purpose, however, was not singing. Married persons, the widowed, bachelors or maidens, and children each had their special group in which members could confide and share the concerns of their souls. A choir could be broken down into smaller "bands" containing two or three persons to permit even more personal interchange, concern, confession, and care for one another. For the Moravians, everyone's daily behavior became a matter of mutual discernment, confrontation, and constant encouragement.

The Methodist movement in seventeenth-century England grew out of a visit from John Wesley to the Moravian community. He returned to form Methodist societies, subdivided into "classes," each with twelve people and a leader. Members learned to confess their faults, make known their temptations, and open their souls to everyone present. To belong, members had to express a desire to be told their faults, even if it were to "cut to the quick." Then it was their task to accept what criticism each person posed around the circle. All were there to help each other work out their daily living through bearing one another's burdens and supporting each other in personal growth.

The Oxford Movement among Anglicans in the 1800s set out to recover the practice of confession in small group meetings. Four activities dominated their efforts. First, everyone was encouraged to engage in rigorous self-examination. This was followed by individual confession of character defects before the group. The third step was to carry out some kind of restitution to anyone whom they had harmed. Finally, all group members took on the task of working with others who stood in need of help. The practice of group confession in the Oxford Movement spread to Episcopal congregations in the United States where it proved influential to several of the founders of Alcoholics Anonymous. Confessing debilitating aspects of one's private story to a group became a regular practice, not only at AA meetings, but also throughout the recovery movement that followed treating addictions and traumas of all kinds. I have heard a number of women recovering from sexual abuse tell their stories without shame, overcoming the isolation of their untold secrets. Sharing their wounds with others brought healing, sometimes tearfully, sometimes determinedly, sometimes joyfully.

The power of such Child-to-Child disclosures within an accepting group can display itself in many settings. There are times in group therapy when suddenly an intimacy and a closeness envelop the process of self-disclosure. Everyone is drawn together around the courage and openness of someone's confession. Yesterday it was Randolf who spoke quietly of his fear, despair, and loneliness in facing his approaching death from an inoperable malignancy. Perhaps nothing isolates us from those around so busy with life as the awareness of our inevitable death. Randolf's confession managed to break through that isolation and establish authentic conversation in which everyone shared openly, Child-to-Child, their own angst, hope, warmth, and appreciation for one another. Bathed in this energy, Randolf's isolation melted into a sense of oneness and solidarity. We all must struggle with death—together or alone.

More Conclusions

By this stage of our discussion, more conclusions are evident. First, the main purpose of confession is no longer the amelioration of sin. As the practice evolved, notions of a final judgment and the avoidance of eternal punishment in hell receded. Once the confessional conversation moved beyond its first level of Child/Parent exchange, its aim was clearly spiritual growth. Instead of preparing us to die, it prepares us to live.

Second, in the process of addressing what troubles us deeply, new meanings to life emerge. New beliefs are formed as we discover ways to overcome or cope with aspects of the human predicament. Confession of sin and confession of faith merge in natural progression. Through the very process of grappling with what troubles us most, we come to learn what is most important, even sacred, to each of us.

Third, a sense of encounter with a Presence greater than ourselves is often a part of confessional experiences. We are somehow met by a quantum of power, purpose, and direction that religious people call God. Those not given to religious language may choose to call it something else, which in no way lessens its force or activity or influence. The practice of confession serves as a potential wellspring of spiritual growth for anyone.

Finally, any recovery of the practice of confession in our time will originate through one or more of these levels we have discussed. It could be happening frequently outside the doors of organized religion. It becomes possible wherever two or three are gathered together, and there is such candor and self-disclosure. Honest confession may take place within marriages, families, study and support groups, psychotherapy, friendships, and even within our business, political, and corporate relationships where it is direly needed. And who knows when and where else?

Practice

Where does our conscience come from? Almost everyone agrees we get it from our parents along with other significant authority figures. Eric Berne locates it in the Parent ego state. In Walt Disney's *Pinocchio*, Jiminy Cricket's melodious advice to the young puppet is: "Always let your conscience be your guide." That's tantamount to saying, "Always do what your Parent tells you to do." That may work pretty well for a puppet but most of us mature to a point where we want to think for ourselves. We want to be like Pinocchio when he became a real boy and sang, "I got no strings on me." But our conscience often attaches strings to our experience—some wise and good, some oppressive, and some downright harmful.

There is an important step I want to add in considering a *relevant response* in your confessions. Don't simply take feeling guilty, ashamed, anxious, or troubled for granted without exploring the makeup of your conscience. Develop your own way of determining what "Parent tapes" may be playing in your head. Often we fail to put words to precisely what bothers us. Never simply let yourself "feel bad." Reflect with care on your internal dialogue— who is talking in your head? Normally the Child in you is reacting to old messages in your Parent ego state. Sometimes you remember them intact. Other times a scene flashes before your mind's eye in which the message was delivered. Sometimes only the feeling remains, and you have to turn your imagination loose to discover associations with figures in your past whose influence drones on in oppressive and outworn ways.

There are a number of methods to determine the source of what's in your conscience. It may be enough simply to interrupt your ruminations, sit down, and establish awareness of who is speaking in your head. This may help you decide if what is being said is worth listening to. You use your Adult for that. If that doesn't work, get out a piece of paper and write down in full sentences what you're telling yourself about the event at hand. Then record your response to what you see or hear or understand. Most of us are surprised at how much clearer an issue gets once we give it our full attention, especially when we take time to write it out or journal about it.

The purpose of this simple exercise is to shift an internal dialogue of Child/Parent confession or rumination to Adult self-reflection. Of course, if this were as simple as I have described, we would all be doing it by now. Most of the matters that trouble us deeply are soundly ingrained in our mental processes. Many, especially the ones that trigger shame or anxiety, were installed when we were so young we can't remember how. Or we heard them so often and from so many people that we take them for granted. This is especially true of religious teachings that start with parents, priests, Sunday School teachers, nuns, ministers, preachers, bishops, sons of bishops, etc. Many of our ideas about God were forged upon the anvil of such relationships. Sometimes, as in Salem, Massachusetts, it is difficult to tell the difference between God and the Devil. Clarity and relief from many internal conflicts can require a number of sittings, considerations, conversations, and conclusions, even with paper and journal in hand, particularly when it comes to what God says or doesn't say. The exercises that follow can be of real help.

Self-Awareness and Internal Dialogue

1. When the above measures don't accomplish clarity of conscience, you may want to externalize your internal dialogue. You can go off by yourself where you will not be disturbed. Get a chair for your Parent ego state, another for your Child. Either one can speak first. If you feel guilty, ashamed, or anxious and are not sure why, get in the Child chair and address your "conscience" in the Parent chair. If you've already formulated what your conscience will say, you can start there. Conduct a conversation by getting up to speak and answer from each chair so that the Child in you has been thoroughly instructed about what you did wrong.

2. It is quite possible at this point that one or more "faces" have been attached to figures who spoke from the Parent chair. If not, get back in the Child chair and listen once more to what has been said. If necessary, speak each Parent message again from that

chair to the Child, then move to the Child chair and permit your imagination to construct the source.

3. You are now in position to determine what kind of response you wish to make to your conscience. It is important to pursue your internal dialogue to some conclusion of your choice. Otherwise you may just return to "feeling bad." Try deciding from the Child chair first. Then check it out from a third chair for your Adult. It is okay to talk to your Child from the Adult position about your objective reflections on what your conscience has said. This proves easier than it sounds after you've done it a few times.

4. There is another step if you remain undecided as to how to distinguish between what you actually believe and what others have told you about God. This is particularly helpful if you have difficulty forgiving yourself for some action or feel at odds with God for one reason or another. Add still another chair for God. Take the Child chair and address "your God" directly in that chair. Then without knowing what will be said in response, take God's chair and answer the way you imagine your God responding based on your own personal experience with a caring Presence in your life. I have worked with people who have needed to "decontaminate" their idea of what God says from what others have told them God says. If God sounds like everybody else or some particularly influential individual, I have encouraged them to make certain they distinguish to their Adult satisfaction any difference between their Parent ego state and their own perceptions of God.

Confessional Partnership

1. Some reflection on the four types of confessional relationships can prove beneficial. How many of them can you identify in your own conversations?

2. Confessional partners can be of assistance in sorting out your internal dialogue. In fact, it is often beneficial to do the above exercise with your partner, who can encourage you to carry the conversation to a full conclusion. Often by ourselves we are prone to stop prematurely, particularly when the going becomes difficult.

3. An effective team of confessional partners can move the conversation easily to the Adult/Adult level when reflecting on matters of conscience. Reactions to one another can be of genuine benefit. Relevant responses for the confessor can receive an imaginative exploration that is always enhanced by connections at the Child/Child level of exchange.

Discussion Group

1. Consider each of the four types of confessional relationships outlined in this chapter. Members of the group may offer examples or experiences of each.
2. Flesh out some of the differences between what Martin Buber called an "I–Thou" relationship as opposed to an "I–it" relationship. Is such intimacy possible with yourself? With others? With the world around? With our Creator?
3. What safeguards may we consider when we look at the task of spiritual direction? How can we guard against the excesses of the past? Are there parallels to the Inquisition, the Crusades, or the witch hunts in our own time?
4. The manner in which we deal with our conscience is worth considerable attention. Discuss different kinds of responses we can make to our internal dialogue. What measures can we take to break the grip of debilitating influences from the past?

Confessional Group

1. It is possible for the confessional group to assist a confessor in the same way confessional partners do. This is particularly true in matters of conscience where Adult-to-Adult reflection can greatly expand self-awareness and imaginative responsiveness.
2. Chair work in externalizing an internal dialogue is well suited to the group process. In fact, the group rapport may enhance the potential for its successful completion and resolution. Members may coach and encourage each other in ways unavailable to individuals and pairs working alone.
3. The group may choose to identify as many instances of the four types of confessional relationships as it can in its experience together so far.
4. Members of the group may benefit by reflecting on potential points of involuntary confession (Parent/Child) discovered in sources of repeated antagonism and resentment toward other persons.

CHAPTER 7

Women in Confession

Julian of Norwich and Margery Kempe

When I asked my good friend Louis Weeks, a church historian, to read the chapters on our confessors, he made a number of valuable suggestions. One idea stood out above the rest: find some confessions by women. Easier said than done.

Of course, there were prominent women of faith, but well into the Middle Ages, it was customary for men to write about them. This delayed women from writing confessions for centuries. To qualify, confessions must be autobiographical self-disclosures addressing key issues in one's private story. I finally came across two women who were born 40 miles from each other in fourteenth-century England. In fact, their paths actually crossed in later life. Both Julian of Norwich and Margery Kempe wrote within our criteria. Well, not exactly, because Margery Kempe couldn't read or write. But after a somewhat prominent career, she reputedly dictated her life story to one or more persons who served as scribes.

Julian Of Norwich

Julian of Norwich was born in 1342 and lived to 1413, perhaps even to 1426. From a family of good standing, she was well educated and well read. People in fourteenth-century England lived in an insecure world. There were fires, wars, rebellions, persecutions, and famine. In addition, there were the plagues of 1349, 1361, and 1369, and the Black Death came to Norwich where Julian lived. The times were marked by the rise of the miracle play, Gothic art, and stained-glass windows. It was a time of religious excess and emotion in which there was often conflict between the crown and the established church.

Near-Death Experience

Perhaps it was the plagues that unsettled Julian's privileged life. At 30 she wrote, "God sent me a bodily sickness."[*] She thought for 3 days that she was on her deathbed. On the third night, not expecting to survive, she received last rites from her priest. Instead, she lived 2 more days; then once again became certain that death was at hand. Her friends sent for her curate who placed a cross before her for comfort. The lower part of her body was already lifeless, and the upper part was beginning to die. As her pain increased, she became short of breath and certain this was the end. Suddenly, all her pain dissolved; she was as sound as ever and astounded by her sudden healing.

During the ordeal, Julian experienced numerous visions. When she recovered, she concluded they were nothing more than delirious ravings. Later she had another vision in which she was convinced she had experienced genuine spiritual revelations. Sharing her encounter with death and the inspirations that followed shaped the remainder of her life. For decades afterward, she continued to receive inspired teachings that expanded the ideas that came in her initial mystical experience.

Later on, Julian began to wish for a "second wound as a gift and a grace." She wanted her body to experience pain in order to share Jesus' "blessed Passion" and suffer with him.[†] A vision of Christ's bleeding head became for her the "spiritual sight of his familiar love." He showed her something small, no bigger than a hazel nut, in the palm of her hand. She saw three things: first, God made it; second, God loves it, and third, God preserves it. She knew she could never have perfect rest or true happiness until there was nothing in creation standing between her and this Creator-Lover-Protector she had come to know.

In 1393, Julian entered anchorage in a special room built onto the side of the church in Norwich. Her cell had two windows; one opened to the church where she could see Mass and receive the holy sacrament, and the other opened out to the world where she could entertain conversation with others and receive the services of those who cared for her needs. Her daily life as an anchoress was built around her threefold vow of obedience, chastity, and constancy of abode. She would never again come out of her cell. Inside, she lived a simple life, making clothes for the poor, shaping and sewing church vestments, meditating, and writing.

---

[*] *Revelations of Divine Love*, Translated by M. L. Del Mastro (New York: Doubleday, 1977), Chapter 3.

[†] *Ibid.*

Meanwhile, she became quite well known on the outside. Through her tiny portal to the world, she conducted consultations with rich and poor alike. She became what amounted to a modern-day pastoral counselor without peer. Margery Kempe, whom readers are soon to meet, was among those who came to see her.

Sin and Shame

Quietly across the years, Julian's lifelong confessional pattern began to take shape. She struggled with the idea of her sinfulness but eventually concluded that she "did not see sin" and decided it had "no kind of substance."* For Julian, pain and suffering came to constitute the royal road to spiritual experience. Those who suffered as Christ did shared his joy in heaven. God showed her that there was no need for shame in our sinfulness; in fact, sin brought honor to human kind in a rather strange way. She reasoned that because for every sin there is an answering pain in reality, thus for every pain, bliss is also given to the same soul. This became her formula: sin produces pain, which in turn yields eternal joy in heaven, so all those who are known by the church on earth for their sins can see "how these sins are no shame to them but have been transformed to their glory."†

Julian thought it was necessary that we fall and recognize that we did. God may allow some of us to fall harder and more seriously than we have on previous occasions, but this is no cause to doubt all of our wisdom and believe that everything we have begun amounts to nothing. If we did not fall and experience how feeble and wretched we are, we would not know "the marvelous love of our maker." At the same time, we can realize that we "never lost any of his love, nor were we ever of less worth in his sight."‡ To Julian, all our efforts to label some deeds well done and other deeds evil were not of great consequence to God, for everything that has being is of God's creation and therefore in some way fitting to God's purposes. She believed God had ordained all things from the beginning. And it was "more worship to God to behold him in all than in any special thing."

So preoccupation with sinfulness and scrupulosity fell by the wayside in Julian's quest to become one with her Creator. She had no hesitancy to acknowledge that in "ourselves we are right nought but sin and wretchedness." But through this "meek knowing," we are broken from all that stands between us and our Lord. This makes way for our Savior "to perfectly heal us, and one us to Him." This breaking and healing process was meant for all humankind. So regarding sin, Julian wrote:

---

* *Op. Cit.*, Chapter 38.
† *Ibid.*
‡ *Op. Cit.*, Chapter 61.

He willeth not that we busy us greatly about our accusing
ourselves for our sins, nor He willeth not that we be
wretched over our self; but He willeth that we hastily
turn ourselves unto Him. … For we are His joy and His
delight, and He is our salve and our life.*

God Our Mother

The feminine experience is already apparent in Julian's perception of God.
Gone are the harsh, judgmental images of a patriarchal God the Father.
Grace, she wrote, transforms our failings full of dread into "abundant
endless comfort." Grace turns our shame into a noble, glorious rising, our
dying full of sorrow into a holy, blissful life. Grace and mercy go together
to form the kind of love we know only in the "motherhood of Christ."

"I saw no difference between God and our substance," wrote Julian, "but
I saw as if it were all God."† This mystical "oneing with God" lay at the center of her experience. She called it "a lofty understanding inwardly to see
and to know that God, who as our maker dwells in our soul." But it was an
even loftier and greater understanding "to see and to know that our soul,
which is created, dwells in God's substance." She wrote with a sense that we
are all somehow "enclosed" within the Creator's presence. In our making,
"he knitted us and joined us to himself." In this joining, we are somehow
"kept as clean and as noble as we were created to be" by God's love.

In these beliefs, Julian anchored herself to Catholic orthodoxy, both literally and figuratively. She held fast to her Trinitarian understandings but
never hesitated to put her womanly spin on its character. She wrote that
in our creation, "God Almighty is our natural father, and God all-wisdom
is our natural mother, with the love and goodness of the holy spirit." She
could speak of the second person of the Trinity as "our Mother" both in
nature and in substance. Jesus became "Christ our Mother" in whom we are
grounded and rooted. In this way, our "high God, the sovereign wisdom of
all" made himself entirely ready in the low place of our poor flesh in order
to do "the service and the office of motherhood himself in all things."‡

Julian's idea of herself somehow "enfolded" into "oneness" with her
Creator, sharing the substantial presence of a motherhood of God in her
soul, caused her to discard any preoccupation with how grievously we may
sin. Whatever we have done, there is a Mother's love that is never damaged, and we are never of less worth in God's sight. She freely employs the
metaphor of mother and child to describe this belief. If we are filled with
shame at falling into wretchedness, God our Mother absorbs our fear and

---

* *Op. Cit.*, Chapter 79.
† *Op. Cit.*, pp. 179, 180.
‡ *Op. Cit.*, pp. 191, 192.

dread, urging us not to flee. Instead, God wills that we own our condition as a child who is hurt and afraid, and run hastily to our Mother for help with all our might.

Gone is the traditional Judgment Day of orthodoxy with threats of condemnation and eternal punishment. In its place stands God our Mother whose arms remain extended and open to all her children. Julian insists it is impossible to seek mercy and grace without already having experienced them. She believes that whatever we seek in God has been ordained and present for us from the beginning. "For I am sure," she wrote, "that no man asketh mercy and grace with true meaning, but if mercy and grace be first given him."[*]

As for the wrath of God so prominent to the Middle Ages, Julian observed that she saw none, except on "man's part." For wrath is "a contrariness to peace and love," and it comes through either some failing of might, failing of wisdom, or failing of goodness. None of these is a failing of God, but a failing on our part.

Self-Knowledge

Julian was convinced that we could never come to know God fully until we first clearly knew our own soul. Deep within herself she encountered a feeling of being "enclosed" by God. A sense of mystical union of the soul with God permeated all her thinking. Our soul was made to be God's dwelling place, and the dwelling place of the soul was God. A sense of "oneing" with God came only through a full knowledge of ourselves. If you wanted to find God, look within.

Julian's solution to the human predicament was to become a seeker. It was the continual seeking of the soul that pleased God fully. She suggested three ways. First, seek the presence of God earnestly, diligently, and gracefully, without unreasonable heaviness and vain sorrow. Second, "abide in Him steadfastly," without murmuring or striving against him. And third, "trust in Him mightily" with an assured faith that he shall appear suddenly and blissfully to all that love him.[†]

Julian's life as a closet feminist in the fourteenth century boggles the mind. She remained loyal to the traditional church of her time while feminizing its theology with the motherhood of Christ. She quietly transformed orthodox ideas of our sinfulness into an occasion for grace and mercy. Perhaps the cell in which she anchored herself outside the church, looking in, fully attached, yet separate, is an apt metaphor for how she lived her life. Some of her ideas, as we shall see, have far-reaching implications for even our contemporary scene. For the present, let us take note that, for her, the

---

[*] *Op. Cit.*, Chapter 42.
[†] *Op. Cit.*, Chapter 10.

confession of sin resolved itself into an ongoing confession of the faith of a seeker.

Margery Kempe

We turn now to Margery Kempe, whose deeply troubled life was very different. Julian was well educated, while Margery could not read or write. Whereas Julian was devoutly chaste, Margery was very sexual and produced 14 children. Julian remained devoted to the church; Margery challenged the patience of more than one archbishop. Where Julian lived out her life in quiet anchorage, Margery traveled the world on three extended pilgrimages, dressing flamboyantly and weeping inordinately. She was, to say the least, a character no one could ignore.

The Book of Margery Kempe lay undiscovered and virtually unknown until 1934 when Miss Hope Emily Allen found it in the library of Col. Butler-Bowdon at Lancashire, England.* Recognized by some as the first autobiography written by a woman in English, scholars have puzzled over precisely how the manuscript took shape. Tradition has it that Margery told her story to two separate scribes at two different periods in her life. It survived in the form of sacred biography in which the lives of holy women were verified by male scribes. Because Medieval texts were seen as communal, scribes who copied them often offered commentaries linking them to the values of their own community. Some scholars identify editorial comments in this work from as many as four different scribes. Others claim the book is fictional or, at best, legendary. But Margery becomes so real that most readers readily accept the story as her own.

Early Life and Visions

Margery Kempe was born in 1373, the daughter of John Burnham, who was five times mayor of the English town of Lynn. For some strange reason, she was never taught to read, which was very unusual for the daughter of so prominent a public figure. Literacy was a normal accomplishment for a middle-class girl of the times. As a result, she was thrown inordinately upon her own mental resources, which may account in part for some of her emotional difficulties. Also, there was the matter of some secret sin of which Margery refused to speak that plagued her for years. One commentator speculates it was something relatively minor, perhaps in the nature of a sexual peccadillo. I suspect it was more than that, given her subsequent history of emotional instability and her preoccupation with her sexual urges. Whatever the case, we will never know, as we shall see.

---

* See *The Book of Margery Kempe*, Edited by Lynn Staley (Kalamazoo, Michigan: Western Michigan University for Teams, 1996). Available online.

In 1393, Margery married John Kempe, a young merchant in town. Although the arranged marriages of the time often left much to be desired, Margery and John appeared to have had a very good one. John was very understanding for a man, and Margery seemed to take considerable pleasure in physical love. She soon became pregnant. The birth was very difficult with prolonged labor. The views of the time surrounding childbirth did not help. Pain that accompanied it was regarded as the curse of Eve. Little to no attention was paid to easing labor or to the possibility of complications, resulting in many women dying in delivery or going "mad." So there was little sympathy for the mother. It was common to believe women deserved all this torment as partial expiation for any sexual pleasure leading to the birth. Eve's sin of having tempted Adam, precipitating humankind's fall from grace, was even regarded as an added reason for such suffering.

Following the birth of her first child, Margery fell ill and "went out of her mind." She became "vexed and labored" with devilish spirits for more than 6 months. She feared death and an eternity of what she had been through—profound pain without dignity or understanding. She asked for a priest in order to confess the hidden sin of her youth that she had kept secret from all. Whatever happened next was most unfortunate. When the priest arrived, Margery began to cry uncontrollably. For some reason, her bawling so upset her confessor that he began to yell at her before she ever got to confess her big sin. Margery panicked and bolted hopelessly to the window, trying to throw herself out. She blasphemed against Christendom, her faith, her God, the Holy Mother, and all the saints in heaven. She slandered her husband, her friends, her father, her mother, as though she "knew no goodness and desired all wickedness."[*]

Margery's husband, John, hired keepers who locked her in a storeroom. There she bit through the veins on her wrists. When she was chained to her bed, she kept crying out for months on end. It was here Margery had the vision that changed her life. One day, she looked up and Jesus Christ was standing there. He said to her, "Daughter, why have you forsaken me when I never forsook you?"

Following these words, Jesus rose in the air into a bright light that opened before her. Immediately she was "stabled in her wits and in her reason as well as she was before." Her keepers were upset. But as soon as John saw her, he trusted her and ordered her unchained. That night she sat down to supper, again the mistress of her own house, as sound as she had ever been. She threw herself into her station in life with renewed energy. The crisis she had been through sounds like more than any simple case of

---

[*] *Op. Cit.*, Chapter 1.

post-partum depression. My guess is she had an acute psychotic episode that was somehow thrown into spontaneous remission.

The Struggle for Freedom

Upon her recovery, Margery filled her wardrobe with the latest styles of the day, becoming Lynn's most flamboyant dresser. She was, of course, John Burnham's daughter and privy to the privileges of the mayor's station in the community. She turned an eye toward the industrious medieval marketplace on the rise around her. First, she went into a brewing business that flourished for 2 or 3 years. She became the biggest beer-maker in town. Then, when business declined, she formed a horse-drawn milling company. It too failed, causing Margery considerable humiliation. In her defense, she must have been somewhat preoccupied during this time, having 14 children, one after another. But she couldn't be just a housewife. Although she failed as an entrepreneur, she looked for something else to which she could devote her seemingly endless energies.

At this point, Margery had her second vision of the Christ. It became clear to her that she should devote herself entirely to Christ's service. This meant chastity, which served for centuries as a means of survival for many religious women, enabling them to escape an endless chain of pregnancies. When she posed her desire to John, he agreed that it might be a good idea someday, but not just yet. The children kept coming. Finally, as Margery's desperation grew, one night when John made advances, she cried out, "O dear Jesus Christ, Save me, Jesus!" And quite miraculously, John didn't feel amorous anymore.

Even with John's cooperation, however, chastity was not easy for Margery. She was a sensual woman with an eye for the men. One day after church, she yielded to temptation and propositioned a young man who attracted her. But he ran away, yelling he would rather be cut up into little pieces for a stewpot than to sleep with her. When Margery confessed her sin to God, God told her she had to have something in her life for which to do penance.

After that, Margery upped her church attendance and did some personal fasting. And she began to cry lengthily, frequently, publicly, and conspicuously. Opinion on the streets of Lynn was split about evenly as to whether her behavior was the work of God or the work of the Devil. So Margery began to search for needed credentials and support against charges of demon possession.

In 1413, John Burnham died, leaving Margery a substantial inheritance. England had gone to war with France; business was bad, and John Kempe found himself deep in debt. Margery announced she would rather see him killed than submit to him sexually anymore. The two of them agreed that if Margery would pay off his debts, he would sign a contract of chastity, and she could be free to pursue her mission to serve God and wear white.

Pilgrimages and Service

Around 1413, Margery began a series of pilgrimages to places she considered holy and to authorities who might confirm her way of life. Her particular form of asceticism involved an uncontrollable need to pray and to weep loudly and at length, which held little appeal for her neighbors or the clergy of Lynn. Perhaps the pilgrimages were, in part, a means of escaping local criticism. Her book gives an account of her travels, her conversations with various people, and her visionary experiences on these journeys.

Armed with newfound freedom, Margery set out with John for the shrine of St. Thomas Becket. She spent the day moaning and crying before the shrine. John retired to a less conspicuous place at the hotel. A monk from the nearby monastery challenged her credentials, and she told him she knew God. Doubting her claim, he asked her to name his "secret sin." She did so without hesitation, "Lechery." Taken aback by her accuracy, he asked whether it was with a married woman or a single one. "Married," she replied. And he acknowledged her to be "a right holy woman." Nevertheless, she and John had to slip out of town before a gathering mob pursued her, thinking she was a Lollard.

Now Lollards were followers of John Wycliffe, who challenged the authority of the Pope and a number of practices dear to the organized church of their time. The Lollard manifesto, known as *The Conclusions of 1395*, advanced a number of ideas distasteful to religious authorities. For instance, it charged that the priesthood of the church was not the priesthood Christ gave to the apostles. A thirst for temporal possessions had ruined the church and driven out the Christian graces of faith, hope, and charity. The monk's vow of celibacy only created an unnatural lust and should not be imposed. Taking the sacraments gave no assurance of salvation. Confession made to the clergy and declared necessary for salvation was the root of clerical arrogance. *The Conclusions of 1395* threatened the very seat of Catholic orthodoxy. It was a dangerous time to be a Lollard or a member of any other group deviating from prevailing practices of the church. The Lollards, the Hussites, and their likes were always one step away from heresy and two steps away from the execution block. So Margery's "service" required solid credentialing in the eyes of the church, especially if she were to wear white as a symbol of chastity and travel with a husband. Although her spectacular demonstrations of personal piety were not uncommon in her day, they served to imply she did not trust that the sacraments of the church provided sufficient means for salvation.

Yet it was more than credentialing that drove Margery to the sanctuaries and shrines. She knew many people suspected she was putting on a show to draw attention. Her certainty of God's special friendship was challenged by doubt from time to time. Recognition of her gifts by religious authorities would prove reassuring. She began with William Southfield, the White Friar of Norwich. She met him in his chapel to determine "if she were deceived by any illusions...." All the time she spoke, this good man held up his hands and said, "Jesus, mercy and thanks be to Jesus." As she was leaving, he said to her, "Sister, have no fear about your manner of life, for it is the Holy Ghost plentifully working his grace in your soul."[*]

Then she went to see Dame Julian, the anchoress of Norwich. She told Julian about her revelations and the compassion God had put into her soul, in order to discover if there were any deception in them. Julian told her to fulfill with all her might whatever God put into her soul, "if it were not against the worship of God and the profit of her fellow Christians."[†] Others she visited bore witness that there was no delusion in her manner of living, but they did counsel her to persevere because they were afraid she would waver before so many enemies and so much slander.

Wherever Margery went on her journeys, she encountered opposition and mockery. On her pilgrimage to the Holy Land, she spent so much time crying and falling off her donkey that her companions deserted her. On the trip to the shrine of St. James in Spain, her fellow travelers became so tired of her talking about religion that they threatened to throw her into the sea. Her visions continued on occasion. In the Church of the Holy Apostles at Rome, she experienced a mystical marriage with God, who expressed his pleasure that she believed in the sacraments of the Holy Church, especially in the manhood of Jesus, and in the suffering he endured.[‡] It was common among women mystics to think of themselves as becoming "the bride of Christ," but marital union with God the Father was a bit excessive. So was her vision of the presence of the Holy Ghost, the mother of Jesus, the 12 apostles, many other saints, holy virgins, and a multitude of angels at the event.

Margery was also filled with a sense of great spiritual and bodily comfort. She sensed sweet smells, sweeter than she had ever smelled before. She heard sounds and melodies daily, especially in times of prayer. She saw many white objects flying about her as thickly as specks in a sunbeam, and they were very delicate and comforting. She felt the fire of love burning in her breast. She was afraid until the Holy Ghost told her it would burn away her sins.

Several readers have questioned including Margery as a confessor, given the radical nature of these experiences. How difficult it must have been to navigate these times as a woman, given the male-dominant oppression one must survive. The grandiose, somewhat hysterical, character of these visions suggests Margery may have suffered occasional recurrences of regression to her psychotic episode in the past. But her struggle to survive with faith

---

[*] *Op. Cit.*, Chapter 18.
[†] *Ibid.*
[‡] *Op. Cit.*, Chapter 35.

makes her worthy of inclusion in this book. This, plus the legendary character of these writings and their communal authorship, should not serve to obscure the plain hard realities of Margery's life. In the summer of 1417, she made her way back from Spain by way of York and London. During the 1420s, she remained at home and began to commit her experiences to writing with the help of a scribe. At some point, her husband John became severely ill, and she nursed him for several years until he died in 1431. By 1433, Margery was ready for another pilgrimage, this time to Norway and Germany. This trip became the subject of the tenth chapter of her second book. She is mentioned in the records of Lynn during 1439, after which we know nothing of her publicly.

Communication and Good Words

Margery had more than one significant clash with the authorities of her day. She describes them with a measure of amusement, despite the fact that the accusations she faced placed her in danger of being burned at the stake. She was constantly preaching and talking about religion as she passed from village to village. On her way home from the pilgrimage to Spain in 1417, she was arrested by the mayor of Leicester, who thought she was a Lollard. She was released when she appealed to the Bishop of York. After stirring up considerable unrest among the local clerics, she was sent to face the Archbishop of York, where she was charged with being a Lollard and a heretic.

The Archbishop inquired why she was dressed in white. Was she a maiden? She answered, "No, she was a wife." The Archbishop put her in fetters and called her a heretic. She told him she wasn't and would prove it to him. The Archbishop said he had been informed she was "a right wicked woman." She told him she had heard he was a wicked man. The Archbishop asked her to lay her hand on the Bible and swear she would get out of his diocese as soon as possible. She insisted that he first give her leave to return to York and say goodbye to her friends. He gave her leave for one or two days. She told him that was too short a time for "I must tarry and speak with good men before I go...."*

And so the battle of wits continued. The Archbishop asked her to swear she would neither teach nor challenge the people in his diocese. She told him "No, she would not swear to anything." A prominent clerk quoted the apostle Paul as saying no woman should preach. Margery answered, "I preach not, sir, I go in no pulpit. I use but communication and good words, and that will I do while I live."†

With that, the Archbishop looked around saying, "Where shall I get a man who might lead this woman from me?" Immediately, a number of

---

* *Op. Cit.*, Chapter 52.
† *Ibid.*

young men came forward offering to do so, but the Archbishop declared them all too young for such a task. He selected a good, sober man from his own household and offered him five shillings to "lead her fast out of this country."

It almost worked. But as luck would have it, Margery went on toward the town of Beverly, meeting many times with the men of the country, refusing their advice to forsake her itinerant teaching and go "spin and card" as other women do. When she ended up again before the poor Archbishop of York, he exclaimed, "What, woman, are you come again? I would fain be delivered of you."

He told her he did not know what to do with her. His steward said to let her go; and if she ever came back, he and his friends would burn her at the stake themselves. Compassionately, Margery offered to leave on her own if the Archbishop would give her a letter upon his seal that nothing was charged against her, neither error nor heresy, provided he again offered his man John to bring her over the water. The Archbishop kindly granted all her desires.

Thus, Margery jousted with martyrdom and escaped. She expressed the desire that her head "might be smitten off with an ax upon the block" to show her love for her Lord Jesus Christ. Still, she decided there was no better way to please God than to think continually in His love. Hers was to be a life of contemplation. She prayed, "Let me never have other joy in earth, but mourning and weeping for thy love...."*

As for her sinfulness, Margery focused her attention upon the great wonder that her Lord would become a man and suffer grievous pains for someone such as her. When in prayer she asked Jesus how she could best please him, he said, "Daughter, have mind of thy wickedness, and think on my goodness." So she prayed many times with the words, "Lord, for Thy great goodness, have mercy on my great wickedness, as certainly as I was never so wicked as thou art good...." For Margery, forgiveness was the paramount purpose of Jesus' life and death. Even in her strongest devotion to him, she remained somehow deeply sexual, praying, "Good Lord, I would be laid naked upon an hurdle for thy love, all men to wonder on me and to cast filth and dirt on me, and be drawen (sic) from town to town every day of my lifetime, if thou were pleased thereby, and no man's soul hindered. Thy will be fulfilled and not mine."†

---

* *Op. Cit.*, Chapter III. Treatise on Contemplation, p. 144.
† *Ibid.*, p. 148.

Faith in a Different Voice

Margery Kempe and Julian of Norwich expressed faith in a different voice from the Catholic orthodoxy of their time. They stood within a tradition of mysticism extending back to the earliest centuries of Western Christianity. Spiritual experience came through encountering a Presence deep within the self. In Julian's case, a kind of "bodily sight" came to her, coupled with words formed in her imagination, and some sort of "ghostly sight" that enlightened her thought processes. Margery saw visions and heard all kinds of conversations in her mind, in addition to smelling odors, hearing music, and feeling physical sensations such as a fire burning in her breast.

Both Margery and Julian embraced self-knowledge as a source of more than the awareness of their sinfulness. Through such heightened self-encounters, their own personal understandings of faith took shape. For Margery, the wretchedness of her own sinful ways paled before the great goodness she experienced in Jesus' suffering. For Julian, any substance of sin melted before the personal pain it created, which in turn enabled her to participate in the greater suffering of "Christ our Mother." Both had little time for searching out and brooding over misdeeds.

Life-threatening crises launched both women on their spiritual encounter. Julian lay on the brink of death, her life slipping away, before her remarkable and spontaneous recovery. Margery experienced despair so profound following the birth of her first child that she tried to throw herself out the window and spent months restrained as a psychotic. For each, visions accompanying their recovery evoked a response of radical change. Julian doubted the validity of her experience at first but eventually became a "seeker." Margery's visions returned after her emotional upheaval was thrown into remission, prompting missions capable of stretching the imagination.

Their lives took quite different courses. While Margery in her white robe caused a stir on widespread pilgrimages with much weeping and public teaching, Julian retired to a life of contemplation, writing, and counseling anchored in a cell at Norwich Church. Julian was self-effacing and utterly humble. Margery was flamboyant, believing herself to be a favorite of God. Julian was quiet and respectful of others, while Margery never hesitated to tell anybody what to do. Julian was loved and respected by all, while Margery was often mocked, derided, and deserted. Julian remained reverent and devoted to the church; Margery was often a thorn in its side and a burr under the saddle of its authorities. Julian's revelations were more of the nature of spiritual reality itself; Margery's were more personal in terms of tasks to perform or missions to carry out.

Both women employed female imagery to describe their spiritual experience. Their gender framed their resolution to their human predicament.

Margery embraced the traditional metaphor in mystical thought of the soul as the bride of Christ. It fit appropriately with her strong and always budding sexuality. She wore her white robe and her wedding ring after she severed her sexual relationship with her husband, later describing her mystical marriage to God the Father. Julian, on the other hand, never used bridal imagery but chose to describe the soul's relationship to God as that of a child to its mother. She focused most of her attention on the motherhood of God and the imagery of Christ as mother, a mother in which every soul is nurtured, nourished, and loved.

Guilt and shame for both women dissolved before the motherly care of a loving God. Julian even spoke about being of the same substance as God. Both women were confident that the passion of Christ would overcome sinfulness, reducing its significance with the promise of heaven's joys. Prevailing ideas of judgment, condemnation, the wrath of God, and a hell of eternal punishment were muted by the sound of a different voice.

Practice

What can we come to understand about confession through the self-awareness practiced by our two women confessors? Both encountered something greater than themselves deep within. As a seeker, Julian found something in her soul that was one with God, even of the same substance. Both women seemed to sense a line of continuity between their higher selves and their Creator. I can imagine their thinking something like this: if I can feel the motherly concern of a woman for her child, how much greater must our Creator feel this compassionate and loving concern for those whom He/She has created? Both understood their own existence in its higher and better moments as reflecting the nature and presence of God.

The Self-Awareness and Internal Dialogue

1. Can you build any similar bridges of understanding? What do you make of your higher moments of purpose and intention? Are there clear times when you see beyond? Have you sensed an inner Presence reflecting something greater than yourself?

2. How strongly are you influenced by your gender in the way you think about the world, other people, and the purpose of life? In your private time, imagine yourself as a member of the opposite sex. Start the day and go through it in your imagination as a man if you are a woman, or as a woman if you are a man. Go about your tasks for the day. Meet your friends, your colleagues, your employees, your students, and anyone else who comes to mind as you usually do. Explore your aspirations,

interests, commitments, spiritual inclinations, and ideas about God through self-understandings that occur in your fantasied gender change.

3. Keeping to the assignment above, explore your role as Parent. While you are at it, if you are married, imagine yourself married to you. These exercises got really tricky for me, and revealing as well. How many of your basic feelings about love, spirituality, and God are altered by a change in gender perspective? Record them if you journal.

4. As a seeker, Julian experienced God as like her, only much more so. For example, if a mother's love for a child could never be surrendered, regardless of what the child did, sin would not lessen our personal worth in God's eyes. Record your thoughts about this.

Confessional Partnership

1. Share any awareness you want to from the exercises above. Your reactions to each other can provide valuable feedback.

2. You may wish to discuss what differences you would perceive in your relationship if your partner changed gender.

Discussion Group

1. Compile as many differences as you can between the feminine experience in confession and the male confessors in Chapters 3 and 4.

2. Consider the role of self-knowledge as a source of knowledge about God. Can we avoid it? Are there limits?

3. There may be reactions to Julian's view of pain and suffering as a royal road to spiritual consciousness and to reward in heaven.

4. Do Margery's antics and questionable behavior disqualify her spiritual experience as hysterical and grandiose?

5. What is the role of gender in spiritual encounter? Did these early experiences of Julian and Margery form a legitimate expression of feminism for their time?

6. What of Julian's dismissal of doctrines that involve the severity of God's judgment upon sinfulness and eternal punishment in hell? What about her ideas of union or "oneing" with God, or sharing the same substance with God.

Confessional Group

1. This is a good occasion for the group to reflect upon how gender has been influencing its conversations. The makeup of the group is important. If your group were (or is) predominantly or completely

of one gender, how different would your conversation become through including the other half of the world?

2. Are there discernibly different ways of perceiving that are gender driven? Consider perceptions of the world, relationships, spirituality, right and wrong, God? How do these perceptions influence your relationships to one another?

CHAPTER **8**

Contemporary Women Confessors

Karen Armstrong and Elaine Pagels

My search for contemporary women confessors yielded two fascinating subjects: Karen Armstrong and Elaine Pagels. Like Julian of Norwich and Margery Kempe, they are opposites in many respects. Karen Armstrong grew up a Catholic in England and became a nun. Elaine Pagels was raised by a liberal Protestant family in the United States and joined a conservative evangelical Christian congregation as a teenager. Armstrong once characterized herself as "a failed heterosexual." Pagels was married and lived in Princeton, New Jersey, with her two adopted children after her husband was killed in an automobile accident. Both women became spiritually homeless and found themselves "seekers" to overcome their painful experiences with organized religion.

Karen Armstrong

On September 14, 1962, Karen Armstrong entered the convent at the age of 17. Her parents were horrified. She described herself as quite shy and troubled by the approaching demands of adult social life. She didn't like being a teenager, feeling awkward, plain, bookish, and unpopular with the boys. She shrank from the idea of being an old maid but found the prospect of marriage equally unappealing. Perhaps the religious life would help her experience a different dimension, live authentically, or offer some radical freedom where no man could tell her what to do.* She says little about her experiences in early childhood but there is the hint she sought escape from an unhappy environment through her spiritual quest.

The Convent

In the convent, Armstrong encountered a harsh discipline. Life there required that she subject her ego to a degree of self-abandonment that she found sadly beyond her capacity. Novices were carefully trained never to tell their troubles to one another. Her attempts at self-discipline brought one failure after another. One of the biggest failures was in her inability to pray. She was told that without prayer, their religious lives were a complete sham. The silence of their days was designed for them to listen to God. "But," she reflected, "He had never spoken to me."[†]

For 7 years, Armstrong kept to herself the shameful secret that unlike everyone else, she could not pray. She remained uninvolved with God, and God appeared quite indifferent to her. "And that," she wrote despairingly, "I became convinced, must be my fault."[‡]

Then there were the accumulating matters of discipline by her superiors. She had difficulty with her needlework. She put one sewing machine out of commission with her awkwardness. Mother Albert sent her to practice on an older machine in the adjoining room. There was no needle in it. When she reported somewhat bluntly that the needle was missing, Mother Albert, already angry, responded, "Don't you know that a nun must never correct her superior in such a pert manner? You will go to that machine next door, Sister, and work on it every day, needle or no needle, until I give you permission to stop."

For 2 weeks, Sister Karen practiced on the empty machine, quelling her objections and trying to believe this was God's way. She felt it was her own "wretched intellectual pride" that blocked her spiritual advancement.

Some respite from her failures came in 1966 when she passed the entrance examinations for St. Anne's College, Oxford. In her novitiate, she was trained to turn off her critical faculties and accept discipline. At the university she was taught to question everything. The two proved increasingly irreconcilable. Her aging superior was bitterly opposed to new ideas, and Armstrong fought with her "tooth and nail." Her accumulated failures in the convent left her exhausted and sick. She wept uncontrollably, suffered nosebleeds, and found it impossible to keep down her food. Then she began fainting. Her superiors considered that emotional self-indulgence.

---

* See Karen Armstrong. *The Spiral Staricase* (New York: Anchor Books, A Division of Random House, Inc.). Earlier she wrote *Through the Narrow Gate* and *Beginning the World*, also autobiographical, but discredits them as ill-conceived and premature here.

† *Op. Cit.*, p. 39.

‡ *Op. Cit.*, p. 43.

However, she didn't feel guilty. Her superiors taught her that guilt could be self-indulgent, a sort of wallowing in the ego. She was more sad, crushed by the repeated failures of her novitiate. Members of the community suggested she pursue her desire for further study.

The Secular World and Psychiatry

In the spring of 1969, Armstrong left the convent to become a graduate student at Oxford. The climate in the world around was one of protest. Her new friends in the dorm were engaged in politics and demonstrations. Armstrong herself even ran for Secretary of the Common Room where her fellow students organized and met. But she was overwhelmed by culture shock. She didn't even know who the Beatles were. Her capacity for affection had atrophied. She shied away from intimacy of any kind, even touch, unable to admit any sexual needs. She had been taught physical restraint, modesty, and "custody of the eyes," which meant one looked down all the time. Now she was trying to live in the world she had been taught to reject.

Her studies demanded she become self-reliant. Life in the convent had taught her to be dependent, and she found she had no ideas of her own. One professor's assignment, to read a Coleridge poem and write what it meant to her, paralyzed her. The idea of thinking for oneself, making up one's own mind, and developing one's own opinions and beliefs, so precious in the higher halls of graduate study, had been quietly wrenched from her grasp by 7 years of disciplined thinking in the convent. She struggled every day to recover her sense of independent choice and personal judgment. But asserting her own thoughts proved to be a slow process.

Meanwhile, the fainting attacks continued. The college nurse assured her that they were almost certainly due to stress. Armstrong could not forget the emptiness she encountered when she tried to rely upon her own judgment. Her knack for writing intricate Gothic essays seemed to please her professors, but underneath her seemingly polished intellectual exterior, she felt there was "a vacuum at the core." She started to have visions and hallucinations. One day while shopping in the Cornmarket, "the world seemed to have lost all connection with fundamental laws that gave it meaning and coherence. It took on the grotesque aspect of a cartoon."[*]

She knew she was ill but somehow it felt appropriate that the world she was taught to hate had turned against her. Finally her physician referred her to a psychiatrist. Entering treatment marked the beginning of what Karen Armstrong described as "years of psychiatric sessions during which we raked over the memories of my unexceptional childhood."[†] Dr. Piet

---

[*] *Op. Cit.*, p. 56.
[†] *Op. Cit.*, p. 73.

served as a "composite figure" for a series of doctors who became her therapists. She granted that her treatment conformed to the orthodoxy of the day and may have in many cases proved effective. But with her, it simply did not work. In retrospect, she wondered if it would have had Dr. Piet permitted her to talk about the novitiate, her loneliness, and the strain of the past few years of religious life, but any effort to do so was interpreted as a distraction. The anxiety attacks, the terror, the occasional loss of consciousness, and the hallucinations served to push her further into isolation. Still, Dr. Piet seemed to be her only chance. She kept returning with the understanding that miracles don't happen overnight. After all, what did she know about psychiatry? This line of thought only made her more uneasy, she confessed, because it was the same kind of reasoning she followed in the convent.

Then came another success in the midst of everything negative. It was in academia where her skills first came to light. Her papers were accepted in the doctoral program at Oxford. She could proceed to write her dissertation. She took a new room with Jennifer Hart, a tutor in modern history at St. Anne's. The Harts had a child named Jacob who had brain damage and suffered from seizures. At times she filled in for Jacob's nanny, and across the period of her studies there, she formed a significant relationship with him. One day as she and Jennifer were talking, Jennifer wondered if Jacob would benefit from going to church. She thought of the liberal Catholic group known as the Blackfriars and asked Armstrong if she would take him on Sunday.

The idea that someone like Jacob might get something out of the Catholic liturgy without accepting the creed was new for Armstrong. As far as she was concerned, religion consisted essentially of beliefs, and if you could no longer subscribe to the creed, you couldn't be a religious person. But all around them the spiritually homeless were experimenting with alternative forms of religious experience. Jennifer understood what Karen acknowledged she did not see at the time. Quite apart from any creed, Jacob needed some form of spirituality and ritual that could bring him a measure of peace. So she took him. And when he was eager to go back, she began to take him regularly. Still she remained haunted by the memory of a Jesuit retreat in which she was taught that faith was not really intellectual assent but simply an act of will. She realized she had given up. She no longer had the emotional or spiritual energy to make that choice. It seemed as if Jacob's religious life was beginning, and hers was ending.

Spiritual Homelessness and Awakening

As Armstrong's treatment continued, Dr. Piet seemed convinced she was just another brainy girl having problems accepting her femininity. She agreed that she probably did have gender issues. Her eating disorder served to neutralize her body, making it neither male nor female. But there was still so much unfinished business left over from the convent. Each effort to discuss it was labeled another "exotic distraction" unrelated to the real issues. Dr. Piet challenged her to stop wasting time, to cut out the histrionics about minutia at the convent: "Let's see what you are really like when you lose control. Surprise me!"[*]

A few weeks later in the autumn of 1971, Armstrong did. She even succeeded in surprising herself. She remembers waking up in the hospital throwing up an overdose of sleeping pills. She did not remember taking them. It was not a lethal dose and she was ashamed. She sensed a veiled contempt in the way her nurses treated her. Dr. Piet was convinced she was angry with him. But Armstrong became even more certain that her mind was irreparably injured in some way. Her treatment had stumbled to a halt. She took a measure of solace in reading Wordsworth's "Ode: Intimations of Immortality," in which he described a childhood decision he made when he realized the glory of the world he knew as a boy had gone forever: "We will grieve not, rather find / Strength in what remains behind."[†] It became her mantra through the crisis that followed.

Armstrong did not feel she could return to live with the Hart household, so she needed a place to stay while she recuperated. She called the convent; but when her superior heard her story, she did not think the community could accept the responsibility of letting her stay there. Suddenly Armstrong was not only cut off from her past; but she also was homeless. Out of desperation, she tried to check herself into Littlemore Hospital. She was escorted through a psychiatric ward and seated next to a male patient with a beer belly who took it upon himself to cheer her up and indoctrinate her to "the loony bin," as he characterized it. Then a nurse suddenly appeared. Armstrong was led back to the doorway where Jennifer Hart stood beckoning. Dr. Piet had already been consulted, and the family eagerly awaited her return. Armstrong remembers this frightening incident as a watershed event. She still saw Dr. Piet and other psychiatrists after she left Oxford. She still had panic attacks, episodes of amnesia, and periods of feeling cut off from the world "in a capsule of unreality." She was hospitalized on at least two other occasions. But from this point on, she recalled being different.

During her third year of doctoral studies, Armstrong turned a corner. She began to eat normally and food tasted good to her. She gained weight. She gave up psychiatry, acknowledging that she had submitted to other people's programs and agendas for too long. Her first "flicker of true recovery" came in 1973 when she went to hear Dame Helen Gardner

---

[*] *Op. Cit.*, p. 123.
[†] *Op. Cit.*, p. 129.

lecture on T.S. Eliot. The topic was a sequence of poems Eliot called "Ash Wednesday." The "Ode: Intimations of Immortality" from which she had taken her mantra was the first poem. It had served her well in the decision to move ahead with her life "with its serene determination to let go of the past and cultivate new strength and joy."* She was profoundly moved. She no longer had to wait for an interpretation as she heard Dame Helen read it aloud. She made her own emotional, intuitive response that reached something "deeply embedded within." In some of the "Ash Wednesday" poems, Eliot described spiritual progress and illumination by the symbol of a spiral staircase. The verse constantly turns upon itself in repetition of the words "I do not hope to turn again." Nevertheless, throughout the poems, Eliot is doing just that, gradually ascending to one new insight after another. Paradoxically, abandoning hope is transformed into acquiring hope.

This paradox of hope had become the clear pattern of her life. Just at her moments of deepest despair, something new emerged pointing the way beyond. It awakened a growing faith that would eventually find its way into her *sacred story*. This is the theme we have noted with all our confessors: our *human predicament always points beyond itself* awaiting our *relevant response*. Once Armstrong abandoned any hope of going back and undoing her past, the way forward became clear. She could stop striving toward what was normal for other people. Their experience was unlike hers. She, too, had given up what Eliot called "the infirm glory of the positive hour." She had experienced the "horror" of what lay beneath our ordinary waking consciousness. What she had was "now" in this time and this place. Somehow this thought set her free to join the poet in rejoicing that life is as it is:

> Because I cannot hope to turn again
> Consequently I rejoice, having to construct something
> Upon which to rejoice.†

For the first time, Armstrong responded spontaneously with her whole being to a poem. With her response came authentic spiritual encounter. Human life must really be this way. In trying so desperately to save your life, you lose it; and in the process of losing your life, you find it. She was not emotionally dead. Her mind was beginning to come to life again. Put the world of black and white and "proofs" for the existence of God behind you. And psychiatry too. If she gazed at reality, however unpleasant, she, too, might learn to rejoice in it.

---

* *Op. Cit.*, p. 139.
† *Op. Cit.*, p. 142

What followed was the first measured period of success in Armstrong's life. Characteristically, it came after an unexpected turn toward failure in her doctoral studies. Her work was suddenly terminated by an advisor whom she and others felt to be arbitrary and unfair. And just as quickly, she received a position teaching in London at Bedford College. For the first time, she made a niche for herself in the world. She began to establish some comfort in visiting her family and even successfully vacationed with them one summer. She found in literature what had eluded her so long in the convent. She no longer studied to promote herself. As soon as she was immersed in a text for its own sake, she was inundated with ideas and words to express them. A renewed delight in the written word came to her like a gift of grace.

Then one day, entering Baker Street Station on the way home, she had a seizure. The attending physician at Middlesex Hospital suggested she had epilepsy. Dr. Wolfe, who became her consultant, told her some weeks later that she had all the classic symptoms of temporal lobe epilepsy. He was astonished that neither Dr. Piet nor any of her doctors had ever suggested an EEG. For Armstrong, this discovery became an occasion for pure happiness. She was not the failure she had always thought herself to be. This reprieve brought a joyous sense of relief that has never entirely left her. She walked away from Dr. Wolfe's consulting room that spring morning in 1976 knowing she had a viable future.

There were men in Armstrong's life but she refused to describe her relationship with them as "love affairs." A love life never seemed to materialize for her. She once described herself as a "failed heterosexual" while having dinner in New York with two gay friends. She characterized her more serious relationships with men as nasty, brutish, and not as short as they should have been (paraphrasing from Hobbes). "Men of my age tend to be big on control," she noted, "and I have found that when I let a man into my bed I have suddenly found my life invaded by a mini-dictator who has to have his own way in the smallest matters."*

The Battle with Belief

The pattern of *transformational stories* in Armstrong's life began to come clear. Whatever her predicament, it served to point beyond itself to the next step on her "spiral staircase." This awareness was to become the first article in her newfound faith. After Bedford College came a stint teaching at a girl's school in Dulwich. By now she had developed a strong distaste for organized religion. She could not tolerate God language and talk about Jesus. Then came another setback. After her third year at Dulwich, she lost her teaching job because the epilepsy continued to produce sporadic

---

* *Op. Cit.*, p. 189.

seizures. Old fears about making money and supporting herself re-appeared. Dramatic improvement in her medication during the summer of 1981 helped but it came too late. She had written *Through the Narrow Gate,* which described her life in the convent, and this won her an invitation to do an interview with Channel 4 television. It took place the day after she taught her final class.

Once again, Armstrong's struggle with failure led to the next step. No sooner had she lost her teaching job than she became a hit on British television. Her assignment there was to liberate people whose minds had been contained within an untenable doctrinal system. She waded into the oppression she experienced during her years in the convent. She realized she had a lot of scores to settle with the church. When she was done, the cameramen went "Phew!" He told her she was "embarrassingly good." Soon she had another job preparing documentaries.

A 6-week series on the life of St. Paul seemed an ideal place to start. How much of the church's preoccupation with doctrinal complexity, its denigration of women and the body, its intolerance and authoritarian corruption could be traced to Paul? Her research began in preparation for a whirlwind filming tour in the Near East. In the process, she met two men who had a profound influence on her. The first was Michael Goulder of Birmingham University, who had recently resigned his Anglican orders because he no longer believed in God. He was selected as her expert advisor but he quickly joined the ranks of others who discouraged her from doing the documentary, telling her that she simply did not know enough. He was tough. He ripped her draft scripts apart over the telephone "sentence by jejune sentence, line by naïve line, and page by uninformed page."* Armstrong learned fast; and by the end of the project, they were friends.

Then she was off to Tel Aviv on a mission to unmask the dogmatic intolerance that plagued the church. There, Armstrong met a liberal Jew named Hyam Maccoby, who disabused her of the New Testament view of the Pharisees. More importantly, he introduced her to the spirit of Judaism in which theology is just not that important. There are no creeds or infallible pronouncements, and one can believe anything one wants within reason. Right practice is what is important, not right belief. "You Christians make such a fuss about theology," he said, "but it's not important in the way you think. It's just poetry, really, ways of talking about the inexpressible. We Jews don't bother much about what we believe. We just do instead."†

Hyam Maccoby planted a seed of expanding appreciation for Judaism and also for Islam and the other great world religions. As Armstrong worked on her scripts, she entered more deeply into a Jewish perspective.

---

* *Op. Cit.,* p. 233.
† *Op. Cit.,* p. 236.

For a Jew, observing one of the 613 commandments (*mitzvoth*) was to turn toward God by giving daily life a sacred orientation. Such practices served to introduce a source of continuing joy and liberation by bringing a sense of spiritual presence into one's activities. Jesus' first disciples were understandably upset when Paul told them God had now abrogated the law and Jesus had become God's primary revelation to the world. The first Christians were all Jews. And Armstrong would never again be able to think of Christianity as a completely separate religion.

In the spring of 1985, Channel 4 sent her to do another series, this one on the Crusades. Her research was both heartbreaking and eye opening. In July of 1099, 40,000 Jews and Muslims were massacred in 2 days during the conquest of Jerusalem. The first victims of this particular crusade were members of the Jewish communities along the Rhine Valley who were given the choice of baptism or death. Armstrong had always thought of the Muslim faith as inherently violent and fanatical. In reality, Islam had been far more respectful of other faiths than Christianity. Even during the Crusades, Islamic generals behaved with greater restraint and compassion than their Christian counterparts, a sobering discovery.

Studying the Crusades strengthened Armstrong's conviction that stridently parochial certainty could be lethal, especially in religious matters. She saw the importance of finding out about other cultures and traditions. As long as we in the West cling to our old distorted picture of Islam, we will live in an increasingly dangerous world. Her heart was beginning to thaw. For the first time in years, she started to feel the pain of other people. She developed a passion to overcome the dangerous assumption that we in the West have some monopoly on truth and justice. But the filming, which began in the summer of 1985, dragged on erratically for 3 years. By the summer of 1988, production came to a standstill, and Channel 4 declared the series bankrupt. And Armstrong experienced another disheartening sense of failure.

Once again, she was back wondering how to make a living. She lost her voice and for 2 years found it impossible to speak in public. But this time she experienced all the feelings that accompanied her downfall. Now she was well enough to go through all the outrage, distress, and pain she should have experienced on those other occasions when she lived through failure. This ability to experience pain and sorrow ushered in the next steps to her spiral staircase. She realized she had unfinished business with God. For the past 3 years, she had steeped herself in the deadly hostility separating Jews, Christians, and Muslims. Why not take a look at what these three Abrahamic faiths, each strongly monotheistic, held in common?

The History of God

Armstrong's decision to write *The History of God* came out of the blue in a way traditional believers would call "an inspiration."* She even compared it to the Ancient Mariner's seeing the water snakes writhing and gleaming around his becalmed ship, redeemed by a spontaneous ecstasy and regard for his fellow living creatures. As the albatross slipped from his neck, the Mariner was drawn out of himself and discovered he could pray again. Neither she nor the Mariner knew what they were doing. Both were saved by the hidden workings of their unconscious psyche. Each knew instinctively a best and relevant response. Her decision to write about God became a defining moment. Not only did the book become a best seller and solve the quandary of how to support herself, but it also served as the occasion to complete her spiritual quest.

Writing *The History of God* brought to an end Armstrong's lengthy battle with belief. Her study forged a faith from her own unique sense of spiritual encounter. The articles of her newfound faith surfaced as convictions formed at points along her journey. First of all, she had to *set off by herself on her own path.* She learned to think, feel, and choose what she was moved to believe deep within herself. This was the same conclusion reached by Elaine Pagels, as we shall see. Both joined Julian and Margery as seekers.

Second, some form of *empathic participation in the lives of others* proved essential to spiritual encounter. All major religions from Confucianism, Buddhism, and Hinduism to the three Abrahamic faiths taught a spirituality of empathy. Empathy involved extending our own self-awareness into the perspective of others. Every religious tradition called for establishing awareness beyond our own ego, experiencing a state of *ekstasis,* or "standing outside" ourselves, as the Greek term suggests. The idea was to move beyond our inherent self-centeredness to assume the frame of reference of others. Empathy formed the foundation for all significant acts of forgiveness. It was preserved in the notion behind myths of *kenosis* or "self-emptying" found in traditions about the nature of God. We are most creative and transcend our ordinary experience when we leave ourselves behind in this fashion. Armstrong had previously experienced empathic entry into poetry and literature. Now she was having the same experience with theology. Like the phrases of poetry, religious ideas, myths, or doctrines communicate truth that eludes ordinary language, expressing what remains inaccessible to simple, rational interpretation. She found herself empathically drawn to the prophet Mohammed. Her book about him possessed such compassionate understanding that the Pakistani scholar

---

* (New York: Ballantine Books, 1993)

Akbar Ahmed described it as a "love story." "If you had met the Prophet," he said to her, "you would have consented to be his fifteenth wife."[*]

Third, most traditions of faith are more about *practice* than belief. They are true—not because they conform to some established metaphysical, scientific, or historical reality, but because they are life enhancing. None of us will discover spiritual truth until we apply spiritual practice to our own life. The religious quest is not about discovering "the Truth" with a capital "T" but about living as intentionally as possible in the here and now. Here, Armstrong echoes something of the "uncertain certainty" that moved Tolstoy to seek a compassionate life of non-violence and care for the underprivileged.

Fourth, the litmus test of good theology is the *empathic quality of compassion*. Do your beliefs make you kinder and more empathic, capable of concrete acts of loving kindness? If your notion of God makes you unkind, belligerent, cruel, self-righteous, if you are given to killing others in God's name, you have a bad theology. In all three Abrahamic religions, there are fundamentalist movements that distort the faith they seek to defend. Fundamentalists seem to possess an innate tendency to emphasize belligerent elements in their tradition and overlook the insistent and crucial demands for compassion. Armstrong was convinced that we have seen too much "religious certainty" lately. Now is the time for honest searching, doubt, repentance, compassion, and empathy. She was struck by a profound similarity between the insights of Jewish, Muslim, and Christian thinkers. She quoted the Islamic mystic Ibn al-Arabi, who cautioned against attaching oneself to any particular creed exclusively: "[O]therwise you will lose much good, nay, you will fail to recognize the real truth of the matter. God, the omnipresent and omnipotent, is not confined to any one creed for he says, 'Wheresoever you turn, there is the face of Allah.'"[†]

Armstrong continued to struggle with the absence of God in her life. Many of the spiritual masters she studied insisted that God was not another being—someone whose existence parallels ours "out there." "And yet," she observes, "the very absence I felt so acutely was paradoxically a presence in my life. When you miss somebody very intensely, they are, in a sense, with you all the time."[‡] We do have partial glimpses of transcendence, although no two experiences of the divine are the same. Whenever we try to hold on to one of these, we unwittingly cut it down to our own size and close our minds to its infinite presence. We do better to open ourselves to the sacred dimension in everything around us, including one another.

---

[*] *The Spiral Staircase*, p. 277.
[†] *Ibid.*, p. 289.
[‡] *Ibid.*, p. 301.

Elaine Pagels

Although her autobiographical material is sparse, Elaine Pagels wrote *Beyond Belief: The Secret Gospel of Thomas* in a confessional stance.[*] *Beyond Belief* is based on her earlier studies of *The Gnostic Gospels*, a collection of sacred books discovered in December of 1945 by an Arab peasant at Nag Hammadi in Upper Egypt.[†] This remarkable archaeological find contains sacred writings from one of the earliest Christian sects. There are 52 texts from the beginning of the Christian era, including a collection of early Gospels previously unknown. In addition to the *Gospel of Thomas*, there are the *Gospel of Philip,* the *Gospel of Truth*, and the *Gospel to the Egyptians,* together with other writings attributed to Jesus' followers, such as the *Secret Book of James,* the *Apocalypse of Paul,* the *Letter of Peter to Phillip*, and the *Apocalypse of Peter.*

In my seminary days, we dismissed any writings of the Gnostics as tainted by Greek thought and the "mystery religions." The Gnostics thought the human soul contained a divine spark that emanated from God. This idea made the human soul and the Divine in some way identical or substantially similar. It also made self-knowledge a source of special knowledge of God or "gnosis." We learned about the Gnostics from Irenaeus and other early fathers of orthodoxy who denounced them as "full of blasphemy" and "lies." Now some scholars suggest that the collection of sayings in the Gnostic Gospels may include some traditions older than the Gospels of the New Testament: Matthew, Mark, Luke, and John. We knew so little about them because at the time of Emperor Constantine's conversion, making Christianity the official religion of the Roman Empire, possession of these books became a criminal offense, and all known copies were destroyed. Somehow the documents at Nag Hammadi were safely hidden from the purge.

Elaine Pagels found in these long neglected texts a rich diversity of early Christian faith. She was the Harrington Spear Paine Professor of Religion at Princeton University. Her undergraduate work at Stanford was in history and her master's degree in classical studies. For her original discussion of these materials in *The Gnostic Gospels*, she received both the National Book Award and the National Book Critics Circle Award, but her involvement in their content was much more than scholarly or academic. It was intensely personal.

The Struggle for Faith

Pagels begins *Beyond Belief* confessionally. She is running in New York City one bright Sunday morning in early February. She stops to

---

[*] (New York: Random House, 2003).
[†] (New York: Random House, 1979)

rest in the stone vestibule of the Church of the Heavenly Rest. She has not been to church for a long time; but while she catches her breath and warms herself, the music and the prayers from within compel her attention. And she thinks to herself: here is a family that knows how to face death.

The night before had been a sleepless one, full of fear and worry. Her son Mark, two-and-a-half years old, had just been diagnosed with pulmonary hypertension, which is fatal. The previous day Mark had undergone 6 hours of further testing by disbelieving doctors who a little over a year ago had completed his successful open-heart surgery. This was too much. They could do a biopsy to see how far this rare lung disease had progressed, but that was all. Why add to his suffering at this point? Pagels and her husband had decided, instead, to take him home the next day.

Standing at the back of that church, Pagels realized that she needed to be there. She felt a desire to weep in a safe, acceptable place, to acknowledge her dread of dealing with what she knew lay ahead. To face the disheartening news from the day before demanded some sort of hope or faith. So Pagels, like Julian of Norwich, became a seeker confronted by the reality of death.

It was another death, years before, that had precipitated her initial struggle with faith. When she was 14 years old, she had joined an evangelical Christian church that had an enthusiastic youth ministry. It provided the assurance she craved at the time: that of belonging to the "right group," God's "one true" flock. Here was where the book of John gained her attention because it was regarded as the most "spiritual" of the Gospels. Nobody grew up in Danville, Kentucky, where I did, without learning John 3:16 by heart: "For God so loved the world that he gave his only Son that whosoever believes in him should not perish but have eternal life." Not only was that verse quoted at every revival service, but the fellowship of Christian athletes hung it behind the goalposts at football games.

As a teenager, Elaine Pagels was about to learn there was a cost to being included among the true believers. The *Gospel of John* alternates between the assurance of God's gracious love for those who "believe" and warnings that everyone who does not believe is condemned already to eternal death. John has Jesus speaking of his own people, the Jews, as if they were alien to him and "the devil's offspring." This belief was played out in her church community when its leaders urged their charges to avoid associating with nonbelievers except to convert them. And Elaine Pagels had a close friend who was Jewish.

She could manage until her friend, at 16 years of age, was suddenly killed in an automobile accident. Her fellow evangelicals grieved her loss with her but insisted that because he was not "born again," he was eternally damned. This distressed her. When she expressed any disagreement with their interpretation of faith, there was no room for discussion. It was at this point that she realized "I was no longer at home in their world and left that church."[*]

The death of her Jewish friend left Elaine Pagels disillusioned and spiritually homeless. It also launched her search for spiritual roots elsewhere. Entering college, she learned Greek and read the New Testament in its original language. She read Homer's poems, the plays of Sophocles and Aeschylus, Piondar's hymns, and Sappho's invocations. Many of these "pagan" writings she also found religiously significant, but in a different way.

After college, she studied dance in New York but was unable to shake her urge to discover "real Christianity." Perhaps if she engaged in further study of the earliest Christian sources, she could discover the faith she sought. She entered the doctoral program at Harvard to do research in early Christian history. There she discovered that Professors Helmut Koester and George MacRae had accumulated file cabinets filled with "gospels" and "apocrypha" from the first two centuries. Among them was the cache of texts from the beginning of the Christian era found in 1945 at Nag Hammadi. She was immediately struck by the rich diversity in these manuscripts. And so began her research leading to the publication of *The Gnostic Gospels* in 1979.

Pagels was surprised at the way some of these writings struck her with an unexpected spiritual power. One passage from the *Gospel of Thomas* represented Jesus as saying, "If you bring forth what is within you, what you bring forth will save you. If you do not bring forth what is within you, what you do not bring forth will destroy you."[†] Instead of telling us what to believe, it challenged us to discover what lies hidden within ourselves. This appealed to her instincts, particularly in light of her youthful encounter with rigid orthodox beliefs that excluded her Jewish friend as a nonbeliever. Other ideas also struck a chord with her. There was *The Teaching of the Twelve Apostles to the Gentiles* (known as *the Didache* or "teaching") written by a group of Jesus' followers who did not think of themselves as true believers separate from the Jews but as "God's people." This was written in Syria some 10 years before the New Testament Gospels of Matthew and Luke. It recognized Jesus as the great interpreter of the law and also contained many sayings that later appeared in the gospels.

The Gnostic gospels expressed many ideas that appealed to Pagels. The special *gnosis* that they sought was a knowledge deep within the self, not unlike the self-knowledge of Julian of Norwich or the knowledge of God

---

[*] *Beyond Belief,* p. 31.
[†] *Beyond Belief,* p. 32.

embedded deeply within the unconscious self of Carl Gustav Jung. Most Gnostics thought of themselves more as "seekers" than "believers" who possessed some kind of final truth. Everyone was encouraged to pursue what became clear as they sought to explore their own unique experience of spiritual presence.

Even more important was the realization there was a rich and growing diversity among Christian groups that flourished for 300 years before the beginning of the fourth century. At that time, with the formation of a universal (Catholic) church, those who belonged were required to profess a complex set of beliefs about God and Jesus formulated by fourth-century bishops into the ancient Christian creeds. The Gnostics and their writings were denounced as heretical. Everything about them was so successfully suppressed by later "official" versions of Christianity that now only in places like Harvard could Elaine Pagels and others learn about them.

Exploring their rich diversity, she soon began to recover a sense of being spiritually at home. It was the same feeling she realized, however dimly, as she stood in the doorway of the Church of the Heavenly Rest. A drama that spoke to her condition also was being played out there. It brought together the same reality of fear, grief, and death, while at the same time nurturing hope. Four years later when little Mark suddenly died at age 6, The Church of the Heavenly Rest offered her shelter, along with words and music, when she gathered with family and friends "to bridge an abyss that seemed impassable." Faith to her had little to do with giving assent to beliefs expressed in one creed or another. She had come to regard herself as like many of the Gnostics she studied, heretics or not, who saw themselves not so much as "believers," but as "seekers."

Among the members at the Church of the Heavenly Rest, Pagels had found fellow companions on a similar journey. She realized how much she loved her Christian tradition and how powerfully it can affect us, even transform us. At the same time, her studies of the Gnostics made clear what she didn't love—the tendency to identify faith with some "single, authorized set of beliefs," coupled with the conviction that these beliefs alone can offer access to God.

John and Thomas

Beyond Belief was devoted to understanding what led to the collapse of the rich diversity Pagels witnessed among the Gnostic writers. She focused her attention on the rise of orthodoxy from the second to the fourth centuries and the "canon of truth" that led to the rejection of heretical literature. Of special interest were the *Gospel of John* and the *Gospel of Thomas*, both of which appeared close to the beginning of the second century.

Some perspective on the formation of the New Testament is helpful. The "canon" (or measuring rod) by which some books were included and others rejected represented an effort to determine the truth about Jesus' life and mission. The four gospels, Matthew, Mark, Luke, and John, became an authoritative part of this canon, ostensibly because they were written by apostles who could give an eyewitness account. Actually, we don't know who wrote them but their style is expressive of the communal authorship of the day. Matthew, Mark, and Luke are commonly called the "synoptic gospels" because they may be seen together. They share so much common material that scholars believe they all drew from a common source that came to be known as "Q." All were written more than 40 years after Christ's death, making authorship by one of the disciples highly unlikely. Mark is dated 68 to 70, Matthew and Luke 80 to 90. John followed over a decade later.

John's gospel is very different from the synoptics. Its account of Jesus' ministry begins with the cleansing of the temple. In the synoptic gospels, Jesus drives the money-changers from the temple during the final week before the crucifixion, an act that provoked those who opposed him and led to his death. John places this climactic act at the start of his public life, as if to suggest his whole mission was to purify and transform the worship of God. In the synoptics, there is a mystery as to who Jesus is. In Mark, the disciples discuss popular notions that he is John the Baptist, or Elijah, or one of the prophets come back. Peter proclaims he is the "Messiah," literally God's "anointed one," designated to become Israel's future king. Other terms such as the "Son of Man" can mean anything from "human being" to someone "invested with divine power." Even the term "Son of God" to the Jew of Mark's time normally meant, like *Messiah*, Israel's human king anointed or chosen by God.

By the time John appears, Jesus has become God himself, not just God's human servant. John begins by announcing Jesus is the Word that was in the beginning with God, that was God, through whom everything was made. This Word became flesh and dwelt among us full of grace and truth. By now, Jesus' significance and place in the scheme of things are clearly linked with the foundations of creation itself. Jesus is described as "the light of the world" present in the primordial light at the origin of creation.

The gnostic *Gospel of Thomas* also identifies Jesus with the divine light that came into being in the beginning, but Thomas reaches a quite different conclusion about its presence. Instead of making Jesus the one true light by which humankind is saved, the divine light that Jesus embodied is shared with all humanity. Because we are all created "in the image of God," the presence of this divine light lies ready to be discovered in every person and has become "what you bring forth within you that will save you."

By the time both John and Thomas' gospels are written, the Church has a more fully formed set of understandings about who Jesus is than we find in the synoptic gospels. John was probably written between 90 and 100.

Thomas' gospel was completed between 90 and 130, with parallel parts in existence in partial or fragmented form at virtually the same time. Pagels compares and contrasts the two as pivotal documents, both known to the early Christian historian Irenaeus. They form a vivid picture of an orthodoxy developing that would exclude as heretical any number of views that later flowered among Christian mystics of many generations.

For Thomas, the kingdom of God has already come among us, and it is our task to recognize that it is spreading on earth. Thomas' kingdom is inside of us. When we know ourselves, then we will be known and will see that we are all children of a loving Father. If we don't see this, we will dwell in poverty. Our task is to "know ourselves," for the light is within each person.

Painstakingly, Pagels contrasts John and Thomas. In John, Jesus is the light of the world; in Thomas, the light is within each person. In John, only Jesus came from God and can provide access to God. In Thomas, we all come from the light and may become seekers on our own by tapping our spiritual resources within. The same understandings would later become a central theme in Jewish mysticism. But to Irenaeus, these views diluted the uniqueness of Christ and were attacked as heresy.

Thomas' emphasis on the Kingdom of God was taken up by Leo Tolstoy in *The Kingdom of God Is Within You*. The book, you may recall, followed his search to determine who among his people possessed faith enough to provide the courage to live well. Discovering such a faith among the common people of the land, Tolstoy urged everyone to give up violence and coercion, and to realize the Kingdom of God is here and now. In the century past, Thomas Merton echoed the same theme and interpreted the kingdom as a mystical presence within the hearts and minds of believers. Both men express the same kind of diversity that thrived within Christianity at the beginning of the second century. Pagels' research led her to conclude there is an impulse to seek God that overflows the banks of any single tradition, but something led Irenaeus and other Christian leaders at the time to discourage the urge to seek God on one's own. John was included in the canon of truth but Thomas was excluded. Slowly but surely, Orthodoxy began to prevail.

Canon and Creed

What led Irenaeus and other leaders a century after Jesus to discourage people from seeking God on their own? Both Irenaeus and his teacher Polycarp shared the vision that the small groups of Christians scattered throughout the world would come to see themselves as one Church called Catholic or "universal." Irenaeus insisted that only the four gospels—Matthew, Mark, Luke, and John—were written by witnesses to events through which God sent salvation to the world. These four documents became the basis for his campaign to unify and consolidate Christianity during his lifetime.

Now Irenaeus found himself in the middle of a controversy. Some, such as the Roman scholar Gaius, believed that revelation stopped at the age of the apostles. Others believed that visions and revelations continue. Irenaeus took the middle ground. Even his old teacher Polycarp, the day before he was martyred, dreamed that his pillow caught fire and prophesied that he would be burned alive. Irenaeus was unwilling to say that God did not reveal himself to particular individuals, but he was troubled by the excesses of some. His patriarchal prejudices protrude in his description of one "foolish woman" who uttered "whatever nonsense happened to occur to her, such as one might expect from someone heated up by an empty spirit."* In all fairness, he did have to deal with many groups and factions that challenged his understanding of the gospel.

John became the greatest gospel in his thinking. John alone understood who Jesus really was—God in human form. It was alright to seek revelation but what you found must be submitted to the Apostolic tradition. Even then, additional safeguards were needed to protect against people who might even read the "right" gospels in the wrong way. How many new heresies could be spawned like that? The answer for Irenaeus was to construct what he called orthodox (literally, "straight-thinking") Christianity.

Irenaeus was a favorite among the early Christian fathers when I was in seminary. He was the first among a succession of those who served as architects building a faith that could stand against falsehood. Slowly but surely, across the next two centuries, these leaders in "straight thinking" delivered the authentic Christian truth by weeding out all heresies that deviated from its plumb line. Irenaeus led the rejection of any approach to studying scripture that included ideas current among the Greek philosophers. Heretics, he warned, read widely and concentrate on the enigmas, mysteries, and parables they find in scripture rather than on passages that convey the plain truth.

The plain truth made John the first gospel, not the fourth, because John alone clearly proclaims Christ's divine origin. God is the Word. The Word is Jesus, and only Jesus offers eternal salvation. For Irenaeus and his successors, those who do not follow this canon of truth are doomed. He ends his five-volume *Refutation* calling upon fellow believers to judge and excommunicate heretics. Choosing the path of orthodox faith and practice ultimately makes the difference between heaven and hell.

The orthodox Church that Irenaeus envisioned lay 150 years in the future. It came to fruition at the Council of Nicea in the year 325. The Council was the result of a massive restructuring of the Roman Empire by its emperor, Constantine, which had begun a decade earlier. Alexander, the bishop of Alexandria, and his successor Athanasius became the new

---

* *Beyond Belief*, p. 93.

champions of Irenaeus' agenda. In 318, they excommunicated a heretic named Arius for preaching that emphasized Jesus' humanity, saying that, while he was divine, it was not in the same way as God the Father. Constantine summoned Alexander and Athanasius to Nicea to formulate a creed for the "universal" Church of the Roman Empire. It was here that the "Nicene Creed" took shape, proclaiming Jesus Christ was "God from God, Light from Light, true God from true God." Jesus was "begotten, not made." The power and control of the Holy Catholic (or "universal") Church was vested in its role as the ark of salvation. There is one God, one Lord and Savior Jesus Christ, one Pope and one Church, all united in one common body of belief.

By 367, Athanasius was in his sixties. Securely established as bishop, he wrote in his annual Easter letter a denunciation of all heretics who tried to introduce apocryphal books into the mix with divinely inspired scripture. He set forth, in order, the accepted books of the Bible he believed to be divinely inspired. These included 22 books in the Old Testament, and 27 in the New Testament beginning with the four gospels, Matthew, Mark, Luke, and John. The canon, the creed, and the ecclesiastical hierarchy had been formed in the line established from Irenaeus to Athanasius. All other books were heretical imposters.

Athanasius took one final shot at the body of Gnostic writings, aiming at those who sought direct access to God through the "image of the God" in which we are created. In *On the Incarnation of the Word,* he held that, although originally God created Adam in his own image, human sin had damaged that image beyond any human capacity to repair. Only Jesus Christ embodies the divine image. And somewhere around this time, an unknown monk near Nag Hammadi decided to defy the orders of his established Church and removed more than 50 books from the monastery library, hiding them away in a jar he buried. There they survived the literary holocaust against heresy that followed, awaiting discovery some 1600 years later.

A Woman's Belief

Elaine Pagels no longer believed everything she thought Christians were supposed to believe. Why not just leave Christianity and religion behind as many others have done? Her spiritual homelessness drove her toward a deeper encounter with "something compelling, powerful, even terrifying" that she could not ignore.* She recognized that beyond mere belief, Christianity involved spiritually significant practices, pathways toward transformation. The force of these practices returned one Christmas Eve when she attended a midnight service at Princeton with her 16-year-old

---

* *Beyond Belief,* p. 143.

daughter Sarah. At age 8, Sarah had joined the choir at Trinity Church, saying, "Music helps my heart." Pagels' mind went back to the Church of the Heavenly Rest, to her daughter as an infant, resting in her arms and raising her head to listen to the choir singing from the loft above. She realized that the celebration she had come to love as a child she could come to love again as an adult.

Since Mark's death, Pagels had found participation in worship difficult. Somehow on this night, the stories of angels singing and the miraculous birth seemed to meld with other stories from the Judeo-Christian tradition like those of Isaac's birth to an aging Sarah, of the prophet Samuel called as a child, and of the rescue of the infant Moses. They all came together for her—this mixture of legend and Midrash about which scholars have little to no historical information—in the joy and solemnity of Christmas Eve. She was moved beyond the pain of her past with love and gratitude toward her daughter Sarah and the whole community gathered there to celebrate Christmas "with intimations of Jesus' impending death as well as the promise of his continuing, radiant presence."* Somehow everyone was brought together for her that night, both living and dead.

For a moment, she was shocked by the thought that we could have made all of this up out of what has happened in our own lives. Then she realized that no one has to do this. Countless other people have already woven the narratives of innumerable lives into stories and music and meanings. They have shaped and reshaped them from generation to generation, and they continue to do so as they carry on a tradition that may shape and reshape us as it intersects our human experience.

The feminine perspective permeates Elaine Pagels' thought, as it did that of Julian of Norwich and Margery Kempe before her. She was taken by the Gnostic writings of Valentius and a number of women heretics who became a burr under the saddle of Irenaeus. When Irenaeus would question them about true beliefs, they would often remain silent or simply state he was wrong. They thought that he had not yet advanced beyond naïve levels of understanding. Irenaeus called them "absolutely foolish and stupid people" and threatened them with excommunication. They simply replied they "no longer believed in the God whom he invoked as an angry judge ready to cast unbelievers into the fires of hell."†

Among the Gnostic writings, there is a unique and special place for women. In *The Secret Book*, the story in Genesis of Eve's birth from Adam's rib becomes the story of the awakening of our spiritual capacities to know God. According to the author, all human beings have this innate ability, although it offers only hints and glimpses of divine reality. Eve became

---

* *Ibid.*, p. 144.
† *Ibid.*, p. 159, 160..

a symbol for the gift of spiritual understanding that enables us to reflect, however imperfectly, upon divine reality. In some versions of the text, Eve is the gift of the divine "Mother-Father" who feels compassion for Adam by sending him a helper, a luminous *epinoia* ("creative" or "inventive" consciousness) to show him how to ascend back the way he came down.

The conclusions reached by Pagels are few and modest. First, like Margery and Julian, she elevates self-knowledge as a legitimate, even essential, aspect of faith. What we have of *The Gospel of Mary* begins with a vision of the risen Jesus telling his disciples, "The Son of Man is within you. Follow after him! Those who seek him will find him."* Pagels focuses her attention on what each individual soul may experience for herself. Orthodox doctrines of God, whether they be Jewish, Christian, or Muslim, normally tend to emphasize a separation between what is divine and what is human. God may be "wholly other" from humankind but revelation need not be seen as diametrically opposed to any form of human perception. Those mystically inclined sons and daughters of Abraham who believe that truth may come through intuition, reflection, or creative imagination should no longer be denied equal or legitimate status.

Second, she makes a telling argument for embracing the presence of diversity that continues to persist throughout organized religion. As guardians of an unchanging tradition, orthodox believers tend to equate faithfulness with adhering to an ancient canon of truth to which nothing should be added or subtracted. Historically, they have often had difficulty acknowledging, much less welcoming, diverse viewpoints. However, from its very beginning, the Christian faith has never failed to spawn such diversity. Not only did orthodoxy fail to suppress it completely, diversity abounds in increasing novelty and varied expressions throughout history. Sanctioning this diversity became a vital part of Elaine Pagels' life and work.

Finally, Pagels calls herself a seeker. In doing so, she joins ranks with Julian of Norwich and other sisters in faith who choose to follow a road less traveled. The word *heresy* originally meant "an act of choice." Christianity, Judaism, and other ancient traditions survive only as each generation relives, reinvents, and reinterprets what it has received from those who went before. We all must make choices. We all must seek insights, intuitions, and intimations that validate our faith from our own experience; ultimately, each person must decide between right and wrong, between truth and lies. Accordingly, Pagels echoes Karen Armstrong in confessing that "Most of us, sooner or later, find that, at critical points in our lives, we must strike out on our own to make a path where none exists."†

---

* *Ibid.*, p. 103.
† *Ibid.*, p. 184, 185.

More Conclusions

So what about the choice posed by orthodox Christianity between becoming a believer or a seeker? Irenaeus' canon of truth served an important, if not essential, role in preserving the vision of a universal church. Without the strong organization preserved by its creed, canon, and hierarchy, Christianity might well have foundered on the anvil of history as Mithraism and other mystery religions of the time. It survived, but often at the price of ignoring the fruits of self-knowledge and discouraging many who sought to pursue and explore the seeds of faith in their own personal experience. Revelation was shut down for generations during the Middle Ages as complete and confined to the past, so thoroughly that a group of monks were said to have searched the Bible to determine how many teeth were to be found in the mouth of a donkey, rather than simply count them.

Neither believing nor seeking is a workable end in itself. Endless belief, set in stone for all times, is an unmodified and inflexible vessel, ill equipped to navigate even the shallowest waters of human consciousness and unadaptable to the constancy of change everywhere in real life. On the other hand, continual seeking, aimlessly creating no workable belief, is a directionless boat without a rudder, tossed to and fro repeatedly in circles of its own wake. Creeds are incapable of bearing the complexity and diversity of human experience. Their aim is to embody some clearly held conception of truth. They may carry a set of symbols, myths, and legends capable of addressing a much broader range of meanings, but they are not a vessel equipped to navigate the deeper waters of diversity, complexity, and ambiguity that surround us.

More is required before the evolving forces that living human systems need to maintain balance, growth, and harmony. Believers must seek, and seekers must believe. Beliefs require seeking actualization in experience, and experience requires conceptualizing in belief. Creeds and liturgy are formed for repetition, creating a solid vessel in which to deliver the possibilities of a renewed and evolving faith to each generation. And the guard is constantly changing. Diversity in both our body of belief and our experience is always emerging throughout history, beneath the wings of any orthodoxy. Such is the diversity of faith we enjoy today.

Most of our confessors struggled with the orthodox beliefs of their time. Augustine chaffed under his teachers to find his own way, although later life led him to champion his mother's orthodoxy and help shape the future of Catholic theology. Tolstoy was so disillusioned with the Russian Orthodox Church of his time that he lost his will to go on living. Vonnegut was enraged when established religious conservatives burned his books the way Athanasius set fire to those of the Gnostics. Theirs was a more masculine experience. It differed markedly from the experiences of faith we encounter among the women.

Our women confessors never seemed to feel confined within the narrow lines of a prevailing orthodoxy. Julian appeared relatively untroubled by anything so compelling as the testosterone of an Augustine or a Patrick. Instead, she came to regard the patriarchal preoccupation with sin and eternal punishment of her time as unworthy of the grace and mercy she came to know in God our Mother. Now Margery was not without her struggles with libido; but after 14 children, like many other women of her time, survival depended upon becoming celibate. She fought long and hard for ecclesiastical credentials to wear the white of chastity and ended up with a spiritual marriage to God the Father. Such spiritual unions among religious women of her day were normally with Christ, but then Margery was never given to the non-excessive.

Karen Armstrong and Elaine Pagels' struggles with orthodoxy are fresh in our minds. Neither was preoccupied with sin and judgment or heaven and hell. Pagels admired the Gnostics' indifference to ideas of the wrath of God. For Armstrong, the measure of any theological doctrine was its compassion and capacity for empathy. Both became earnest seekers in search of a workable faith. Our body of belief is incomplete apart from the feminine experience budding beneath whatever orthodoxy prevailed, leaving its own marks of self-knowledge throughout the diversity of religious history.

This rhythm of seeking and believing is woven into the faith of every age. Beneath the continuity provided by canon, creed, liturgy, theology, and hierarchy that governs the institutional church, the human spirit has always produced seekers. Spawned under the wings of Mother Church, they learn to fly on their own. This is the character of a full confessional experience. In whatever human predicament we find ourselves, there is always a pathway or direction that can usher us into a fresh spiritual encounter.

Practice

Self-Awareness and Internal Dialogue

1. Are any of your own personal beliefs changing as you react to the confessions of Karen Armstrong and Elaine Pagels? Have you located in yourself some kind of rhythm between seeking and believing? What positive confessional experiences have you had so far? Take time to register in writing any beliefs you have been formulating as you go. While you're at it, you may wish to consider any beliefs you have been challenging or discarding.

2. At crucial times in their lives, both Elaine Pagels and Karen Armstrong reached a point where they felt compelled to strike out on their own. They left behind old ideas and troublesome beliefs in order to pursue their own pathway of personal experience and

spiritual commitment. Can you point to such instances in your own life? Take time to chart your course through whatever experiences come to mind.

3. In the quiet of your private time, locate where you are at present. Is some sort of quest, spiritual and/or compassionate, taking shape in the way you approach others? In your work? In your family life? Note, journal, or "brood upon" what occurs to you, permitting your attention to follow whatever comes to mind.

Confessional Partnership

1. Take time to share anything of your choosing from the self-awareness exercises above. Often, aspects of positive confession can be developed and refined in conversation.

2. Confessional partners may adopt measures of accountability that serve to solidify our choices and give us a boost to report back on various quests, tasks, and pursuits that we have assumed. Reporting back to one another builds our confidence in ourselves and in each other. We are more apt to take constructive risks in the context of a confidant and more apt to avoid unrealistic folly.

Discussion Group

1. These two women confessors are an interesting study of parallels and contrasts. An opening discussion might build a list of them from the group: for example, a nun and an evangelical Christian, for a contrast, and their mutual emphasis on empathy and compassion for a parallel.

2. Both women have emphasized points in their lives where they felt compelled to strike out on their own. The differing circumstances and various ways this can happen in life could prove worthy of considerable discussion.

3. There are a number of other powerful themes that could stimulate conversation, including:

   a. Both seemed to see the essence of religion more in its practice than in its belief in formal creeds or theology.

   b. Karen Armstrong suggests that compassion should become the litmus test between good and bad theology. Are there other considerations of equal importance that you would suggest, and why?

   c. What about the prevailing unequal status that Pagels describes between the self-knowledge of the seeker and existing

Orthodox beliefs? Is there a rhythm of seeking and believing that we can make workable?

d. Should we sanction diversity within and across different faiths, as well as our commonality? What are the limits or boundaries?

4. The discussion leader or various members of the group could read Karen Armstrong's *The History of God*, or portions thereof, feeding their impressions into the discussion, particularly the final chapter.

Confessional Group

1. Some sharing of the current status of positive confessional conclusions among members would be a good exercise at the start of this group. Getting into words any awareness, practice, or new belief that has come as a result of your experience thus far can prove beneficial—not only to you, but to others as well.

2. A word is in order about conversations in which you share what you believe with other people. They often involve a strong measure of intimacy and self-disclosure, especially when it comes to things that matter a great deal to us. Sharing a growing faith is a very sensitive matter for most of us, often more difficult to talk about than the negative things we confess about ourselves. Acceptance is fully as important here as in any matter of shame or embarrassment.

3. We mentioned above using accountability in confessional practice. We can set out to accomplish some intention and report upon the results at the next meeting. Some people develop specific quests that take time, effort, and encouragement. Maintaining a running account of your experience with other members of the group will provide ongoing support in such endeavors.

CHAPTER 9

The Enneagram

Sooner or later I knew I had to tackle the Enneagram. I was skeptical about this ancient tool that some say originated in Babylon as early as 2500 BC The term *enneagram* comes from the Greek word *ennea*, which means "nine," and *grammos*, the Greek word for "figure." It is a nine-pointed figure set within a circle replete with mystical symbolism. The Enneagram has been widely used by Christians, Buddhists, Muslims (especially Sufis), and Jewish mystics following the *Kabbalah* for well over a thousand years. Some think it was derived from the nine divine attributes that Neoplatonists like Plotinus and other Gnostics in the third century believed to be reflected in human nature. If so, these found their way into the Christian tradition as their opposites—in the form of the Seven Deadly Sins to which fear and deceit were added. (See Figure 9.1.)

I was skeptical because some of the primary laws of mysticism seemed far-fetched to me. There was the Law of Three represented by the central triangle of Three–Six–Nine, standing for the trinity of forces present in creation. These forces are represented in the Christian trinity of Father, Son, and Holy Ghost, and in Hinduism's three divine forces of creation: Brahma, Vishnu, and Shiva. This triad can also be called creative, destructive, and persevering, or active, receptive, and reconciling. At any rate, when you divide one by three you get 0.333333..., which repeats infinitely. In some mysterious way beyond my imagination, this repetition demonstrates mathematically how the trinity of forces works together to help events survive through time, providing a new influx of energy to perpetuate their life.

Although I was a math (and chemistry) major in college, this mathematical proof still makes no sense to me. The Law of Seven is equally

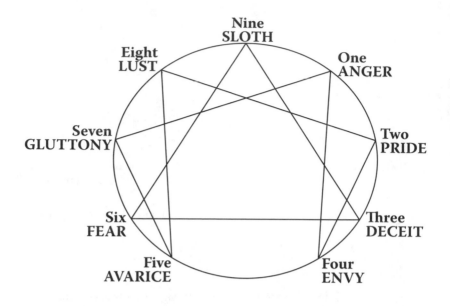

Figure 9.1 Oscar Ichazo's Enneagram of the Passions (Deadly Sins).

mystifying. The Law of Seven or The Law of Octaves, preserved in the musical scale as seven notes with the repeating "Do," somehow governs the succession of stages by which events are played out in the material world. If you divide the number one (1) by the number seven (7), you get another infinite repeating series of numbers that look like 0.142857142857..., none of which contains a multiple of three. This division somehow demonstrates mathematically how the Law of Three and the Law of Seven interact in specific ways along the diagram's inner lines. I'll stop here because I suspect you may be as bewildered and unenthusiastic about such data as I am.

Armed with this confusion and cynicism, I forced my way into the finer points of the Enneagram. The idea behind both the Seven Deadly Sins and the Enneagram is that all of us have some measure of each tendency within us, but one of these features crops up again and again as characteristic of our human predicament. This feature becomes the root of our imbalance, serving to keep us trapped in our ego. I resisted the notion of some modern writers that these nine tendencies can be considered "personality types."* Psychiatrist Claudio Naranjo called them "ego fixations."† I selected the descriptions by Helen Palmer, who uses the term "personality types," but also refers to them as nine "features," or "types" of "mental

---

* See Riso, Don Richard, and Hudson, Russ. *The Wisdom of the Enneagram* (New York: Bantam Books, 1999).
† Naranjo, Claudio. *Character and Neurosis* (Nevada City, CA: Gateways/IDHHB, 1994).

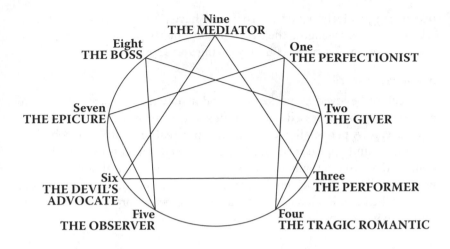

Figure 9.2 The Enneagram of personality types.

and emotional preoccupations" to which we may fall prey. Her wording is neutral and workable for most of us, using neither "sin" language nor the over-polished refinements of an established "personality type." (See Figure 9.2.) Her simplicity preserves the genius of the Enneagram. She maps out the behavioral tendencies of each type in minimally suggestive language and depicts the possibilities of response and movement toward change and balance, freeing each of us to adapt its potential for use in our own unique life experience.

The Nine Types[*]

1. The Perfectionist

You are critical of yourself and of others. You tend to feel ethically superior, that there is only one correct way. You are concerned with right and wrong, with correcting and controlling yourself and others, and can have problems with repressed anger and impatience. The sin derivative is anger. Evolved Ones can be critically astute and morally heroic.

2. The Giver

You tend to demand affection and approval. You seek to be loved and appreciated by others and may become devoted to meeting their needs. You may also be manipulative and seek to become indispensable to someone else. Twos may show a different "self" to each good friend and can

---

[*] Palmer, Helen. *The Enneagram* (San Francisco: HarperCollins, 1991), pp. 36–45.

become aggressively seductive. They may have problems caring for themselves and acknowledging their own needs. The sin derivative is pride. An evolved Two can become genuinely caring and supportive of others.

3. The Performer

You seek to be loved by performing and achieving. You are competitive and may become obsessed with winning and comparative status. You are often a Type A personality and confuse your real self with your job identity. Image and appearances are important, and you can look more productive than you actually are. Threes can become workaholics and may be highly driven for personal advancement. The sin derivative is deceit. Evolved Threes are often effective leaders, competent promoters, and captains of winning teams.

4. The Tragic Romantic

You are tragic, sad, artistic, and sensitive. You tend to be attracted to the unavailable. Your ideal is never here and now. Your attention may be focused on an absent love or the loss of a friend. Fours may be personal and emotionally honest but also feel moody, self-conscious, and sorry for themselves. The sin derivative is envy. Evolved Fours can be creative in their lifestyle. They may be committed to beauty and the passionate in life. They are also able to help other people through their pain.

5. The Observer

You tend to maintain emotional distance from others. You protect your privacy, don't get involved, and may do without as a defense against involvement. You may feel drained by commitment and by other people's needs. Fives tend to compartmentalize obligations and stay detached from people, feelings, and possessions. The sin derivative is avarice. They may tend to hold on to their own resources and minimize their needs. Evolved Fives are capable of making excellent decisions, may become quite visionary, and can be both independent and innovative.

6. The Devil's Advocate

You may be fearful, dutiful, and plagued by doubt. Thinking may replace doing because you can be afraid to take action. You suspect exposure to others will lead to attack. You tend to identify with the underdog. You can be anti-authoritarian, self-sacrificing, and loyal to a cause. Phobic Sixes tend to vacillate, feel persecuted, and cave in when cornered. Counterphobic Sixes may feel trapped and confront what they fear in an aggressive way. Their sin derivative is fear. Evolved Sixes will work for a cause in the way that others labor for personal gain. They can be good team players, loyal soldiers, and faithful friends.

7. The Epicure

You may tend to look and feel eternally young like Peter Pan. You can be dilettantish, superficial, and adventurous, a dance-away lover who takes a gourmet approach to life. You may have trouble keeping commitments, desire to keep your options open, and want to stay on an emotional high. Sevens are generally happy and stimulating to be around. They have a habit of starting projects that they fail to see through to completion. The sin derivative is gluttony. Evolved Sevens are good synthesizers, theoreticians, and Renaissance types who are capable of focusing their talents on worthwhile goals and becoming highly accomplished.

8. The Boss

You may tend to be extremely protective, to stand up for yourself and your friends, to take charge, and to love a good fight. Being in control is important. You are capable of open displays of anger and force. You have respect for opponents who stand up to you and fight. Eights are given to contacting others through sex and toe-to-toe confrontations. They often maintain an excessive way of life: too much, too late at night, too loud, and so on. Their sin derivative is lust. Evolved Eights excel as leaders, especially in an adversarial role. They can offer powerful support to other people and make the way safe for friends.

9. The Mediator

You may tend toward obsessive ambivalence, seeing all points of view and readily replacing your own wishes with those of others, or your own goals with non-essential activities. You are willing to go along in order to keep the peace and want everything to be without conflict. You may have a tendency toward narcoticizing yourself with food, television, and drink. Nines often know other people's needs better than their own, tend to space out, and are uncertain whether or not they want to take part or play on the team. They may be agreeable, but their anger comes out in indirect ways. Their sin derivative is sloth. However, their motive is drawing back to avoid conflict rather than simple laziness. Evolved Nines are excellent peacemakers, counselors, and negotiators, and tend to achieve well when on a chosen course.

Resolving Impasses

There you have it—the Enneagram. You have read it through as I did the first time I saw it. That is all I had to do to become engaged in a new level of self-awareness. I am a Three, a Performer; there is no doubt about it. I had never thought about myself exactly that way, but nothing better characterizes my more troublesome mental preoccupations and struggles. I hope you had a similar experience, that is, found your number so clearly. If you didn't, go back and try again until one of these basic types engages you enough to gather your self-knowledge around it. That is the first step to test its value to you.

We can use the Enneagram to address the makeup of our human predicament in a way that invites exploring all kinds of possibilities for expanding our self-knowledge. We begin by establishing confessional ownership of the most troublesome aspects of the basic type that describes us best. From there we can map out some of the chief ways we might search for a relevant response. Instead of offering us some static view of "sin" or a "perverse tendency" that we must either quit or struggle with endlessly, it provides us with a starting point to consider many responses.

Each of the nine types points beyond itself to possibilities of an "evolved" expression of its essential characteristics, so there are ways we can turn what troubles us most into something of genuine benefit to ourselves and others. This supports the notion in traditional mysticism that each point of the Enneagram was derived from one of the nine attributes of God that the Gnostics believed were embodied in the human spirit. Each of the Seven Deadly Sins, in turn, was formulated as the opposite of a divine attribute. The Enneagram preserves the notion that sin always points beyond itself to some potentially spiritual resolution. It fits with the idea in the *Gospel of Thomas*: "If you bring forth what is within you, what you bring forth will save you. If you do not bring forth what is within you, what you do not bring forth will destroy you."

Everything in the Enneagram points beyond itself. Each of the nine types has its wings on either side that are said to influence or "flavor" your chief feature. Then there are dynamics from other types that can go into action when we are placed under stress, and still others that come into play when we are in a secure or non-stressful situation. These, in turn, open up even more possibilities to move through whatever impasse has been governed by the primary mental and emotional preoccupation of our type. The circular character of wholeness, completeness, or balance in the Enneagram suggests an increasing number of responses through which we may change and evolve. But I am getting ahead of myself at this point.

A Personal Journey

I want to take you through some of my own reactions to the Enneagram. I hope that walking through it again with you can serve to demonstrate how you can make your own journey into its possibilities. The only way is to write with some measure of confessional openness about its impact upon me. Perhaps my efforts can demonstrate its potential for self-knowledge as a guide for your own use. Karen Armstrong had inspired me to approach it empathically and honestly for what it has to offer despite my cynicism and preexisting prejudices. It soon became quite a trip.

I am a Three—a Performer. My struggles with performance date back to my earliest years. I was born into a family of musicians with great expectations that I too would excel in that field. My father was an accomplished organist and pianist, and could play virtually any musical instrument. My mother played the cello in numerous string quartets. I started taking piano lessons at the tender age of 5. We lived in Hartsville, South Carolina, which was small enough for me to walk across town to my music lessons. My teacher was a tall and extremely attractive dark-haired woman named Mrs. Prugh, who kept a damp rag in her studio to wipe the dirt off the keys after I played. She was patient with me, patient beyond belief, mostly out of loyalty to my father, I suspect. I hated to practice, but practice I did. Endlessly, it seemed.

Most of all, I hated the pressure to get it right, perfect. With each new piece assigned for recital, I can still remember my mother saying to my father, "Play it for him, Dwight, so he can hear how it will sound." And he did. And I would listen, but I could never make it sound like that. I can still hear my father's voice from the other room as I practiced, "F sharp, David!" Once on the way to a lesson across town, I became so anxious that I soiled my britches. I crawled into some bushes, but not in time. Now what would I do? I couldn't go to the lesson like that, and I was ashamed to go home. I still have occasional dreams about toilets and getting clean.

I took piano until I was 11 years old. I was determined to perform and perform well. And I did on occasion. My career as a pianist came to a painful end when I was 11 at one of those countless music contests in which you are rated Superior, Excellent, Very Good, Good, and so forth. My father was a professor at Coker College in Hartsville. The auditorium was semicircular, with a main floor and a three-tiered balcony like the Met in New York. It was packed, and my father was there too, watching, and listening. I played a sonata by Mozart, which I hear occasionally nestled among the classics playing on FM radio when I drive. For the life of me I cannot remember its name. I played through to the first rest and tried to adjust the piano bench a little closer. I lost my concentration but I kept going, painfully, determinedly, heartlessly, and far from perfectly. But I finished and left the stage. The tears came, and they still come sometimes when I hear the same piece. I never played the piano again. To me it was the major failure of my young life. And I never got over it. A Very Good.

So I am a Performer. I am competitive. I am conscious of status and comparisons. I am driven by the parental message "Always do your best." In some other areas, I could be better than "Very Good," which only served to drive the bar higher and higher. I raised my children the same way. Even now when we share what happened playing golf, the question is always, "How did you do?" I never knew there was another one until my old friend George Bennett told me his father always used to ask, "Did you have a good time?" The worst thing a Performer can be is a quitter. And I was a quitter—I utterly failed as a pianist.

Dealing with Failure

So I received an old trombone and was encouraged to join the high-school band. You could in the seventh grade those days—the marching band. Performers are determined. I still blocked in reading music, but with enough practice and memorization, I began to excel. By the age of 14, when we moved to Danville, Kentucky, I got even better. Doc Owens, our band director, put on an annual concert each spring with the Danville, Burgin, and Lancaster bands. I was given a solo, accompanied only by piano. I practiced and practiced. I had no idea how anxious I was. Performers often wonder what they are feeling. When I arose to play, alone before all those people, my performance anxiety was through the ceiling. My mouth went dry. Now if you have ever tried to play a trombone with a dry mouth and lips, you know you can't. Every third note I blew air. I stood there half-playing my way through "The Song of the Evening Star" from *Tannhauser*. When I finished, I left the stage humiliated, overwhelmed with shame. My only memory afterward was Red Brandenburg hunting me out and trying to make me feel better by saying I did "Very Good."

Doc Owens told me I showed a lot of courage standing up there and finishing. What else could I do? But no more solos. My only musical accomplishment after that was to disgrace the family by playing trombone in a small dance band around central Kentucky. But I still balked at reading music. We faked a lot of what we did, listening to recordings and "aping" them. Performers aren't supposed to quit. When I became a senior in high school, Doc Owens again talked me into doing a solo and entering the State Music Contest. By now my skills were pretty good. As for my performance anxiety, Doc suggested a large lemon and a glass of water in case my mouth went dry again. So armed with fruit and liquid, I made it through the District, sipping and sucking, before, during each rest, and after. Then the Regional Contest. Success again, and on to the State.

Now the State Contest was at the University of Kentucky. I was determined to leave the lemon behind and mounted the stage armed with only a paper cup filled with water, which I placed as unceremoniously as possible behind me on the grand piano and turned to face the judges and all the musicians who had survived their Districts and Regionals to compete for the golden orb, a Superior. Performers are competitive and determined. And now I was determined to master my performance anxiety and do well. I played through to the first rest. I didn't have to have a drink; I can make it to the second rest. Once there, I felt I could get to the third rest. At the third rest, it's now or never; I can finish without a drink. And I did. I finished! It was then I turned around, only to notice I had inadvertently knocked over my cup of water before I ever started to play. How close can one come to ultimate disaster? And survive?

I wandered around alone for a while. There were visions of what could have been. I could see myself frantically bending over the closed top of the grand piano trying desperately to slurp up a few drops of moisture and regain my composure enough to continue. Finally, I mustered sufficient courage to go downstairs and view the ratings that had been posted. There were 16 trombones (not 76), and at the top there were two Superiors. I was one of them.

Instead of joy, there was only relief. True to form, I soon abandoned the trombone. By now I had learned to approach most significant activities in life as a Performer. There was work. I could excel there. At age 11, I began delivering newspapers all over Hartsville—318 *Charlotte Observers* daily and on Sunday. At 12, I began working for Mr. Hoskins at the Piggly Wiggly. I stocked, sacked, and carried out groceries to cars after school on Thursdays, Fridays, and all day Saturday. There is little performance anxiety in good, old-fashioned, hard work. This was before child labor laws in South Carolina. I worked from seven in the morning to midnight on Saturdays with a half-hour off to eat lunch. At ten o'clock each night, the fire whistle blew to signal closing time, which for us marked the beginning of the hardest work all day. We swept off the front sidewalk; emptied the windows of vegetables and perishables and dressed them for the weekend; swept and oiled the wooden floors; cleaned out the meat cases, swept up the sawdust and scraped down the cutting blocks; cleaned the saws, cases, and counters in the meat market; swept out the back room; and carried out the trash into the alley.

In short, I became a workaholic. There was scouting—I became an Eagle Scout. There was school—I never matured to the point that my own children did early on, learning I did not have to do everything the teacher told me. My performance grade-wise was always important, even after I moved to Danville, Kentucky, in the ninth grade, where making good marks was a marginal accomplishment among peers and highly suspect by anyone with athletic ability. I don't know what I would have done without sports. My early training in music led me to doubt my ability to perform in the "manly arts" of fighting and competition. I had always hated bullies and shied away from fisticuffs whenever I could. In Danville, football and basketball were king. I will always be indebted to my old coach Ernie Wofford who asked me to come out for football my sophomore year.

Newcomers were hazed rather thoroughly in preseason practice. I had two things going for me as a Performer: (a) my work ethic, in which I would attempt to undertake any assignment; and (b) the strange liking I took to bodily contact, which met some need deep down inside to strike back at those who tried to push me around. And, I suppose, I desperately needed to prove to myself (and to others—the Performer's concern with "image") that I was no "sissy."

My test came early on when I was backing up the line on the scrub team. I overheard John Acton, a senior tailback with whom I later played in college, tell big Ben Williams, who played tackle across from me, to "step aside" and let him just run right over me, so I knew it was coming. As a sophomore, I wasn't very big yet. I had that David/Goliath kind of feeling without sling and stones. I can still see him coming at me with knees high and feet flying. There was no time to adjust piano benches or get anxious. I got as low as I could, came up and met him, and managed to stand him up in the air for a moment, then slam him sideways to the ground. That would not have been possible if he had not been "hot dogging" and showing so many foot movements that he was leaning slightly backward when I struck him. I shut my eyes on impact, and, when I opened them, they were met by a bewildered gaze in his. I had made it into that accepted circle of athletes at Danville High School. Even if I didn't drink, I was accepted. I loved the camaraderie and competition of team sports. Two years later, I showed some early evidence of becoming an evolved Three, according to Palmer. I was captain of a winning football team.

Stress and Security

The issues of being a Performer have followed me all my life. They circle back at each new stage or situation, like Karen Armstrong's spiral staircase. Each time they do, they tend to present an increasing number of doorways to different responses. We are ready to consider this range of responses now. Once you have decided upon your type or chief feature, the one that is operative under usual conditions, you are ready to explore your involvement with two other types: (a) one that comes into play when you go into action or are placed under stress; and (b) the other that emerges when you are in a secure or non-stressful situation. This is depicted in Figure 9.3. Your *stress point* is in the direction that the arrow points. Your *security point* is the one away from which the arrow points. My Stress point is a Nine; my security point is a Six. You can readily determine yours.

So could I really identify Nine-like behavior when I was under stress? I can certainly be very ambivalent and draw back to avoid conflict. Many times I can recall going along in order to keep the peace. I can get paralyzed with indecision. One favorite saying is: "When you don't know what to do, nothing is usually a pretty cool thing." Not only was I uncertain whether I wanted to play musical instruments for recitals or contests, I quit the music team out of extreme anxiety. I suspect that I may have resolved some of my issues as a Performer by evolving as a Nine through my years spent in the practice of psychotherapy. There I was forced to learn first-hand that "It" was not all about me and how I did. It was more about other people and what I could help them do. And become. In the process, I think I can now qualify in such evolved Nine "achievements" as peacemaking, counseling, and negotiating.

Then there is a matter of my security point, which is Six. I have to confess immediately that I am a workaholic and I am afraid not to achieve. So when there is nothing to do, I become anxious and restless. Perhaps this is why bypass surgery followed my retirement from the seminary by barely a month. I fear doing nothing. There is a recurrent dream with very few variations. I'm a senior in college, and it is midway through football season. There are not many more games, and I am not playing as well as I had expected. I must try harder to do something noteworthy on the field. Sometimes it is the last game, and I am on the bench. I walk by Coach hoping he will realize I'm not in and put me in. I am not certain as a Three that I can really enjoy the security of not having to achieve. Good team players still carry out assignments, and loyal soldiers still must do battle. Faithful friends still stick by others dutifully. I can bolt to such evolved activities to avoid doing nothing, but how secure is that?

I suspect that this is the point—at least it is for me. Authentic security is not to be found within the security point for many Threes. I agree with Palmer, who thinks the "security cult" among Enneagram enthusiasts is on the wrong track. Its members suggest a strategy for moving toward health is in cultivating the better aspects of one's security point. Their assumption is that a security reaction is innately superior to an action/stress reaction.

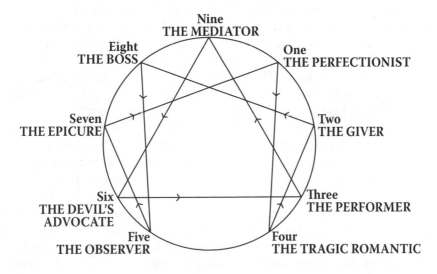

Figure 9.3 Toward action, away from security (toward stress, away from nonstress).

Palmer reports interviewing an equal number of people whose character has been positively formed by developing the best aspects of their action/stress point. This was certainly true for me. In my case, the issue goes even deeper, and I suspect it may for many others. Here we need to deal with two other aspects of the Enneagram that offer pathways to the formation of character.

The Wings*

The *wings* are the points that appear on either side of your basic type. As a Three, my wings are Two and Four. Together we belong to one of the three "core personalities" formed on either side of the Three—Six—Nine triangle of "core points." For reasons equally mysterious as the Law of Three itself, the wings to each of these three points (in my case, Two and Four) express an internalized and an externalized version of their core point and serve to influence or "flavor" its expression. Each of the three core personalities has its own focus of concern—with our group it tends to be preoccupation with image and difficulty determining what we feel. The wings of Six (Five and Seven) share an underlying paranoia or fear, and the wings of Nine (Eight and One) share a core disposition toward anger. But only the Three–Six–Nine core points find internal and external expressions of themselves through the other two wings in their group. However, the wings of any point are influential. For example, a Nine who would prefer to express anger indirectly or passively would lean either to the Eight side (the Boss), becoming blunt and stubborn in a passive/aggressive approach, or the One side (the Perfectionist), becoming critical and nitpicking in indirect ways.

If this material doesn't "click" with you, take your time with it. I had to go over it a number of times to "get it." As a Performer (Three), I certainly did a lot of Giver (Two) activities to get approval and love. I gave it all I had at work and at play. I can still remember watching Mr. Hoskins at the Piggly Wiggly to see if he noticed how hard I was working. Image is important. No Boy Scout ever forgets his mother sewing on merit badges or pinning an Eagle Scout medal on his chest. And who else always helps old ladies and the infirm across the street? If I am completely honest, I don't believe many people go into the ministry or the helping professions who are not in search of love or approval. Most people who devote themselves to meeting the needs of others have gotten the task fairly mixed up with meeting their own needs. We think if we can busy ourselves helping someone else that our own problems will go away. They don't. They just get worse, especially when we try to fix what's wrong with us in somebody else. For this reason, people in the helping professions usually require close supervision and often personal psychotherapy. I know I certainly did. If we

---

* Palmer, Helen. *The Enneagram* (San Francisco: HarperCollins, 1991), pp. 36–45.

will just learn to deal with some of our own needs, blind spots, and one-sidedness, then we might get into a position to be of help to someone else.

Performers like me often engage in external expressions of the Giver (Two), seeking affection and approval through meeting the needs of others. We may even work to become indispensable. We can do this as parents with our children and have profound difficulties letting them go. People in the helping professions can do it with clients, patients, parishioners, students, and anyone else who comes through their doors. We can give those around us assistance, knowledge, insight, help, money, attention, time; but until we learn to get beyond our own needs for affirmation, our caring remains manipulative and shallow. We can also lose sight of our personal needs for attention and self-care. Unless we can own these tendencies in full self-awareness, our efforts at genuine care and support of others tend to crumble beneath the weight of seeking approval and affection.

So Performers efforts always fail to produce the love and approval we are after. When performing, I could never be good enough or succeed in performing long enough to satisfy even myself. Moreover, when I performed well, it never seemed to matter that much to others. Some were even envious and became guardedly jealous or oppositional. When I externalized my performing to Giving (Two), the results were even more frustrating. Some people never even acknowledged my efforts. Others came to expect them and were incensed if they weren't continued or increased. People are not necessarily grateful when you assist them. I will never forget Ernest Carver's exclaiming in group therapy one day after working through a very difficult problem, "I just hate being helped!"

With such failures as a Three and at my Two wing, I would eventually be driven into internal expressions of the Four wing—the Tragic Romantic. I could manage never to feel satisfied that I was loved enough. Inside, I could feel loveless, alone, and insecure. Strangely enough, I became much more certain of my father's love after his death, and I confess my lowest points in life have come when my striving to win someone's affection impaled itself upon the shadow of my self-seeking and fell lifeless before me. I could feel abandoned, alone, and maudlinly sorry for myself. And no one "sees how hard I tried." I put the last in quotation marks in gratitude to Eric Berne, who taught me to understand the many moves of a psychological game he called "See How Hard I Tried." The person who is "It" (me in this case) always ends up feeling the same inner loneliness and tragic sadness of love lost or never present. I can hardly do this number with a straight face any longer. But on occasion, even now, if the circumstances are right....

My hunch is that most Performers share some similar fate. Efforts at Giving (Two) never succeed in accomplishing the sense of being lovable for which we search. The fate of the Tragic Romantic (Four) prevails, bearing the sadness of a futile search for affection that fails to materialize. This

Three needed to deal with the tendencies in both wings before I could lessen the grip of always having to perform and begin to evolve anywhere.

Simply pursuing some evolved expression of either your security point or your stress/action point may not be enough. In my case, it was necessary to deal with my continuing involvement in my two wings. Only then did the way become clear to move in the direction of more evolved levels at any point. My wings presented a system of concerns so intricately intertwined they had to be addressed together. I know this to be true in retrospect. This larger, more systemic picture provided by the Enneagram may be obscured by a more limited attention to particular strivings.

My experience here is difficult to put into words. The "sin" of a Three is "deceit," self-deceit and deceiving others. For a performer like me, that's one reason the idea of honest confession proved so powerful. Across the years I have come to realize that regardless of how well I perform, I seldom keep performing at the level of the "image" I seek to project. Yesterday, for example, I made a real mess of my work with a young woman who has an eating disorder, the details of which I will not reveal. By the same token, when I stop deceiving myself, I must acknowledge that I have never failed so miserably as I have felt I did, even at the time of my catastrophic recital in Coker College auditorium at age 11. I am never so good or so bad as I have thought myself to be on occasion. At times, I can be quite grandiose about the importance of both my deeds and my misdeeds. Here is where the "sin" of pride enters the picture from my Two wing. Givers learn early to deceive others with efforts that allow people to perceive both their abilities and their contributions in ways that far exceed either. Sometimes they themselves come to believe these exaggerations. Humility always lurks in the wings, awaiting the return of a realistic awareness that it isn't all about us, what we do, and how we are perceived.

This crucible of reality awaits us relentlessly in each outbreak of seeming success or failure, guarding our humanness and protecting our capacity for humility—which literally means "living close to the earth." We can ground ourselves with realistic pride in doing what we become able to do well and, at the same time, accept our earthy humanness, refusing to engage in efforts to prove our worth to others or ourselves by fulfilling some set of grand expectations. Our worth does not follow from what we do for others. It arises from what we are and become within ourselves. Here the message of Thomas' Gospel points the way, "If you bring forth what is within you, it will save you. If you do not bring forth what is within you, it will destroy you." This can occur in Threes like me when we stop denying our feelings and find suitable ways to contain and express them. Anger was always difficult for me to own and acknowledge. The more I know about my anger, the less I "lose my temper." I also hate to admit when I'm afraid;

but when I do, I am not as afraid. Denying my sadness creates depression, until I give vent to it with clear waves of grief. And so on.

Up Close and Personal

It is evident how up close and personal the Enneagram can take you in your most intimate relationships. This is where I start reigning myself in concerning what aspects of my life I will choose to expose in print to anyone picking up this book, and what I will keep to myself or disclose in a confessional partnership with a confidant or confessor. You may be facing similar choices regarding matters of your own growing self-awareness. All of us are entitled to our right to privacy.

Before I claim mine, there are some advantages to making confessions in family relationships. Genuine self-disclosure may prove invaluable when the bonds of trust and loyalty are strong enough to permit. For instance, as a Performer, I have always had difficulty saying, "I'm sorry." There is a stubborn streak that emerges in matters of importance to me. Sometimes I think I would rather be right than happy. This is particularly true when I argue with my wife, Margaret. Only recently have I come to understand some of the depth of what is at stake for me as an evolving Performer.

At the heart of being a Three is the need to take pride in performing at a high level, whatever it is, and being recognized as doing so. That puts me on the defensive in so many ways in my marriage. When Margaret is critical of something I do, don't do, or haven't done yet, a performance alarm goes off deep inside. It is a familiar and primitive mixture of anxiety, guilt, and shame. Some failure to perform at the level I wish to is about to be exposed. If I am into the Two wing of Giver, what was offered was unsatisfactory. I was stupid or inept or incompetent. If I am into the Four wing of Tragic Romantic, I have proven to be inadequate or unlovable. If the issue is substantial, and sometimes even if it isn't, I must defend myself. I must explain, justify what I have done or failed to do, appear blameless or innocent, or unjustly accused or angry in an always-futile effort to protect the fragile self-image of high-level performance.

It is important that I know these tendencies in myself. Unless I confess them, they may govern whole chunks of valuable time and energy between Margaret and me, unbeknown to either of us. If I can declare them openly, the need for all the defensiveness starts to crumble before significant measures of mutual acceptance that suddenly emerge through coming to understand one another. Saying "I'm sorry," for me, becomes easier once I have evolved beyond having to protect my flawed performance. When we start to share this kind of confession, differences can be accepted, resentments dissolved, and forgiveness becomes a practical reality. More about this in a later chapter.

Practice

Many books are written about the Enneagram. My own preference is that you use this ancient tool with just the information I have given you. Make your own application to your own life in your own way. If you have difficulty settling on which of the nine types fits you best, there is some help. Riso and Hudson include a simple two-page scoring test that will help you narrow down the possibilities.* They claim it is 70% accurate. It will take you 5 minutes. I must add, however, that it failed to identify me as a Performer. If you need more help than that, the authors include 15 statements characteristic of each of the nine types at the beginning of each chapter. Like many others, Riso and Hudson employ more positive terms for these types than Palmer: the Performer is an Achiever; the Epicure an Enthusiast; the Perfectionist a Reformer, and so on.

Self-Awareness and Internal Dialogue

1. Once you have settled on your particular type, I recommend that you follow a simple set of steps. You may choose to do this during some quiet time alone. Or you may want to do it with pencil and paper to jot down whatever occurs to you, especially if you journal. By now you have established the best way for you to go about self-reflection, so hang on; you may be in for quite a journey.
2. Proceed as follows: first, register as much evidence as you can that would support a hypothesis that you are one of these basic types. Second, explore your two wings, the types on either side of your chief feature in the same way. Third, follow the arrows on the diagram that indicates your stress point and your security point. Note carefully any ways in which these come into play at various times in your life.
3. Then repeat the process, paying attention to ways that you have evolved beyond the basic behaviors of your type, its wings, and its stress and security points. Don't be discouraged if you have to read the instructions again and again, as I did. The end result can be worth the effort.

Confessional Partnership

1. Take time to share what you wish from your experiences with the Enneagram. Usually partners can find some ways to help each other.

---

* *Op. cit.*, pp. 14, 15.

2. As you have come to know each other, you have formed impressions that will confirm, add to, or raise questions about your partner's conclusions. You have the added opportunity to explore ways in which your types fit with each other. Where do you connect naturally? Where do you experience differentness and conflict?

Discussion Group

1. It would pay the leader of the day to bone up sufficiently on the Enneagram to lead discussion and answer questions.
2. Conversation about its validity and accuracy may develop. Some may be even more skeptical than I. Using it is not a class requirement.
3. Some people may need a little assistance in working their way through the Enneagram. Members of the group can help each other with coaching and interpretation.
4. For some reason, most people like to share, at some level, what type they believe they are. This normally happens quite spontaneously. You can also consider how different types may go together in various kinds of relationships.

Confessional Group

1. The group may engage in the first three tasks of the Discussion Group. Members may share their reactions.
2. Check your impressions of your type with other members of the group for their feedback.
3. Be sure to examine some of the possibilities for considering relevant responses in the confessional use of the Enneagram. The group provides a forum for feedback, reactions, encouragement, and accountability.

CHAPTER **10**

The Truth of the Matter

When Martha Key introduced herself as "a liar," she sensed things about lying I had never considered. I had always thought lying was a simple matter of not telling the truth. But Martha Key instinctively knew lots more about it. She knew that a lot of lying involved liberal measures of self-deception, denial, and habitual lying to oneself. Even more important, lying to oneself or others avoids facing our human predicament as difficulties accumulate and escalate. Sooner or later, there comes a day of reckoning. At some level, she sensed what the Enneagram makes plain: by failing to address what troubles us most, we cease to evolve and grow as human beings. Not only do we evade the responsibility of making a relevant response; we miss out on the opportunities for spiritual encounter that may accompany such efforts.

Lying

So I felt the need to bone up on lying because I had never really examined the subject for myself. The dictionary simply defined a lie as a false statement made with deliberate intent to deceive. Most studies that I came across emphasized three elements: (a) the consciousness of falsity, (b) the intent to deceive, and (c) a preconceived goal or purpose.[*] A substantial number joined Martha in including the liar among those deceived in one way or another. In the process, I learned a number of things about lying. Here are some of them:

---

[*] I found the following article a very helpful summary: Ford, Charles V., M.D., King, Barry H., M.D., and Hollander, Marc H., M.D. "Lies and Liars: Psychiatric Aspects of Prevarication," *American Journal of Psychiatry* 145(5):554–562, 1988.

1. Lying lends itself to a number of classifications, which probably attests to its ubiquity as well as the range of moral feelings surrounding it. There are aggressive lies and defensive lies. There are "white lies," "altruistic lies," and lies that can be regarded as "normal" or "abnormal" (including a number of forms of pathological lying). Lies that are not determined by situational factors tend to be regarded as pathological because of their unconscious motivation.

2. The concepts of lying and telling the truth are mutually interdependent. One cannot exist without the other. Children can neither tell the truth nor lie until their mental processes have matured to the point they can distinguish between their inner world of fantasy and imagination and the outer world where reality can be tested. This is at age 4 to 5.

3. A number of psychologists consider lying an important part of psychic development. Separation from one's parents both physically and mentally, particularly from the mother, is essential to establishing our boundaries as distinct and individual human beings. Attachment theory assumes that as infants we are unable to determine where we end and Mother begins, mentally, physically, and emotionally. An important step in learning to be our own person is to establish a separate mentality. If we can tell a lie and Mother acts as if it is truthful, we have established the separateness of our own thoughts. Mother cannot control them. In this context, a lie may be one means to differentiate ourselves and establish our identity.

4. An undetected lie may also reveal parental shortcoming and disestablish our notion of an idealized, omniscient parent. However, the idealized imprint remains in the growth of self-regulation through the sense of there being an all-seeing ego, the superego. This sense of being overseen may sow the seeds from which self-control, and later, conscience grow.

5. Developmentally, issues of lying and telling the truth are often reactivated during adolescence. In our struggles for separation and maturity, we often revert to behaviors involving secrecy and deceit as we seek to become autonomous. Privacy is often at stake. Some believe no other period in life better demonstrates that lying is as much a part of normal growth as telling the truth.

6. A combination of parental influence and cultural factors shapes the way we approach matters of truthfulness and lying. No family is ever entirely truthful. Psychologists report they observe varying degrees of truth and falsehood in all family life. These range from continual lying to the child, as in repeatedly breaking promises, to

conversations about Santa Claus, storks, politeness ("I'm so glad to see you."), and other "white lies." The more secrets there are in the household, the more parents suppress or distort their past, or the more hypocrisy there is in the practice of religion or the observation of laws, the greater the possibilities of contagion for long and continued untruthfulness.

7. Some point out that lying may well become a form of repression or denial in response to traumatic experiences. The phenomenon of dissociation is one solution to an overwhelmingly traumatic event. Memory of the truth is erased as though it never happened. Lying may well become a way of concealing and, ultimately, denying what we cannot assimilate in other ways. Then our health and well-being turn upon addressing the aftermath of what we no longer recall.

8. Honesty and truthfulness are important social values for groups in general and society as a whole. Duplicity and deception can undermine mutual trust at every level of social life. Street gangs and Boy Scouts often share a common oath of trustworthiness in order to maintain good faith in their dealings with one another, which may or may not be extended to others and probably won't to those considered enemies.

So, to tell the truth, the need for honesty and the need to lie are acknowledged as omnipresent realities throughout life on earth. Like it or not, both are part of the complexity and perplexity of the human predicament. On the one hand, good faith in relationships at every level is based upon credibility—being able to trust the accuracy and intent of what we are being told. On the other hand, lying is a common and accepted practice, both at home and in the marketplace. At home, courtesy demands we greet others, suppress reactions, and receive unwanted gifts with "white lies" or distortions of the truth. At work, there is the classic paradox of employment. If employers hire only experienced workers, then no one seeking employment could ever gain experience. The classic solution is to lie about previous experience. People lie to avoid embarrassment, to spare feelings, to get their way; they lie to avoid disapproval, punishment, rejection, or loss. They lie to children, they lie to voters, and they lie to the IRS.

The capacity to lie, particularly where security and self-protection are concerned, may be innate, even in the animal kingdom. I witnessed it last spring when Mr. Robin discovered me too close to the family nest behind my cabin and lured me away, feigning a broken wing. He dragged it, with me following, half way across the yard before abandoning his ruse and flying away. Then there is Koko the Gorilla's famous lie, demonstrating a similar capacity among Great Apes in the course of language studies. In a temper tantrum, she had torn a steel sink out of its moorings. When confronted by her handlers, she pointed to her tiny kitten companion, signing in American Sign Language, "Cat did it."

While civilization, justice, and our common good turn upon being honest with one another, our propensity to lie, even to ourselves, is a trait acquired in virtually everyone's childhood. There is a cartoon that appears regularly in *The Family Circus* depicting mother charging three children with a question like, "Who left peanut butter smeared all over the counter?" "Not me," "Not me," "Not me," comes the chorus of responses. And while these three answers are given, virtually in unison, a shadowy figure of some other child with "Not Me" identifying him on his back darts from the room. I doubt there is any parent who has not tolerated with acceptance such self-protective lying. We would probably question the health and well-being of a child who made a practice of turning in himself, herself, or anyone else under such circumstances.

Self-Encounter and Honesty

Self-encounter and honesty form a difficult partnership for us, both cognitively and emotionally. As a parent, I have often been a partner in scenes that foster deception and deceit. I can recall hassle times during trips when our children were young. From the back seat came Andrew's voice, "Liz hit me for no reason." In such disputes, Andrew no doubt knew that an action coming in retaliation to a provocation had acquired some measure of justification, as a result of many inquests into who was at fault. As parents, we usually sought to establish the causal chain of events so as to affix blame in the proper place with commensurate punishment. We attempted to be quite scientific, as our parents were before us, in determining who did what to whom first to start the uproar. The futility of our efforts led us to abandon such interrogation as fruitless because we always got different testimony from the parties involved.

Several years later, when exposed to systems theory, we came to understand why. In the intricacies of family life, there is no first horse on the merry-go-round. In every relationship, such ongoing and repetitive patterns of behavior are sustained by individuals with differing perspectives acting in concert with one another. The blame game is a moot court conducted over and over again in a futile search for a first cause that is unidentifiable. The real culprit is the elaborate system of relating to each other over years of practiced conflict.

Nowhere is this more evident than in the consulting room game Eric Berne called "Courtroom" frequently played out in marital therapy.* Each

---

* Berne, Eric, M.D. *Games People Play* (New York: Ballantine Books, 1964), pp. 96–98.

partner enters the process trying to convince the therapist that the other is at fault. Each takes a turn as prosecutor or defendant, stating their case before the therapist in search of finding a favorable ruling. Defense follows accusation, and counter-accusation follows defense. Whose fault is it really? Both partners have long since learned to say "Not me." When confronted directly, each will normally confess some part in their repeated difficulties, often 50 percent, but seldom will either take any responsibility for resolving their differences. Instead, both resume their "Not me" stance and return to the endless circle of shifting blame to one another as soon as possible.

By the time any of us survive childhood, we have learned to deny, conceal, omit, forget, distort, and perceive in ways that protect us and further our self-interest. We can carefully construct different stories of the same event because each of us sees "what happened" with our own eyes and ears and unique perceptions, all geared to preserve what is important to us. For this reason, confession has never been a simple three-step process of declaring our wrongdoing, seeking forgiveness, and changing. Not even for the great ones. Augustine struggled for years with his lust, Tolstoy for even longer to find the courage to live.

When our privacy, our confidentiality, or our well-being is under some threat, we learn to distort the truth in our own favor. A recent study revealed that most spouses keep secrets from one another about what they are spending. Lying about the cost of an article of clothing, some personal purchase, or questionable expenditure is a well-established practice. Similar deceptions over some failure at work or some aspect of a child's behavior are equally prevalent. But lying is stressful and can prove increasingly difficult to sustain.

Lying is not an easy or natural behavior for the human organism. The polygraph or "lie detector" test is based upon the principle that telling the truth is natural and compatible with normal or stress-free functioning of mind and body. Fear of having one's falsehood detected produces both psychological and physical arousal. There are measurable changes in one's respiration, heart rate, blood pressure, and skin conductance. Our biophysical discomfort increases in direct proportion to the size of the threat posed by the answer required.

I can recall an incident with my father shortly after receiving my driver's license. With several buddies, I left the confines of Boyle County, which was "dry," and drove "over the hill to Nicholasville" where we could purchase beer. The return trip was punctuated by the thump of accurately thrown empty cans against various road signs. To my credit, I was exceedingly careful and drank little, although I risked much. We were in the family car.

The next morning, to my horror as I opened the car door to run an errand, I discovered that one rather full beer can had been spilled across the floor of the backseat before finding its mark out the window. The odor was as unmistakable as it was unacceptable. My father had already used the car that morning. More swiftly than I drove the night before, I was behind a friend's house with soap, water, and bucket, belatedly and desperately undertaking to reverse an impossible situation.

Oh, the anxiety! Returning home later, I waited for the inevitable questions of what, where, when, and why? They never came. And to this day, I remain deeply grateful to my father who graciously avoided putting me in a position where I would either have to lie or face dire consequences. He knew. I knew he knew. He knew that I knew that he knew. And I knew that he knew that I knew that he knew. And that was enough.

A full confessional experience involves a lot more than simply telling or not telling the truth. In fact, I can think of any number of instances where the truth may be just as deceptive or manipulative as a lie. I think of Emma who told the truth repeatedly and repetitively. Over and over again, those who knew her listened to her confess her failures to connect with her husband. She withdrew from him when he was warm and affectionate. She avoided sex at all costs. She couldn't comfort him when he was discouraged. She failed to support him when he was troubled, retreating to her room feeling guilty, ashamed, and depressed. Mea culpa.

It was all true, and the truth sustained her depression. She systematically drew back from life, fearful of traveling, of finding a job, of altering her ongoing retreat from involvement with others. Emma's tearful confessions trumped any efforts by friends, fellow group members, therapists, doctors, and medication to intervene with her ongoing honesty about her failures and self-contempt. The truth of the matter is that the truth was completely co-opted as license to resist and avoid any challenge to change. Emma had long since blurred into consistent denial any self-awareness of her underlying motivation.

Some similar distortion often masks the truth concerning what goes on in many domestic disputes. I think of the alcoholic game "Drunk and Proud" described by psychologist Claude Steiner.* Harry is a successful, hard-working guy who is given to "good times" and "binge drinking." He announces to his wife that he is going to "have a couple" before they go to a party at the Smiths. If she objects, she's an impossible shrew. And if she says nothing, she's a patsy and a victim. When they arrive, Harry proceeds to be the life of the party. He has "tee many martoonies," is out on the veranda necking with somebody else's wife or secretary, or is gone somewhere with his buddies. Wife goes home alone.

---

* Steiner, Claude M. "The Alcoholic Game," *Transactional Analysis Bulletin* 7:6–16, 1968.

The payoff comes when Harry returns home with a full hangover. And he tells the truth. "I am truly sorry; I made a fool of myself," he confesses. "I've got to stop this. I know you're right. Please forgive me and I'll do better." She's forgiven him before, seventy times seven, and turned all four cheeks to this treatment. If she forgives him again, she's stuck in the role of victim. If she refuses, she's an unforgiving, impossible shrew, and Harry can say, "Other people think you're so great. If they could just see you now."

In this case, the truth is confessed abusively. It is used angrily to humiliate, although Harry is unaware of or out of touch with this fact and displays genuine remorse. Clinicians hear such confessions frequently in cases of physical abuse where the perpetrator evidences authentic sorrow and begs to be forgiven and taken back. Repeatedly.

The truth can provide sanction for rehearsing exciting revelries of conquests and failures lamented in sad repetition of unchanging drama. Radford is a charming and successful salesman who has left behind a trail of three wives, all of whom he abandoned for some other woman who managed to attract his attention, and he felt compelled to love, too. In fact, he has lived his life "between two women," destined to leave one for the other. He can do this, incidentally, whether or not he is married. He freely confesses his compulsion, even addiction, to this repeated story, filled with remorse over hurting everyone involved, including himself. The truth hurts. But the truth of the matter is that the script continues unamended by any awareness of his secret satisfactions in serial conquest, let alone any concerted intention to change.

Honest confession involves something different from simply telling the truth. It entails assuming responsibility for our part in what is going on in our lives and the lives of those around us. Honest confession involves a determination to tangle with the source of our estrangement in a concerted effort to find a relevant response capable of breaking the grip those behaviors have upon us. In the big issues (and in the smaller ones as well), we can blur the truth of the matter, escaping from authentic self-encounter and understanding others. We can deny what is painful, threatening, or shameful in order to protect ourselves from too much truth, but not without lingering feelings of anxiety that persistently return, begging for our attention.

What makes self-encounter move toward honest confession is the way we manage the chain of thoughts that follows an event that disturbs us. Whatever our negative experience, its pain or discomfort commands a near-universal response: What went wrong? Was it something I did? Or was it he, or she, or they? Or was it something else? The task of sorting out some kind of understanding among these various possibilities can become complicated quickly.

Honest Confession in the Garden

Let's take that primal experience of Adam and Eve in the Garden of Eden. They eat the forbidden fruit of the Tree of Knowledge. Suddenly they are naked and filled with shame. They run and hide. Suppose we could change places with them for a little while. We would surely wonder why this happened to us. What went wrong? Probably each of us would begin to wonder whose fault this was? Am I to blame? Or was it you? Or was it someone or something else? Where our thoughts move from here is crucial to a full confessional experience. We can shrug our shoulders and try to dismiss what happened as "bad luck." Neither of us really understood what we were getting into. That doesn't feel so good because we are still naked and ashamed. If what happened is too painful, we are capable of disassociating the whole experience, denying it ever happened, even shutting out its memory. That leaves us even more anxious. Instead, most of us would begin an instant-replay of the event at hand. What did I do wrong? Rumination follows and preoccupation with guilt or shame, or both. The parental authorities in our head usually offer free and unsolicited consultation concerning our culpability, which may prove helpful to self-reflection or generate "Not me" responses. The latter automatically activates all of our skillfulness in shifting blame.

This search for who is to blame is as old as Adam and Eve. Adam says the woman gave him the fruit. Eve says the serpent beguiled her. Everyone, it seems, instinctively develops this "not me" response to shift blame to others, even in the earliest stages of life on earth. If we stop there, we may momentarily escape judgment, but we miss out on the whole process of human growth before us. The chain of questions that goes through our minds is a legitimate one of universal proportion and significance. If I'm Adam, I ate whether or not you gave me the fruit. And if you're Eve, you ate, whether or not beguiled. And here we are, both naked and ashamed, and we just as well share responsibility for the number we did together. Neither of us is to blame. There is no single cause to which we can ascribe the state of being "at fault" for it all, no first horse on the merry-go-round.

It won't work to shift the blame over to the serpent either. If we are Adam and Eve, there is always someone or something else in the context of our relationship. We can't just vow to stop talking to snakes. Symbols are eternal, and there will always be beguiling snakes around to step on, trip over, and talk to. We have to find something to do with serpents, as the snake charmers in Far Eastern cultures do, or the snake handlers in far-eastern Kentucky do. Both to me represent a flagrant case of riding a metaphor to death, but the symbolism is intriguing.

Nor can we shift blame to the "stupid rule" that we "can't eat the fruit of that stupid tree." Blaming something else like God, or City Hall, or Parents does not work either. We are all born into a garden with rules and regulations, some of which are stupid, some of which are not so stupid, and some of which are essential. The Tree of Knowledge is a symbol of our human task to deal with the "no-nos" in our garden so that we can sort out stupid and damaging ones from the needed and necessary ones. The guilt, shame, and anxiety that result from breaking one or more of these rules are the price of admission to a quest for our full humanity. It is a trip we have to take. We can run from it, avoid it, deny it, or postpone it, but the anxiety of the unfaced and unresolved remains within, taking one form or another until we respond. Whenever any of us finally stops and refuses to turn away, we enter into a journey of authentic self-awareness with all the emotional and cognitive demands it places upon us. A full confessional experience begins with all its questions suddenly acquiring legitimacy and value when taken together. Am I to blame? Of course not. I am not so grandiose an Adam (man) that I am the sole cause of all this, but I am responsible for my part in it. Playing the blame game is a waste of time and energy. I need to sort out what I am responsible for and make my own response to the situation.

Are you to blame? Of course not. You are not so grandiose an Eve (woman) that you can make me disobey, or eat, or go along with anything. We need to sort out our respective parts in what we did together, and each assume joint responsibility to work out things, which lays the groundwork for both of us to make a different response. The more we understand about trees, and beguiling snakes, and the place of parents and siblings and rules in all this, the better our chances of making new and different responses. Ignorance is never bliss. We also don't want to ignore the possibility of encounter with a Presence that is greater than we in the midst of a full confessional experience. What began with painful admissions leads beyond to something else. In the process, God may come a-walking into our Garden, and we can come out of hiding.

From Myth to Movement

The fall myth captures the anxiety that launches the confessional process. As Reinhold Niebuhr suggests, anxiety is the precondition to sin. It always accompanies guilt or shame, whether we recognize it or not. I think of Fritz Perls when I think of anxiety. The term has so many definitions among psychotherapists. To Perls, anxiety is muffled or repressed excitement. To turn back from it is to turn back from life itself. I can still hear him talk about surrendering our selfhood when we recoil from contact with something new at the boundary of our awareness.

Living in the Now

Fritz had a way of heightening everyone's anxiety with his full attention pasted to what is going on "now." I first met Fritz Perls as he ate breakfast in the dining room at Eselen during the spring of 1968. Sam Keen and I had driven down the Big Sur to see him. There he sat, large as life, intently chewing each bite of his breakfast as he surveyed the expanse of Pacific Ocean before us. He hated for anyone to interrupt his meal with chatter of any kind. Sam Keen and I had wandered in hoping to meet him and discuss coming to some of his workshops while on leave during the year ahead. Quite innocently, and in complete ignorance of my travesty, I stuck my hand out awkwardly and said, "Dr. Perls, my name is David Steere, and this is Sam Keen."

"So?" came his gruff and indignant response, neither looking up nor stopping eating, which left me standing there with hand extended, reduced to ashes. I had studied tapes of his workshops and read *Gestalt Therapy Verbatim* but was not prepared for anything like so anxiety-producing a welcome.*

Mustering all my courage and puffing up big like Toad, I replied with as much counter-gruffness as I could manage, "You crusty old bastard, we've flown 800 miles to meet you; are you going to talk to us or not?"

"Sit down," he said, the edge beginning to drop from his tone, "I start to get interested."

A memorable meeting, but not at all unusual, as we would soon learn.

Fritz Perls is the architect of the "awareness continuum" in which he encourages us to enter fully into every aspect of our experience in the present moment The idea is to own and take responsibility for everything presented to our awareness in the here and now. How am I experiencing the "now?" Whenever I turn back from the reality of the moment and leave it hanging, unfinished and incomplete, I interrupt an innate need for cloture and completion of that event. I am left dangling like a piece of music interrupted somewhere before its final chord. Imagine singing the scale—"do, re, mi, fa, so, la, ti…"—and stopping. Can you do it without silently adding the final "do"? Everything in us begs for a cloture to any configuration of our experience. The German word *Die Gestalt* means "the configuration"—the relative disposition of the parts or elements of something that gives it form, shape, boundaries, beginning and end (in this case, completing the scale).

Unfinished Gestalten in our experience leaves us dangling and anxious. When we rush ahead, or skip back, or avoid in any way completing our awareness of an experience, we create "unfinished business" for ourselves, begging for cloture. When we entertain full awareness of our "now," we assume responsibility for bringing that experience to completion. We own

---

* Perls, Fritz. *Gestalt Therapy Verbatim* (Lafayette, CA: Real People Press. 1969).

everything that enters our present. Our head doesn't ache; we ache in our head. "It" or "You" don't make me angry; I make me angry. Whatever I experience becomes mine to own: my headache, my anger, my fantasies, my wishes, my fears, my anxiety, my shame, my guilt, my memory, my lust, my cruelty, my rage, as well as anything else novel or threatening or a part of my darker side that I may wish to avoid or deny.

Fritz Perls introduced me to the practice of being fully present in the "now." He had a theory of neurosis, and we're all a little neurotic. To deal fully with anything that makes us anxious, we have to work our way through several layers of resistance in which we may characteristically avoid its impact and meaning. There is a level of *phony games* we play with ourselves and others, like "courtroom" and similar means of escaping responsibility or saying "Not me." Beyond phony games, we encounter a *phobic layer* of resistance to owning our involvement in what is going on. If we can handle the fear this arouses and don't retreat to the phony level of denial, then we enter a third layer of "deadness." This is the layer of *impasse,* and we are stuck. We get nowhere, and every tendency is to abandon attention and escape into something familiar. But if we stick with the present, we enter a layer of *implosion* in which the deeper part of ourselves forces its way into our awareness, bearing whatever we have managed to conceal from ourselves, sometimes for years. In the implosive layer, this awareness of something grows in unavoidable magnitude. There follows what Perls describes as the *explosion* into full awareness of what has been avoided, suppressed, or denied. What has lingered long as unfinished business erupts, bringing with it cleansing relief in full awareness of what could not be felt or expressed or owned or known.

As I look back, I realize that it was Fritz Perls who introduced me to the notion that the problem contains within itself its own solution or resolution if we face it fully. The kinds of explosions Perls describes often erupt as expressions of joy and creativity as well as anger and grief. Often, the emotional release is profound transforming the accompanying anxiety into renewed energy to get on with life, full of fresh purpose and heightened imagination. Fritz would probably shudder in his grave at my crediting his raunchy influence for some of my understandings of confession. In retrospect, the seeds of my interest in "coming clean" with confession were beginning to grow. The notion that we can move through our stuck points to gain a sense of completion and cloture stayed with me.

The Shadow Knows

Another piece of my thinking began to fall into place in 1970 when I was asked to chair our General Assembly's Committee on the Use of Drugs. It was my job to assemble experts who were Presbyterian, pastoral, theological, psychological, and knowledgeable to study our nation's budding drug problem and to find effective measures to combat it. The group spent a year traveling the country from the East Coast to the West Coast, visiting treatment programs, rescue operations, research centers, and recovery-communities to observe what was being done. We received a liberal education from Berkeley, California, to the Maryland State Psychiatric Research Center.

One member of our committee was a psychiatrist named Wally Panke. In addition to his psychiatric training, Wally had completed his Ph.D. in the Psychology of Religion and was an expert in the history of mysticism. He worked at the Maryland State Psychiatric Research Center with another psychiatrist named Stan Graff doing research on the use of lysergic acid diethylamide (LSD from its early code name LSD-25) to treat alcoholics and patients with life-threatening malignancies. Wally was interested in the potential for mystical experience under the careful administration of this drug. His doctoral dissertation reported research with a group of ministerial students at Harvard Divinity School who ingested the drug on Good Friday and carefully recorded their experiences. He also had a grant from the federal government to study the creative effects of LSD on 40 "gifted subjects," administered under controlled conditions that included 20 hours of preparation, a thorough program of pre-and post-testing, and 15 hours of debriefing afterward. Eager to learn more about this project, I became one of the subjects.

On the appointed day, I took my place on the couch in a small treatment room accompanied by Wally, Helen Bonney, a trained music therapist, and a medical student who observed. I downed a small vial of the odorless, colorless, tasteless substance, 350 micrograms of LSD, a goodly amount by Wally's account compared to the 25 to 30 micrograms normally found in street drugs. The range of potential experiences had been carefully rehearsed. There were the psychedelic effects of flowers growing huge, pictures coming to life in movement, pungent odors or tastes, the switching of senses, like seeing a sound. There were periods of psychodynamic clarity and strong emotions looking at familiar photographs. Then there was the model psychotic experience in which, at one point, I went into a state of pure paranoia. Of course, I had experienced paranoid thoughts before. The difference was like the difference between a swimming pool and the ocean—one can cope with something the size of a swimming pool.

I had been instructed in pre-session training to move straight into such a demanding experience. If a monster appears, don't run; move toward it. This directive paralleled Fritz Perls' notion of finishing contact at the boundary of your experience, completing the Gestalt. Yeah, sure. Just move into my paranoia. I was convinced that Wally was the devil and Helen was a witch. Wally had horns and Helen was no longer the lovely lady I had known. I would never see my wife and children again. My only chance was to lie still and pretend to go along with them. But somehow I confessed to both of them that I was completely paranoid. And Wally convinced me to take another 50 micrograms of LSD. I returned to the couch and listened through the earphones to the music they had selected.

At one point, I was locked in a struggle of seemingly cosmic dimensions. I stood by myself on some primordial plain. Arrayed against me as far as I could see from horizon to horizon stood the entire heavenly host. I experienced the full measure of my stubborn defiance, shaking my fist in the air and shouting, "You can never have me, never. You can never control my soul."

Part of the preparation had alerted me to the possibility of an encounter with death, or, in one form or another, what some had described as "ego death." Whatever I experienced later came in the form of a complete surrender to the inevitable, to whatever came next, moving into it whether or not I was fearful. For a while, I was submerged in an oceanic world of cellular life, swimming creatures, and expanding underwater plants that took on pristine beauty. Later I was somehow a part of everything. I was a particle of a tree, part of a flowing river, a leaf blowing in the wind, a waterfall, a cloud, the rain, strangely at one with everything. I was lifted up through eons of unfolding awareness.

At one point, I had a sense of warfare, continuing battle, and weary souls plunging back into the fray. At another, I had an ineffable sense that all the suffering, pain, and death around me formed notes to some larger chord with the rest of life sounding a tone of completion or fulfillment pleasing to the ear. At times I think I was nuts. Wacko. Lost in some drug-induced display of Prophetenwahn. At other times, I cannot resist the thought that I experienced something similar to what Carl Gustav Jung called the *collective unconscious*. At points, there were medieval gargoyles, a Buddha-like figure with water pouring in many directions from its abdomen, and many figures of the "sacred feminine," as we have come to call it now. There were Madonnas, children, grownups with children's bodies (that I later noticed for the first time in certain periods of European art), wise men and earth mothers the likes of which I never recall seeing before. For years afterward, I wandered through churches from Mexico to Spain to Italy to the Soviet Union to Europe with a fascination and almost hypnotic attraction to such figures.

At the pinnacle of the eons through which I was lifted, there was a pure, warm, white light that enveloped my awareness. I couldn't say "enveloped me" because the "I" that I was had now become a part of or one with all this. At this point I knew nothing about white lights, near-death experiences, or that mystics in the Middle Ages produced such altered states of consciousness through meditation. I was about as un-mystical as they come. Wally Panke had constructed a Mysticism Scale from his studies. On the post-test was the question, "At any time during your session did you see a white light?" I checked "yes" and was introduced to the possibility of such experiences. We now know that numbers of people with near-death experiences report something similar. And of course, medical researchers have recently sought to account for these reports in terms of certain alterations in brain chemistry at the time of death. Always the chemical explanation.

I experienced sensations similar to the white light only once more. Ten years ago, I was in the Near East visiting a number of archaeological sites in Israel and Jordan with my friend and colleague Gene March, who taught Old Testament at the seminary. Somehow by then, even the churches and mosques in Jerusalem, which Christians, Jews, and Muslims have erected on virtually every "holy" site, had lost their fascination for me. Then we arrived in Egypt. Margaret and I had heard of "Pyramid Power," and we eagerly descended the long stairways to the center of Cheops' gigantic tomb. Search as we did for such energy, none was forthcoming. We went through the Valley of the Kings and the temple at Luxor. Nothing. Then we went to the National Museum in Cairo where all the artifacts and treasures from the age of the Egyptian dynasties are housed. For 3 hours I wandered around lost in a bright, warm state of consciousness that brought tears. The bright, tingling sensations in my spinal cord were similar to ones I recall in the white light experience with LSD. The clear, fresh feel of the air had a whiteness about it that was ubiquitous. Wherever I went, the same sensations bathed my awareness. Somehow I was strangely at one with all that was there, wherever I wandered. No one in our party shared my feelings, and everyone drifted off quietly, leaving me to my own wanderings.

When my wife finally dragged me out, I told her of my incredulous experience. We wondered if it was something I ate. The next day I returned on my own. Again I wandered, entranced in the same experience for 3 more hours, in tears. The impact of events like this wanes in the passage of time and other experiences; but even when their lingering effect has faded before our doubts and the accumulation of everyday consciousness, their recall remains, and their influence often works new directions in our lives. Only with the perspective of time can we connect the dots that comprise them.

I know now that, somewhere in the process, I became a closet Jungian. My choice was between chalking up the entire experience to some chemically-induced illusion or considering the possibility that something like what Jung calls the collective unconscious lies deep within the recesses of my mind and your mind. It begs for our attention through dreams, fantasies, myths, symbols, art, legend, and the like. Most confessions born out of our shame or guilt carry us beneath the surface persona we try to present to the world and like to think of ourselves as being. They involve us in the part of our personal unconscious Jung called the shadow.

The shadow contains all the hidden or unconscious aspects of ourselves, both good and bad, either repressed or unrecognized. "No" may well be the key word we learn during childhood to develop a sense of autonomy. We say "No" to establish our separateness from others. "No, I don't want this; I want that." "No, I am not this way; I am that way." "No, I am not bad; I am good." So we create the shadow as a container for everything we don't want to be. It becomes the unconscious repository of all the "bad" qualities we deny. Every time we think or say "Not me," our shadow lengthens. We reject in ourselves what others consider "bad" or "shameful," seeking to shape consciousness in the direction of our desired persona, and we become progressively estranged from our darker side.

In this respect, shame works in our service to drive us into dealing with our underside. The shadow contains all the disowned and unclaimed aspects of our personal unconscious. Through following awareness into this reservoir of repressed desires, uncivilized impulses, morally inferior motives, childish fantasies and resentments—in short, all those things about ourselves we are not proud of —we begin to lay conscious claim to hidden motives and neglected strengths heretofore unrealized.

It is a dangerous thing to barge through life unaware of our shadow side. Lamont Cranston was right: "The Shadow knows what evils lurk in the hearts of men." Through denying what is within ourselves, we unwittingly project it upon others and seek it in them. Instead of searching for self-awareness and bringing out what lies within, we constantly give away parts of ourselves to others. Unaware of our own inner authority, we blindly submit to the authority of others; out of touch with our own tenderness, we desperately seek it in someone else; denying our own aggression, we fear it in a stranger. The good fathers of Salem were troubled by the "shapes" of barmaids hovering over their beds at night and burned witches at the stake, completely unaware that what they dealt with were projections of their shadow self. Honest confessions of our human predicament are constantly complicated by the necessity to deal with our shadow, which can emerge to control our lives at unpredictable moments and in ways that bewilder us.

Now this is both good news and bad news. The bad news is that our shadow adds to an already difficult task of self-confrontation in which we must deal with what we would long deny and refuse to accept as part of us. The good news is that it forms the passageway through which we can enter the collective unconscious filled with archetypal figures containing the wisdom of the ages. Jung pursued these repeated themes through the dreams, the fantasies, the art, the legends, and the mythologies common to all civilized cultures.

Jung's effort to identify a Spiritual Presence at the center of the self, working its healing and reunification, adds significantly to our understandings of a full confessional experience. On the other side of all the negative aspects of self-exploration, one encounters the archetypal presence of God. In the midst of all we have repressed, this God-image is at work to unify the inner being of the self. This image seeks conscious expression in ways that are the direct opposite of any act of unconscious repression. Although Jung, always the scientist, denied having any data or knowledge about what is normally called "spiritual," he did state without hesitation that we have good reason "to suppose that behind this veil there exists the incomprehensible absolute object which affects and influences us."*

The mandala became Jung's symbol of the Self, the archetype of unity and totality that stands at the center of self-healing. He believed this archetype informed the ideas of monotheism throughout the world's great religions. In this sense, the Self is the "God Within" or the way in which God seeks God's goal through each individual soul.† Jung was fascinated with the Gnostic idea that we encounter God deep within our pursuit of self-knowledge. He thought the Gnostics expressed "the other side of the mind"—the spontaneous, unconscious thoughts that most orthodoxy required its adherents to repress. And when five extraordinary texts from the documents found at Nag Hammadi were smuggled out of Egypt and sold on the black market, a Dutch professor named Gilles Quispel procured them for the Jung Foundation in Zurich. Among them was the *Gospel of Thomas* that Elaine Pagels studied with such intense interest.

So I can look back and trace the seeds of understanding this intrinsic relationship between the confession of sin and the confession of faith in a number of personal influences. There was Fritz Perls' insistence that our unfinished business of the past interrupts the present, begging for cloture. There was the world of the unconscious Wally Panke introduced me to with LSD that demanded self-exploration and movement through very threatening recesses of our minds, even awareness of death itself, and beyond that, a sense of ongoing being, joy, and Spiritual Presence. There was Carl Jung, who mapped the inner chambers of our mental processes that await the serious confessor who explores the shadows of the unconscious and the repressed to find God.

How early might I have had such thoughts? I don't know, but the memory of being 11 years old comes to mind. I was at one of the countless concerts I was required to sit still through as the son of a professor who taught in the Music Department at Coker College. This was in a different setting than usual, out behind the college auditorium where my musical

---

* Jung, Carl G. *Memories, Dreams, and Reflections.* Translated by Richard and Clara Winston (New York: Pantheon Books, 1963), p. 251.
† Jung, Carl G. *The Collected Works of C.G. Jung.* (Princeton: Princeton University Press, 1953–1978) Vol. 10, p. 588.

career met its disastrous end. We were in a natural amphitheater, seated on the semicircular hillside facing a tree-shrouded stage built into the setting above a circular pool that reflected the still, peaceful recesses that occasionally grace higher education.

We were listening to my father's choir present its annual spring concert in early May. My father conducted, of course. Choral work was his first love. I always felt his piano and organ recitals, also numerous, were more like drudgery for him. They lacked the flesh-to-flesh expression of human voices joined together in relationships beneath the sounds they made. In other forms, music was something you had to get right through countless hours of laborious practice. Here it was a shared experience of connecting with others to create something with a measure of intimacy.

I sat with my buddy Ed Watt, who lived next door. He was 4 years older, and I normally followed his lead because he taught me many things, including how to make concerts pass faster. That afternoon our task was to rate each number the choir sang from 1 to 5 in order to select the piece we liked the most. The Coker choir was an all-girls choir because Coker (pronounced Cokaaahhh) was an all-girls school. Nowadays, we would call it a Women's College affiliated with the Baptist Church. My father also wrote a number of anthems, and the choir sang two toward the end. One of them I remember and can still hear in my head today.

The anthem was entitled "Judge Me, O God." It was based upon the Forty-Third Psalm, King James Version, which begins:

Judge me, O God, and plead my cause against an ungodly
  nation.
O deliver me from the deceitful and unjust man.
For thou art the God of my strength; why dost thou cast me
  off?
Why go I mourning because of the oppression of the enemy?

My father cast his own interpretation upon the meaning of this psalm through the music itself. I can still hear the carefully chorded chant that followed in progressive repetition of sound and search: "Judge me, O God, Judge me, O God, Judge me, O God, Judge Me, O God." As this continues in the background, this ongoing celebration of seeking out God's judgment, a crystal-clear soprano voice breaks forth above it in solo:

O send out thy light, thy light and thy truth; let them lead me;
  let them bring me unto thy holy hill, and to thy tabernacles.

Even at our ripe young ages of 11 and 15, Ed and I both put down "fives." We didn't talk much. But we knew we had heard something new and different in the midst of all the fear of fire and brimstone we grew up with in Baptist South Carolina. It was a musical impression with a sense of continuity conveyed in sound and chord that judgment and enlightenment go together. "Judge me, O God, Judge me, O God, Judge me, O God, Judge me, O God." And above that:

> Why art thou cast down , O my soul? And why art thou
> disquieted within me?
> Hope in God for I shall yet praise him, who is the health of my
> countenance and my God.

Whatever liberties my father took with the text, his meaning rings as clear to me today as the voice of his soprano soloist does in my memory. He understood that whatever our shame or guilt, the judgment surrounding honest confession is to be welcomed as the doorway to spiritual encounter and faith.

Practice

Self-Awareness and Internal Dialogue

1. Select an incident in which you experienced some measure of guilt/shame/anxiety. Reflect on it with your eyes closed, your body relaxed. Let your thoughts unfold in the present, accepting one after the other, setting them free to occur. Note any appearance of your shadow or darker side, taking time to own each thought. Search the full range of responses within you, including the appearance of any sense of spiritual presence.
2. When you are done, record your thoughts on paper or in your journal. Pay particular attention to any relevant responses that occurred or are occurring that you could choose to pursue.
3. If you have difficulty staying in the present, intersperse the phrase, "Now I am experiencing …." at regular intervals, filling in the blank. This kind of self-exploration anchors your attention firmly upon the stream of your associations, inviting possible avenues for their completion and cloture.
4. You may also choose in your quiet time to reflect on issues of lying and truthfulness that concern you. Use the same awareness of the "now" as you explore your chosen concern through whatever emerges to claim your expanding attention.

Confessional Partnership

1. You may introduce Fritz Perls' awareness continuum into your confessional conversation, reflecting upon the narrative event you describe by beginning sentences with the phrase "Now I am experiencing ...." as your partner listens.
2. This can be a demanding experience, and also an intimate one. You can use the awareness continuum at any point in ordinary conversation, taking brief forays into the "now" by beginning each sentence with the phrase "Now I am aware ...."
3. You may also wish share concerns you have with matters of truth and falsehood in your life.

Discussion Group:

1. Certainly the topic of lying will emerge as a significant concern for many. As a discussion leader, you could prepare questions around topics such as:
   a. How far should we carry "white lies"? Do they become problematic at some point? Should we make an effort to avoid them? How?
   b. When is lying justified? When giving disinformation to our enemies in wartime? In matters that involve national security? Protecting our privacy? Sparing another's feelings?
   c. What about truthfulness in family life? Conversations about Santa and storks? Embarrassing questions from children about your past? Should couples tell each other everything if asked?
2. Members may want to discuss any number of important issues, such as strategies for managing children's lying, questions about what to tell a person with a life-threatening illness, or the difference between perceptions based upon our own self-interest and out-and-out lies, if any.

Confessional Group

1. The group may choose to share experiences with lying or encounters with their shadow.
2. Don't overlook the positive confessional potential in sharing experiences with relevant responses and growing encounters with Spiritual Presence beyond our darker side.

CHAPTER 11

More Confessors

Bill Wilson and Recovery

Bill Wilson's personal confession appears at the beginning of the *Big Book,* the equivalent of a bible for Alcoholics Anonymous (AA). His confession marks the beginning of one of the most influential confessional movements of our time. The sheer number of relevant responses made in recovery points to a gaping neglect in the practice of honest confession throughout organized religion. Perhaps nowhere else in our society has the *private story* underlying addictions been so thoroughly explored and transformed.

Alcoholics Anonymous

As confessions go, Bill Wilson's begins with a rather lackluster account of his descent into alcoholism.* His drinking began when he discovered liquor as a lonely soldier overseas during the Great War (World War I). He returned home to become a successful broker on Wall Street but his success was short-lived, and he lost everything in the stock market crash of 1929. His story consists of one failure, or fight, or lost job after another, with intermittent efforts to stop drinking, hospitalizations, depressions, thoughts of suicide, and unsuccessful treatment programs. By the time an old friend, Ebby Thatcher, knocked on his door, he had been drinking around the clock for several weeks.

The trail of events leading to this meeting extends all the way back to Carl Gustav Jung. Jung had a particularly difficult patient named Rowland

---

* recovery.org/aa/bigbooki/ww/chapter_1.html, pp. 3ff.

Hazard, whom he treated unsuccessfully for alcoholism. Finally, having exhausted every recourse, Jung decided there was no hope for him in medicine or psychiatry and suggested that perhaps he could find help in a spiritual experience, leading to a genuine religious conversion. Jung had recorded several such cases. So Rowland returned to America and joined an Oxford group founded by Frank Buchman. This group, you recall, sought to establish early Christian patterns of confession through a moral inventory confessing your defects, making restitution to those you have wronged, relying upon God, and helping others. Eventually, he persuaded his friend Ebby Thatcher, who was on the verge of hospitalization for alcoholism, to join him. To everyone's amazement, Ebby achieved sobriety in these Oxford Movement meetings. The requirement to help others stop drinking eventually led Thatcher to call upon the most hopeless alcoholic he knew, Bill Wilson. His mission: to help him do the same.

Ebby was obviously a changed man. His skin appeared fresh and glowing, and he refused Bill's offer of a drink by saying simply, "I've got religion." Here was Thatcher, who the summer before appeared to be nothing more than a religious crackpot, sitting before him looking bright, clear, and ready to share his experience. The two talked for hours. Ebby declared forthrightly that God had done for him what he could not do for himself. Bill Wilson's old irritation with temperance pledges, pious preaching, and churchly teaching welled up from his past. He had always believed in some power higher than himself, some Spirit of the Universe behind it all, but that was about as far as he had gotten. His friend made a novel suggestion, "Why don't you choose your own conception of God?"

Thatcher's suggestion began to melt Bill Wilson's icy cynicism. If it were only a matter of willingness to believe in a power greater than himself, then there may be some hope. Nothing more was required to make a beginning. Growth could start from there. For the first time, he saw the possibility of building in himself what he saw in his friend. Soon thereafter, he entered the hospital with signs of delirium tremens. There he prayed from his bed, "If there be a God, will He show himself!"* Suddenly his room was filled by a blinding white light. He seemed to be on a mountain, filled with ecstasy. A great wind blew and enveloped him, not with air, but with the spirit. It blazed with the tremendous thought, "You are a free man." He offered himself to God then and there, placing himself without reservation under God's care and direction. A profound sense of peace and serenity that he had never known before came over him. "I admitted for the first time that of myself I was nothing," he reflected; "that without Him I was lost. I

---

* Aa/bigbook/ww/chapter_1.html, p. 5.

ruthlessly faced my sins and became willing to have my newfound Friend take them away, root and branch. I have not had a drink since."*

Bill Wilson had taken the first step but this was only the beginning. A *relevant response* involved far more than that. His friend Ebby Thatcher served as his confessor and became fully acquainted with his problems and deficiencies. Together they made a list of people he had either harmed or resented. He expressed a willingness to approach these individuals and resolve their differences as best he could. Thatcher stuck with him through his recovery and stressed the importance of continuing the practices they had begun throughout his life, particularly the need to help other alcoholics as Thatcher had helped him. The seeds of what was to become the twelve Steps were planted. Bill and his wife soon began devoting themselves to assisting others in overcoming their drinking problems. When all else failed, work with another alcoholic would save the day. Still Bill Wilson struggled with sobriety. Whenever the urge to drink seemed overwhelming, he found a drunk somewhere with whom he could share his newfound message of hope, but no one seemed to listen. This urge was what brought about the fateful meeting with Dr. Bob Smith, a prominent surgeon in Akron, Ohio, on May 12, 1935.

Both Bill Wilson and Dr. Bob had been exposed to the Oxford Movement with its confessional groups that had spread from England to the United States. Dr. Bob's group in Akron was considered atypical because it stressed helping problem drinkers through Bible study, prayer, and religious literature, bringing them to accept Jesus Christ as a way to a relationship with God. Most of Dr. Bob's ideas about accepting Jesus Christ, visiting hospitalized drunks, and witnessing came from his Christian Endeavor meetings as a youth. At the time he met Bill Wilson, he still had not been able to stop drinking. Bill Wilson had been sober for 6 months but was still struggling to maintain his recovery by abusing other alcoholics with his sermonizing, none of whom he seemed able to reach. Both were filled with mounting frustration.

On Mother's Day in 1935, Wilson was in Akron, Ohio, on another unsuccessful business trip. He ended up wandering alone through the lobby of his hotel, passing the bar, and realizing he was about to get drunk. In desperation, he called a minister he located in a church directory, seeking the name of a fellow alcoholic who needed help. The minister sent him to Dr. Bob Smith, the most available alcoholic he knew. This time, instead of dumping his evangelistic message on Dr. Bob, the two became engaged in a conversation they shared for 4 hours. Bill Wilson quit preaching, realizing he needed this alcoholic as much as Dr. Bob needed him.

---

* *Three Talks to Medical Societies* by Bill W., Cofounder of Alcoholics Anonymous, (New York: Alcoholics Anonymous World Services, 1973), p. 10.

They immediately formed an ongoing friendship. Together they worked to put Bill Wilson's discoveries into practice. Dr. Smith reputedly achieved his sobriety June 10, 1935, which is considered the date on which AA was founded. Both began working with other alcoholics at Akron's City Hospital, and the Twelve Steps as we know them today began to take shape. Bill Wilson's companions insisted that he assume the task of writing them. He later credited the religious influence of Samuel Moor Shoemaker and the Oxford Movement for the ideas that formed their substance: full self-examination, confession of character defects, restitution for harm done, and work with others. The Twelve Steps as they found their way into print are as follows:

1. We admitted we were powerless over alcohol—that our lives had become unmanageable.
2. Came to believe that a Power greater than ourselves could restore us to sanity.
3. Made a decision to turn our will and our lives over to the care of God as *we understood Him.*
4. Made a searching and fearless moral inventory of ourselves.
5. Admitted to God, to ourselves, and to another human being the exact nature of our wrongs.
6. Were entirely ready to have God remove all these defects of character.
7. Humbly asked Him to remove our shortcomings.
8. Made a list of all persons we had harmed, and became willing to make amends with them all.
9. Made direct amends with such people wherever possible, except when to do so would injure them or others.
10. Continued to take personal inventory and when we were wrong, promptly admitted it.
11. Sought through prayer and meditation to improve our conscious contact with God *as we understood Him,* praying only for knowledge of His will for us and the power to carry that out.
12. Having had a spiritual awakening as the result of these Steps, we tried to carry this message to others, and to practice these principles in all our affairs.*

I found it interesting that Bill Wilson chose not to describe his mystical experience in the hospital as clearly in the first chapter of *The Big Book* as he did later in *Three Talks to Medical Societies,* published in 1973. Clarity often comes or fades with the perspective of time. We know that

---

* From *Al-Anon's Twelve Steps & Twelve Traditions* (New York: Al-Anon Family Group Headquarters, 1989), p. 3.

he struggled with questions as to whether his hospital experience was a genuine religious one, or had he simply teetered on the edge of a psychotic break, perhaps from delirium tremens. His friend Dr. Silkworth assured him that "hopeless alcoholics" often report such conversion experiences before being "turned around" toward recovery. Silkworth referred him to William James' *Varieties of Religious Experience* for a description of people who are "once born," growing up in an unbroken line of developing faith, and "twice born," experiencing some profound upheaval or radical break with the past, which produces spiritual conversion.* James observed that truly transforming spiritual experiences are often founded upon calamity and collapse. Just as Bill Wilson questioned his spiritual encounter during detoxification, I have doubts about my experience with LSD. I don't think either of us would repeat our experiences as a means for spiritual growth, even as their clarity diminished across time. By the same token, I doubt that either of us would simply delete them from our lives were that possible. I know I wouldn't.

Recovery

What is it that makes the Twelve Steps work? Of course, they don't work for everybody. What worked for Bill Wilson became the model for recovery from alcoholism. His spiritual encounter in the hospital is prominent in the first three steps, which stress the "twice born" experience of religious conversion described by William James, James Leuba, Edwin Starbuck, and others—what AA calls "hitting rock-bottom." Dark forces of depression become overwhelming. At some critical point or tragic moment, a sense of spiritual presence claims an individual's full attention, becoming imperative and irresistible. In Bill Wilson's case, there was a sense of Spiritual Presence that came like "a new-found Friend," actively pointing the way to overcome his alcoholism. The Chinese word for "crisis" also means "opportunity." There is little doubt that for many people, such times of crisis and upheaval can serve as an opportunity for spiritual encounter. It brought Bill Wilson a sense of peace and serenity he had never known, but this encounter with a Higher Power was only the beginning.

Bill Wilson had already established a confessional relationship with Ebby Thatcher, who patiently guided him through a moral inventory, confessing the harm he had done to others, planning amends, and starting twelfth-step work (helping other alcoholics). The dynamics of forgiveness that mark all successful confessional relationships were in place: Ebby Thatcher accepted all Bill Wilson's alcoholic failures and misdeeds realistically. Bill

---

* James, William. *Varieties of Religious Experience* (New York: Macmillan Publishing Company, 1961).

Wilson accepted his addiction and his abuse of others, as well as his ability to accept forgiveness and start over. Still, something was missing. It proved to be Wilson's need for a continuing confessional relationship. By his own account, Dr. Bob provided this when they formed a lasting friendship and began to work together. My guess is that they developed what Daniel Siegel calls a *contingent relationship* in which each shared the experience of *being accurately perceived, understood, and responded to* by the other.

The recovery movement has evolved in many ways. The Twelve Steps of AA soon proved applicable to a much broader range of addictions and compulsions. In 1970, I visited the Synanon community in Los Angeles, which had developed a flourishing treatment program for drug abuse based upon the Twelve Steps. I sat in on the "Synanon Game," an open meeting for recovering residents where anybody could be confronted with some breach of community rules or practices, along with evidence of old behavior associated with one's addiction. I recall one man being accused of "slacking off during kitchen duties and standing around scratching all the time." I was reminded of Count Von Zinzendorf's "bands" among the Moravians or John Wesley's "classes" in seventeenth-century Methodism, essentially confessional groups where everyone's daily behavior became a matter of mutual discernment, confrontation, and encouragement.

Treatment programs for substance abuse were only the beginning for the recovery movement. People with compulsive sexual behavior formed Twelve-Step groups for sexual addiction. Overeaters formed Overeaters Anonymous. Recovery practices proved viable for victims of sexual abuse and were widely employed by Adults Molested as Children (AMAC). Recovery provided effective means for treating a range of eating disorders. Others followed suit: Sex and Love Addicts Anonymous, Relationship Addicts Anonymous, Self-Abusers Anonymous, Workaholics Anonymous, Survivors of Incest Anonymous, and so on—all made significant use of group process and confessional relationships to support one another.

As Recovery grew, so did its principles. Ideas about God *as we understood Him* evolved to include Christians, Buddhists, Jews, and Muslims, as well as many who identified with no religion. Agnostics and even some atheists have been able to lay aside alien predispositions and practice Twelve-Step work with a measure of trust in an undefinable higher power. Some even accept the group or the program itself as a higher power sufficient to help them attain sobriety. The prevailing attitude among members is that if you set out to practice the recovery program fully, some viable relationship to a Higher Power will present itself along the way. This belief is not unlike our hypothesis that a full confessional experience with heightened self-awareness and a responsible search for a relevant response creates the potential for spiritual encounter.

So successful was Twelve-Step work in curing alcoholism that it attracted the attention of one of the great minds of the past century. Gregory Bateson wrote a fascinating article in 1971 entitled "The Cybernetics of Self: A Theory of Alcoholism."[*] Both Bateson and the term *cybernetics* require some introduction. Bateson was a noted anthropologist, social scientist, and "systems thinker" who rose to national prominence in the study of organized systems. The term *cybernetics* was coined by Norbert Weiner to designate studies concerned with understanding and managing how organized systems work, whether they are machines, like a computer, or persons, families, communities, or whole ecosystems. The science of cybernetics dates back to the now-famous Macy Conferences in New York from 1946 to 1953 chaired by Norbert Weiner, bringing together experts in the field such as Heinz von Foerster, John von Newman, Warren McCulloch, Gregory Bateson, and Margaret Mead, whom Bateson married. Imagine the brain trust in that union.

At first, Bateson became interested in understanding the human brain and corporate behavior in terms of computer technology. However, he soon abandoned this early fascination with computer models and all such applications from the mechanical, material world of things to the world of living organisms. Whenever we do that, he became convinced, we are "inevitably stupid bound." He felt such efforts lead to a dangerously naive, one-sided perception of the complexity and balance sustaining all living and human systems. Walter B. Cannon, you recall, wrote *The Wisdom of the Body* to describe an *active intelligence* at work throughout the human organism healing wounded tissue and combating invading infections. Yet he insisted to Anton Boisen that he did not believe in a similar wisdom of the mind. Karl Menninger wrote *The Vital Balance,* picturing the way our body constantly monitors the delicate balance throughout our organ systems required to maintain health without any awareness on our part.[†] Still, all our research cannot account for who will get sick and who won't. The nearest Menninger can come is to suggest that disease is similar to the "Plimsoll mark" on the hull of a ship that indicates how heavily it may be loaded and safely navigate the added stress of storms. Illness, both "physical" and "mental," disrupts this *active intelligence* with "more than tolerable functional stress."

Bateson extended this same *intelligence* beyond our bodies into those systems involving the complexity and balance required by all living and human relationships. Every forest, river, mountain, or prairie is its own

---

[*] Bateson, Gregory. "The Cybernetics of the Self: A Theory of Alcoholism," *Psychiatry* 34:1–18, 1971.

[†] Menninger, K.A. *The Vital Balance,* with Mayman, M. and Pruyser, P. (New York: Viking Press, 1963).

ecosystem, populating its growth and various species with its own well-reasoned balance of food and resources necessary to life. If we kill off the thrushes and woodpeckers in a wood, the worms they eat would increase to a new stopping place, endangering the trees or destroying the forest itself. The potential for disaster, present in the constant interaction between human intelligence and this larger intelligence in nature, is well known as modern technology disrupts rain forests, the ozone layer, the atmosphere, the seas, and the climate.

The same *active intelligence* in the natural order is operative at every level of human relationships. Intelligent activity exists at the center of human efforts to grow and learn, to build relationships, establish family life, develop communities, form societies, govern nations, and preserve humankind. What we think of as *mind* is present in all *intelligent activity* that works to maintain everything in creation, seeking its health and well-being. Bateson chooses to speak of it as *Mind* (capitalized). *Mind* as an *active mental process* governs evolution, not through survival of the fittest as Darwin thought, but as *survival of those who fit*—those living creatures who can successfully "fit in" or adapt to this larger Mentality surrounding them. Whenever anyone operates without self-corrective awareness of what they ignore in the larger picture contained by *Mind*, they become trapped in illusions of objectivity, power, and control. More about this later.

Now, what does all this have to do with AA and alcoholism? The alcoholic's addiction is fed by just such an illusion of power and control. Bateson points to an "alcoholic pride" with which the drinker approaches his problem as a simple matter of willpower, ignoring the disruption of intelligent activity both inside himself and throughout his relationships that serves to perpetuate his drinking. He can stop any time he wants to, discounting either the existence or the significance of his problem drinking.

In *cybernetic* studies, two kinds of relationships can be identified in the organization of living systems. There are *symmetrical* relationships in which the behavior of A and B is similar and the pattern established between the two is such that whatever one does stimulates more of the same in the other. We see this operating in an arms race between two nations, in social efforts to "keep up with the Joneses," in athletic competitions, and in arguments of mutual accusation and denial as in "Courtroom" or the "blame game" that escalate out of control.

A second type of systemic relationships can be described as *complementary,* in which A and B behave in ways that are sufficiently different as to fit together mutually and create a stable situation. Some common examples of complementary relationships are dominance and submission, sadism and masochism, nurturance and dependency, and spectatorship and exhibitionism. While warring factions of Palestinians and Israelis rush to acquire more weapons and bombs in an increasingly unstable symmetrical relationship, those who seek peace try to bring them into a complementary relationship with the United Nations relying on peacekeepers to oversee a truce and some lasting solution to their political differences. The ultimate survival of all living systems, of course, requires some kind of sustaining complementary relationship that makes for a stable universe; otherwise, our existing symmetrical relationships would escalate endlessly and uncontrollably.

Bateson points out that "alcoholic pride" is built upon the notion of "I can" as opposed to "I cannot": "I am in charge and self-reliant. I can control what I drink, stay sober, and work things out myself." This creates a symmetrical relationship between the alcoholic's willpower and the ever-present urge to drink, each struggling to gain control. All the while this internal struggle goes on, the alcoholic constantly confronts symmetrical relationships around him. There is the mutual camaraderie of competitive drinking leading to "one more" and "one more." There is the growing criticism of excessive drinking by spouses and friends who oppose it as a weakness in one's character. Criticism usually serves to mobilize further resentment, resistance, and denial, thus exacerbating the increasing symmetrical struggle for self-control within. The battle escalates: the harder one tries, the greater the anxiety, the more difficult the struggle. The experience is similar to trying to "make" yourself go to sleep when you can't; the harder you try, the more agitated you become. We "fall" asleep in a complementary relationship with the rhythms of an active intelligence within.

As the battle for self-control spins beyond the alcoholic's grasp, the one haven from the onslaught of symmetrical opposition to drinking is the relationship to alcohol. Escape comes through the complementary surrender in drinking. Whether alone or surrounded by the fellowship of drinking buddies, the alcoholic gains temporary relief. Fleeting as the sense of well-being may be, alcohol increasingly becomes the source upon which one depends for solace, community, and respite from the symmetrical struggle everywhere else.

Religious conversion offers the alcoholic a dramatic shift from all his habitual symmetrical relationships to an almost purely complementary relationship to others, the universe, and God. Bateson believes that the first three steps in AA serve to establish a counter-complementary surrender to one's complementary relationship to alcohol. The process of hitting rock bottom ushers in all the panic of a system gone completely out of control. Life is unmanageable, like a car skidding wildly out of control on the ice, an apt metaphor, he suggests, for the popular term "skid row." A complementary relationship with a higher power, with God, with AA, and with Twelve Step practices, offers a relevant response with promise.

Here, Bateson, the scientist, becomes the theologian describing the AA reorientation to life in a complementary relationship to others—the universe—God. Bateson's "confession of faith" in accord with these understandings appears near the end of his article. The following is my summary of this confession. His words are in italics; the remainder is my own interpretation in an effort to simplify and illustrate:

1. *There is a power greater than self.* Our efforts to live together successfully require its Presence, whether or not we acknowledge it. I can still hear Reinhold Niebuhr saying, "Power corrupts, and absolute power corrupts absolutely." Bateson continually stresses the dangers and disasters that follow from ill-founded efforts to lay claim to unilateral control of ourselves or others, ignoring the self-corrective wisdom of the larger systemic *Mind* surrounding us. With good reason, those who framed the U.S. Constitution were wise to include a system of checks and balances, distributing authority between the executive power of a president, the legislative power of a congress, and the legal power of a judicial system. No one's will is supreme. Ideally, the combined wisdom of all three may discern and determine our destiny as a nation "under God."

2. *This power is felt to be personal and and to be intimately linked to each person.* We can connect with this higher power as an active Presence, both within ourselves and around us, participating in its purposes and living within its intentions, through communication that is personal.

3. *A favorable relationship with this power is possible.* In personal terms, what Bill Wilson described as his "Inner Friend" can point the way to practices that encourage a relevant response to our predicament, whatever the situation. We may discover a sense of purpose and participate in what many call the "will of God."

4. *By resisting this Power...* (persons may) *bring disaster upon themselves.... The unit of survival—either in ethics or in evolution—is not the organism or the species but the largest system or "power" within which the creature lives.* The practices of recovery in AA seek to help one overcome the disastrous consequences of "alcoholic pride" with spiritual practices similar to those in organized religion that inspired them. The idea of attuning our lives in a complementary way to this Higher Power is preserved in the Abrahamic religions. In Islam it is "submission" with the practice of its "five pillars": in Judaism, covenanting with God and keeping the commandments; in Christianity, embracing the "new covenant" in God's love, loving your neighbor as yourself.

5. *This power does not unilaterally control with reward or punishment. As individuals, we are systemically determined by the forces to whom we respond. Steps one and two [in AA] are the appropriate*

response to the manifestation of this power. These steps candidly call for the recognition that none of us can unilaterally manage the darker side of our lives by ourselves. Through awareness of a Higher Power to which our lives may be attuned, we find grounds for hope.

6. *A healthy relationship between each person and this power is complementary.* This is in precise contrast to the "pride" of the alcoholic. Our health and survival is found through establishing relationships in families, organizations, communities, societies, and nations bound together in complementary relationships attuned to this Higher Power. Ditch stubborn efforts at every level to "go it alone" apart from self corrective input from companions.

7. *Not all transactions between human beings ought to be complementary.* It is clear, however, that the relation between the individual and the larger system of which we are a part must necessarily be so. Well-managed symmetrical relationships may foster growth, discovery, and production in everything from knowledge to "building better mousetraps." However, these very relationships only survive when provided sufficient stability through adapting to some form of complementary relationship that sustains them. For example, a symmetrically competitive free market stimulates obvious growth and prosperity but, without some higher cooperative controls, can create economic disaster as in the Great Depression. This has become plain in the economic policies of excessive de-regulation that precipitated the recent collapse in the international stock market since I first wrote these words.

8. When we choose to operate with false notions of power and control over ourselves and others, ignoring the *active intelligence* at work both inside and outside our skin, we live without the self-corrective awareness consistently available from this Higher Power. Not only do we fail to adapt and find our fit together in the natural order of life; but we become opponents given to exploiting others, fighting endless wars, plundering our environment, ignoring the needy, and quarreling with one another. *It is doubtful whether a species having both an advanced technology and this strange way of looking at its world can endure.*

In considering the Recovery Movement, we have come full circle in a rather interesting way. It began with the Oxford Movement where church

---

* From Bateson, Gregory. *Steps to an Ecology of Mind.* (Northvale, NJ: Jason Aronson Inc., 1972, 1987), pp. 331–337.

members were seeking to restore the practice of confession in small group meetings through rigorous self-examination, the confession of character defects, restitution for harm done, and work with others in need. Bill Wilson, Ebby Thatcher, Dr. Bob Smith, and other founders of AA were all exposed to the Oxford Movement in varying degrees. The Twelve Steps were conceived under its influence. What AA eventually did most successfully was to take the practice of these steps outside the context of organized religion to make them available to alcoholics from every imaginable persuasion to no persuasion at all. God was detheologized to "a higher Power" or God "*as we understood Him.*" Alcoholics could practice honest confession with any number of conceptions about a spiritual presence in their lives so long as they surrendered alcoholic pride and took up the task of making a relevant response to their predicament.

Once again, orthodox religion performed its vital function of spawning beneath its wings help for the spiritually homeless both inside and outside the organized church. It remained for Gregory Bateson, the consummate scientist, to retheologize Recovery with his understandings of God as Mind, capable of containing all the processes of the universe, working as the Presence of an active intelligence at all levels of creation. As the Muslims say, "God is great"—great enough to hold in balance the myriad of intelligent systems at work beneath an overarching surveillance governing our survival, seeking our cooperation through participation in this wisdom that awaits only our awareness and response.

Practice

We all have crises in our lives. There are so many ways of "hitting rock bottom" that the experience is seldom, if ever, restricted to a select few. You may choose in your quiet time to assemble from memory an archive of your personal crises. Sit back, close your eyes, and let them come. You may have felt lost or abandoned as a child or been treated in a way that seemed totally cruel and uncaring. You could have had a scrape with death, or thoughts of killing yourself, or felt so hopeless you just couldn't go on. Any number of events can become a crisis: having to move, losing a job, breaking up with your first love, the death of a loved one, prolonged or crippling illness, or some rejection or betrayal that hurt to the quick. You may even be facing such a crisis in one form or another right now.

> Exercise 1. Trace your recovery through these events. How did you do it? What helped most? Are there different or changing patterns that you have developed to cope with crises? Can you point to parallels in your experience with any of the Twelve Steps? Was there some form of spiritual encounter? When and how did it come? Did

you make some form of confession? To another person? Was there some effort to make amends on your part? Did you at any time help someone else through the same or a similar experience?

The possibility of making amends is worth special attention. This step assumes that a measure of restitution is possible. There may be predicaments where this is impossible. If someone has intentionally or negligently, even accidentally, done great harm to another person, the possibility of making amends may evaporate before other issues. I have worked with several people who felt responsible for someone's death. Seeking some measure of forgiveness for oneself eclipses any consideration of making restitution. Some form of self-acceptance despite having done the completely unacceptable must come first, before we can find even the energy to consider amends of any sort. There are events in life for which we can never make restitution. Having said that, there is a sense in which amends and forgiveness go together. Forgiving ourselves clears the way to consider some relevant response to restore a broken relationship. Often this also involves accepting others, despite what they may have done. Although no effort to make amends can bring about the reconciling force of mutual forgiveness, the effort demonstrates the reality of forgiveness on one's part and openness to reconciliation.

Exercise 2. The possibility of introducing some practice of making amends into our confessional responses may appeal to you. It does to me in a number of ways. For starters, I have always found it difficult to say, "I'm sorry." That means admitting clearly, "I'm wrong here, and I regret it. Please forgive me." However, simple apologies can play an important part in any concerted effort to make amends, especially with the difficult task of maintaining day-to-day relationships in family life. Try adding the words "I'm sorry" to your efforts to work out everyday conflicts, even when you know you are both at fault. Apologizing beats courtroom and other accusatory games and hassles. Do it authentically, owning your "half" or "part" without requiring the same from the other. I once knew a couple who took a cake over to a neighbor's house to say "I'm sorry" and spent the rest of the evening reestablishing their long friendship.

Exercise 3. Select some person you feel you have wronged and make amends. Consider what kind of gesture, act, or overture could serve to establish your regret and your intention to reestablish your relationship on a different basis. This can be a family member, friend, or colleague with whom there is estrangement. There are both verbal and nonverbal ways to make amends. Sometimes our actions speak much louder than our words, delivering in a more elegant way sufficient restitution of what has been missing or neglected.

Amends can serve to right old wrongs even without comment. In the fourth grade, I was suspended, sent home for bringing a pocketful of BBs to school to throw. I didn't know why I was intentionally being so bad. I now realize it had something to do with my teacher, Miss Snell, being a former student of my father's at Coker College. I was locked into my struggle to play the piano, without words to say anything about my feelings (which I now know were desperate, angry, scared, and lonely). Each time Miss Snell turned to write on the board, BBs ricocheted off desks and walls, back and forth between my buddies and me. At recess, the BBs were augmented by pockets full of tiny rocks selected with care from the playground. The rock fight continued beyond any point of tolerance or concealment until six culprits ended up in Mr. Parish's office, their pockets unceremoniously emptied on his desk.

Mr. Parish was our principal. He moved us to a classroom, seated us one behind the other in a row of desks, and walked up and down the aisle where the six of us sat, our eyes firmly fixed upon the back of the head in front. With each step, he flipped his dreaded rubber hose against the palm of his hand. That was the hose with which he beat Hank Walker nearly to death for less than we did (as legend had it). One by one, my friends deserted me, testifying that I started it. Miraculously we escaped the hose. The others cleaned erasers after school, and I went home with a note to my parents (a fate worse than even the hose).

I didn't know what to expect, except the worst. Mother used to apply her hairbrush to my posterior; my father used his hand, which I feared more. I don't remember my punishment or my parents signing the note or my returning it. Strangely enough, my only memory is of my father's coming home for lunch and cooking cheese sandwiches with me—grilled cheese sandwiches, my favorite. Shortly thereafter, I recall getting up one morning to learn my father was taking me to the Sumpter County Fair— with a busload of Coker girls he was chaperoning—to see the Citadel play Presbyterian College in football and watch me race bumper cars around the enclosure five times and eat three bags of peanuts. In retrospect, I got the message loud and clear but not in words: "We expect a lot better out of you. And I realize I haven't been the father to you I needed to be. I'm sorry for my part. I'll pay better attention to my end of the deal from now on." I believe this is where I learned how amends and forgiveness go together.

More recently, I discovered an unexpected opportunity to make amends delayed over half a century. At age 10, I received what I always referred to as the best Christmas present I was ever given. It was a tiny, pure-white American Eskimo pup named Baby Snooks, a gift from Uncle Arthur and Aunt Betty Lou. She soon became "Snookie" to everyone. In retrospect, I see how Snookie was judiciously timed to coincide with the arrival of my younger sister Carolyn, who came the day after Christmas. Snookie was my constant companion throughout the next 15 years of my life. She stuck with me through the disastrous end to my piano career. She slept with me during those tender years when Mother's attention was necessarily shifted to the new infant in the house. She ran beside my bicycle at 4:30 each morning as I delivered 318 *Charlotte Observers* all over town, went camping with me, rode with me in the back seat when we moved to Danville, Kentucky, and the world I knew came to an end. Slowly, as I matured, I left her behind more and more. But she was always there when I came home, eager to take up where we had left off. I can never hear the song "Puff the Magic Dragon" with dry eyes. But what plagued me with guilt and shame for over half my life was my failure at her death. She was sick and obviously at the end of her life. I came home but I could not put her down. I refused. I let her lie there an inordinate amount of time and left her to die alone.

Four years ago, I learned that we sometimes get a second chance to make amends. My daughter Elizabeth and her husband Peter shared three dogs. Two were American Eskimo dogs; one of them was a dead ringer for Snookie and a namesake, based upon pictures Elizabeth had seen and the stories that went with them. Facing an itinerary of foreign travel that eventually led to their living in Guam, Panama, and Spain, Elizabeth asked Margaret and me to take them. They were older dogs— Princess was 12; Coconut and Snookie were 14—but we didn't consider that we were agreeing to preside over their decline and death. Little Princess went first with kidney failure after a desperate battle to save her. That was difficult. Then came Coconut, who also had kidney failure, was incontinent, and nearly blind. His death was difficult yet something of a relief. But Snookie was as healthy as a horse. We became inseparable. We wrote together in the mornings and saw clients together in the afternoons. For 2 years it was as though I had my Snookie back. I made him mine. Elizabeth remarked on a visit that he seemed different from the dog she had to leave behind. He thrived in every way for 2 magnificent years as if returned to me from a previous life. I often dream of Snookie now, and the two pets seemed to have merged into one, the same presence continuing in my life.

Then one day the inevitable happened. While Margaret and I were away for the weekend, Snookie fell desperately ill. Our kennel master took him to Sam Vaughan, our vet. Sam called us with the news as we returned. There was nothing to do but what I had failed so completely to do the first time. Gently I bathed him (only now am I conscious of the gender differ-ence) and more gently held him as Sam administered a lethal injection. Somehow I had come full circle with my sense of guilt and shame. This for me was the only amends possible.

CHAPTER 12

Predicament and Presence in Practice

"Called or not called, God shall be there." Words to that effect were carved in stone above the door of Carl Gustav Jung's house. Confession begins in heightened self-awareness when aspects of our private story emerge in the painful predicaments of life. It may lead to much more than simple relief from shame or guilt. Full confession pursues a relevant response to these troublesome experiences—one that explores our unfinished business, our shadow side, the vices of our cognitive emotional habits, our estrangement from our true self, or whatever terms we choose to characterize these troubles—creating the possibility of new experiences capable of transforming our lives into something different, richer, and better. Confession points to the constructive practice of a compassionate life based upon acceptance and forgiveness, both for ourselves and for others. For Jung and a host of others, the potential for spiritual encounter awaits us at each step.

Spiritual Encounter

In the Old Testament, Elijah waits to hear from God. He listens to the earthquake but hears nothing. He listens to the wind but still hears nothing. He watches the fire but still nothing. Finally, he hears a still small voice deep within. And that is God. To talk about such a Presence, we have to conceptualize it in terms of some experience we hold in common. This can be done only by means of analogy, metaphor, or simile. Even then, the commandments warn against the inevitable problems such imaging will bring, saying, in effect, "Don't make any one of these into some graven image before which you bow down and serve." Pretty good advice.

By far the most common image we have of Spiritual Presence is a god up there *above and beyond* in the heavens, looking down upon us. The earliest known Christian posture for prayer was not on our knees, head bowed to the earth. It was standing erect, eyes raised to the sky, arms spread reaching upward as if to fill lungs and life with an awareness of the Creator. Who hasn't looked to the "heavens" on a night filled with stars and felt some kindred feelings? My friend Bill Peterson used speak of the image of an "oblong blur in the sky," frustrated at trying to capture what exceeded the capacity of his imagination so completely. This notion of a presence *above and beyond* ordinary time and space came to dominate the classical creeds of Christendom with their transcendent God, the sovereign God, eternal, omniscient, and omnipotent, beyond the boundaries of all natural processes in the created world. This became the prevalent view in orthodox Christianity, one shared by many philosophers and theologians in Islam and Judaism as well.

Problems for Orthodoxy

This supernatural view of a God beyond all natural processes of human life did little for the mystics and the Gnostics who searched for spiritual encounter deep within themselves. Our confessors joined them, seeking faithfully to pursue what came to awareness in their own personal experience. Margery Kempe and Julian of Norwich constructed their own ideas of the motherhood of God from their experience as women. Tolstoy felt compelled to search out for himself a faith worth living for among the common folk of the land. Even Augustine wrote his confessions from "what he knew" and "what he didn't know" within his own experience.

Orthodoxy, on the other hand, tended to represent spiritual presence in terms of some interruption of or intervention into the natural processes of life from another realm entirely. This quality of "wholly (holy) otherness" is what grants revelation authenticity, as in a miraculous appearance or an unexplained healing. The Catholic Church still confers sainthood only upon demonstration of two such miracles—while sadly, we learned recently in our newspapers that a study following 1,800 patients at six medical centers financed by the Templeton Foundation found no benefit to heart patients when strangers prayed for their recovery.[*] Even worse, patients who knew that people were praying for them had slightly more complications, a finding that their physicians could not explain. Perhaps, someone suggested, they concluded they were worse off because they "needed" prayer. Dr. Harold Koenig, director of the Center for Spirituality,

---

[*] Malcom Ritter, Associated Press, "Strangers' prayers no help to heart patients," *Courier Journal*, Louisville, KY, March 31, 2006, p. A3.

Theology and Health at Duke University was quoted as saying that science "is not designed to study the supernatural."

Supernatural understandings of spiritual presence are fraught with such problems, especially for those who seek to influence the course of human events through appeals for some display of divine power and control. No small number of believers have lost their faith or had it severely shaken when their "god up there" doesn't come through "down here." Main-line orthodoxy, of course, has always vested particular times, places, and people as occasions for revelation from beyond. For Jews, it can be Moses receiving the Commandments on Mount Sinai; for Islam, the prophet Mohammad writing the Koran; for Christians, the life of Jesus Christ. Then the task becomes one of recovering and perpetuating this sense of special presence through ritual, writing, and practice.

Orthodoxy, by its nature, undertakes to bind us to a set of beliefs across time. When Irenaeus set out to establish "right thinking" in a certain choice of scripture and creed, he sought to unite all Christendom into one Universal Church. Although he did not succeed, the idea of a body of truth delivered from above and beyond once and for all prevailed. God's self-disclosure or revelation came through the special person of Jesus Christ. Eternal Presence above made itself known *then and there* in a manner for-ever relevant to all persons, in all times and places. For Irenaeus, no less a matter than our eternal welfare was at stake in believing this. Salvation in the afterlife depended upon our acceptance of this revealed truth, to which nothing should be added or subtracted.

Although orthodoxy never succeeded in uniting everyone, the idea of a special presence *then and there* did survive and prosper. The Christian faith looked to its scripture and creeds delivered from one generation to another as a permanent source of truth. Its accepted scripture grew to be considered inerrant. It became the Holy Bible. Islam and Judaism share a similar notion of their sacred writings. Fundamentalist beliefs from *then and there* can determine inerrant convictions in the *here and now,* such as who is entitled to what Near-Eastern real estate, or who shall live and who shall die for the apostasy of converting to another faith, or desecrating verses from a holy book, or drawing cartoon images of a sacred prophet.

The orthodoxy in which we are reared can affect us deeply. My first parish as a young pastor was in the knobs of central Kentucky where there was no indoor plumbing. Shortly after arriving, I went to the outhouse out back one day, only to discover old and somewhat worn copies of the King James Version of the Bible there, where discarded telephone books and Sears and Roebuck catalogs used to suffice. I must confess, I removed them when I came to consider the service to which some of my favorite passages of scripture could be put.

So what is it about the tendencies in orthodoxy that proved so trouble-some to those seeking a full expression of their confessions? First of all, the notion of God up there, above and beyond the natural world, focuses our anticipation of presence upon the unusual or the unexplainable. Such events are spectacularly absent from our cussed struggles, day-to-day, with self and others. Notions of a supernatural presence can appear hopelessly remote to the ordinariness of our everyday life. If we are like Elijah and keep looking for it in earthquake, wind, or fire, we may miss the persistence of a still, small voice within.

Moreover, the orthodox emphasis on knowing about God through scripture and creed can serve to direct our search away from any relevant response to the concrete realities of how we live and treat each other. What used to frustrate me to no end, teaching in a seminary, was the tendency among some students to think the only way they could actively express their faith was to say something religious, quote the Bible, or take a stand against something they perceived as wrong. The orthodox emphasis upon forgiveness as something already done for us *then and there* can leave one relatively unscathed by any idea of forgiveness as a practice relevant to living a compassionate life based upon accepting and forgiving one another. More about this later.

Still, orthodoxy has succeeded in delivering its rich tradition of scripture and belief from generation to generation. None of our confessors started from scratch, without the benefit of its heritage. Russian Orthodoxy launched Leo Tolstoy on his personal search for an authentic faith. A Catholic convent started Karen Armstrong on her way. Evangelical Protestants had an impact upon Elaine Pagels. All three made the decision to strike out in search of a workable expression of faith that ended in their own unique spiritual encounter.

In this way, the mainstream of orthodoxy continues to serve its purposes well. We can encounter its liberating power at times in the most unlikely places. I recently heard Sue Monk Kidd, who wrote *The Secret Life of Bees*, interviewed at the University of Louisville Kentucky Author Forum. Her Jungian leanings in search of the sacred feminine deep within the womanly unconscious led to the selection of Jungian analyst Jean Shinoda Bolen to interview her. Sue Monk Kidd was making the point that receptiveness to her ideas often springs up in the most orthodox of circles. She was invited to speak at a traditional Catholic school for young women. Upon her arrival, she was greeted by a summons to the office of the headmistress. Scenes from her parochial-school education flashed before her mind's eye, enveloping her with anxiety. What possible offenses or cautions awaited her? When asked about what she would present, she replied that she encouraged women to look for new ways to experience a sense of spiritual presence in their lives. "Well, it's about time we got something new," came the response, "All we've had so far is two men and a bird."

Encounter Here and Now

In a heightened state of self-awareness, our confessors experienced spiritual encounter in the "here and now" instead of the "then and there." Alfred North Whitehead provides us with a most vivid picture of a God *here and now* in what he terms *Process Philosophy*. His work was widely adopted in religious circles, becoming known as *Process Theology.*[*] For Whitehead, every real-life object must be understood as a series of events and processes. Not just living creatures, but rocks and clouds and fossil fuels and earth and concrete and wetlands—everything is in process. Process, not material substance, is the fundamental constituent of the real world. Substance is but the form taken by the energy of process extended across all actual occasions in time and space, so any point in time is an abstract idea, similar to trying to mark water in a flowing river. In a way, every location involves an aspect of itself in all other locations. Every spacial/temporal standpoint mirrors the whole world. Explore anything deeply enough, and everything is there.

Reality is the *here and now* in its constant ongoingness. Central to spiritual encounter is what Whitehead calls an *actual occasion*. Into each actual occasion he introduces the metaphysical notion of a sense of Presence joining in our process of becoming. Here creativity becomes the principle of novelty surrounding each wave of goings-on that turns everything into something else. We can never have the same experience twice. All must move beyond this moment to the next, which is always different in some way. We are driven by bare desire to advance toward greater beauty, spurred on by feeling, curiosity, alertness, aliveness, and ardor. But pure novelty possesses no character of its own. For Whitehead, something more has to be there, something originating in that ultimate notion of the highest generality at the base of all actuality. Without some higher Presence, creativity by itself would twitch in vain like a frantically fibrillating heart. Each actual occasion serves as the potential for God to supply the eternal, objective ideas for which lesser creatures may aim.

The *actual occasion* serves as the basic unit of human experience through which process theology approaches the succession of moments that make up a lifetime. Spiritual presence is firmly embedded in each

---

[*] See Whitehead, Alfred North. *Process and Reality*, (New York: Macmillan, 1929). Also Cobb, John B. *A Christian Natural Theology, Based On the Thought of Alfred North Whitehead*, (Philadelphia: Westminster Press, 1965) and Harthorne, Charles, *Whitehead's Philosophy: Selected Essays 1935–1970*, (Lincoln: University of Nebraska Press, 1972).

actual occasion, whether or not we realize it. However we might experience the present moment, we are constantly swept beyond it and enveloped in the opportunity for limitless novelty. We enter each actual occasion with all our assumptions and understandings (*prehensions* to Whitehead) based upon the past. These tend to determine our response, our attitudes, our feelings, and our way of being in the world. But God is present here and now as *aim* within the invitation to limitless *novelty* before us. God lures us to what is new and different, and best for us. Creativity without God to teach it could have no power and so would not exist. By the same token, Whitehead's God could not exist without the process that acts out His suggestions. This relationship between creature and Creator becomes essential for both to fulfill their common purposes. In this way, you and I participate in the intentions of God and may even bear some influence upon them.

Central to our predicament as human beings is the necessity to cope with constant change. Upon the occasion of my retirement from the seminary, three of my favorite graduate students gave me a large stone smoothed on one side, into which are carved the letters C-H-A-N-G-E. It stands today on my desk to remind me of the constancy of this fact of life. From the moment of birth, life demands one change after another. Rudely thrust from the safety of our mother's womb, we must breathe on our own. Then we must learn to crawl, and walk, and talk, and read, and work, and socialize, and grow up, and leave home, and make it on our own. Sometimes those around us observe that we are going through a "stage." By that, they mean we are in some sort of transition, learning to cope with a new set of demands brought on by anything from "teething" to "starting school" to "adolescence." Physicians, psychologists, and lots of others have written volumes about these stages from birth to aging to death, including stages in the life of couples, in family life, in divorce, in the formation of new and blended families, even in dying and death. It is the challenge of our human predicament to live through these stages as richly, fully, and successfully as we can or, as Whitehead would say, to connect with the aim or purposes of God in search of what is best here and now.

Practice

You may wish to experiment with Whitehead's understanding of the *actual occasion* as a framework for your own contemplation. Start right now in the moment at hand. Lend full attention to the flow of novelty that presents itself to your mind's eye. Listen to your inner promptings for what is creative. Feel your imagination at work, shifting attention to the next relevant matter. Be awake to where your experience points. You have placed yourself in a position to encounter spiritual presence here and now as *aim or lure toward what is new and best for you.* I am reminded of the movie *Field of Dreams* where Ray Kinsella is prompted to build a baseball diamond in an Iowa cornfield by an inner voice whispering, "If you build it, he will come." Well, I doubt that's how it happens for very many of us, but who knows the inner workings of anyone else's mind?

This exercise is designed for Internal Dialogue and Self-Reflection but is applicable to Guided Imagery, Meditation, or Contemplation for Groups. Confessional Partners may choose to experiment with it, building on some actual occasion between them. Here are some other exercises that follow from the ideas we have been discussing:

1. Change Inventory—If the certainty of change is set in stone as a permanent part of life, you can count on it. As I write this at 75 years old, I know very well that not all progressive processes are welcome and good. I have recently given up competitive tennis because of stenosis in the lumbar region of my back for which the best orthopedic surgeons and neurosurgeons consulted do not recommend surgery except as a last resort. So I have changed to golf with my two sons and still struggle a bit hitting that little ball, although my game has improved considerably from my start at ground zero. Mentally I don't believe I have ever been healthier, although I doubt that everyone else would agree. Only recently have we learned that our brains go on creating new cells throughout the aging process. And learning. More about that later, too. As these thoughts unfold, I am starting my own Change Inventory. There are brand-new thoughts, some of them far from pleasant. Others are very rich in possibilities. How about you?

   Make your own inventory of the changes you are aware of in your present life and your thoughts about each one, then your feelings and your sense of novelty or new directions. As you go, grant your imagination free reign. Sometimes writing with your non-dominant hand will give this a boost. As you lean toward your future, be alert to novelty and aim and growing purpose.

2. Life Map—We have been dipping our oars into a moving stream with its different currents, bends, banks, and ports. Our lives are always coming from and going to as time rolls on. Life Mapping could appeal to you if you liked the previous exercise. There are several ways to do it. Start with a large, clear sheet of newsprint and drawing instruments (crayons, pencils, even paint and brush if you are a latent artist). Chart the course of your life from birth onward in any manner that appeals to you. This is for you. Don't let anyone else look over your shoulder. Be willing to see what comes out. That's one way.

Another is to divide the large piece of newsprint into a series of frames from top to bottom like the comic strips in your Sunday paper. Depict your life in the series of frames before you, picturing its course from one scene or phase to another. If you need a second page to finish, don't hesitate to use it, even a third. When you are done, place your life on the wall before you and see how it looks. Let it show you whatever it will. Still another way is to divide your life into chapters. You can do this on your large newsprint or on a number of pages, each devoted to a chapter. Jot down what belongs in each chapter as the story unfolds. Record whatever comes to mind in each place, stage, phase, time, event, or series of events. Note the major changes in each chapter.

When you have completed whatever way you created your Life Map, step back and note the major changes you have experienced. How have they shaped you? What organizing themes appear? What happens over and over? What really changes? What kind of story is unfolding before you? Showing and telling with a confessional partner or a trusted friend will really help you draw together whatever meaning this exercise may have. Take time to identify elements from the four levels of narration discussed earlier. Recall how Karen Armstrong's transformational stories revealed that each failure seemed to open a new door of opportunity toward the next step in her life. Perhaps you can construct a sacred story with the emergence of elements of a faith all your own.

Confession and the Unconscious

Sigmund Freud spent his lifetime studying ways we often act for reasons that have little to do with our conscious thoughts. Like the gnostic *Gospel of Thomas,* he suggests that what we bring forth in our self that lays beneath our ordinary awareness can either destroy us or save us. Freud explored the unconscious parts of our mind that are capable of influencing our motivation and our behavior in any number of ways. To him, the unconscious is the dwelling place of the unacceptable and the traumatic, for all our experiences that are too painful or threatening for the conscious Ego to process, assimilate, and recall. Beneath that lies the id, a seething cauldron of primitive libido and sensual desire, joined in his later thought by a second drive toward destruction, death, and return to non-existence.

Me and My Shadow

Jung would agree. Our *shadow* becomes the reservoir of all the repressed desires, uncivilized impulses, and morally inferior motives and fantasies that lie unclaimed or disowned in our personal unconscious. Both he and Freud sought to bring the unacceptable to the daylight of conscious awareness. Otherwise we remain at the mercy of what we fail to own and understand about ourselves. In effect, both joined our confessors in searching out what troubled them most from the darker recesses of the mind, but with some very important differences. For Freud, this was a rational task for the intellect, one of mastering the unknown through self-understanding and self-control. Where there is Id, let there be Ego. But for Jung, it became a search for the reunification of the self, drawing together the most negative and the most positive aspects of our being in a way that suggests the full confessional experience we have been describing.

Jung thought there was a *principle of opposites* at work in the psyche. Every wish immediately suggests the presence of its opposite. Every evil thought must be measured against some corresponding thought of good. Any act of kindness stands against the background of an act of cruelty. What a strange mixture we can experience. Once I stood on a fifth-floor balcony overlooking the ocean, holding one of my grandchildren. Suddenly, I was gripped by the fear I could lose control and drop the infant over the edge. Perhaps that is why we shudder when Michael Jackson holds his child over the railing above the street, suggesting the unthinkable, or step back with a tremor in our legs from a great height, feeling drawn by a fleeting, yet alien, impulse to jump. We understand sanity only through some acquaintance with what is insane.

Jung added a *principle of equivalence* to the understanding of how our minds balance energy between both impulses. Both can exist side by side as wishes in the unconscious. When we hold the baby close, or step back from the height, or reject crazy or unacceptable thoughts, we spend that energy toward good and positive purposes. What happens to the energy invested in the opposing wish depends upon our attitude toward it. If we can acknowledge it, face it, and keep it available to our conscious mind, energy is freed for the general improvement of our psyche. And we grow. Harry used to worry about shouting out a curse word during church until he confessed it to his friend, his therapist, and his counseling group. Now he reports that the idea scarcely ever occurs to him.

When we pretend we never had an evil thought or wish, when we deny or suppress them, the wish forms a *complex,* a cluster or pattern of suppressed thoughts and feelings around some theme usually represented by an *archetype.* Jung is the originator of the term "inferiority complex," which we bandy about so freely. Our shadow side is composed of many such complexes. They become troublesome when we pretend that we are only good. When we deny our capacity to lie, to be cruel, to cheat and steal and kill, these impulses go into some complex in our shadow. Across time they develop a life of their own and can come back to haunt us in nightmares and on occasions when we say things such as, "I don't know what got into me," or "I just lost control," or "I simply wasn't myself."

With this awareness we can extend our confessional practices into the realm of the unconscious. We can begin to expose what we deny and accept the unacceptable. We can free life energy for new choices in situations of guilt or shame or anxiety. We can open up the possibilities for relevant responses and personal growth beneath the mystifying return of those more troublesome aspects of our life. Fritz Perls' idea that anxiety signals repressed excitement when we encounter threatening experiences at the boundary of our awareness begins to make practical sense. Whatever unfinished business disturbs our well-being begs for cloture to complete the Gestalt. It serves the dual purpose of introducing us to the long shadow of what we repress and of freeing our energy for whole-hearted participation in our chosen purposes.

So, confessing the alien "Not Me" within us not only disestablishes its power to emerge and overwhelm our good intentions, but can also serve to open the doorway through which may pass the energy to pursue whatever higher intentions we hold in equivalence. Our attention may shift into the presence of Whitehead's "aim" or Jung's "God Within" or Bill Wilson's "Inner Friend."

Practice

As a therapist, I learned long ago to encourage people to pursue further what troubled them, beyond where they usually stopped. I remember one CEO of a large company who wanted to be closer to his wife. She complained he was emotionally unavailable. And he was. He had become almost completely task oriented at work, at home, and at play. Everything became a job to get done, even sex. He worked hard at our conversation, carefully considering every measured response. When I asked him about this, he reported that he was selecting and checking his words carefully to make certain there were no mistakes or false impressions. He had learned to do this long ago managing a company where any misstatement could return to haunt him with a host of problems. When he loosened up and began to say what was "on his mind" without such careful censoring, he would abruptly stop and accuse himself of "just rambling." Only when I encouraged him to ramble even more did he begin to master the art of self-disclosure. To "think out loud" or to report whatever comes to mind was the first step toward accepting and exploring his own internal thoughts and feelings, which, for the most part, remained guarded and protected from everyone, including himself. Most of us carry some measure of inhibition about such free and spontaneous self-encounter. April calls it her "thought police." Sometimes it takes a good, accepting confessional partner to help us escape their vigilance.

Exercise 1 — The next time you turn in confession to what troubles you most, make a special effort to go beyond all your usual stopping points. All you have to do is pick up the next relevant thought that comes to mind. It could prove to be a blind alley, in which case, simply return to what last focused your attention and ride your associations a little further. Be increasingly mindful of the number of responses that appear as possibilities, any shifts in your emotional tenor or mood, new angles through which to view your experience; in short, open yourself to whatever novelty presents itself to your awareness. You are free to select any response that fits. If you can't reach a satisfying possibility to pursue in one sitting, set some time aside later to have another run at it, and keep this appointment for quiet time with yourself. Often, just what we are looking for appears quite spontaneously when our attention has been withdrawn for a while. Don't cheat on yourself with a bunch of old irresolute ruminations that lead nowhere in between times. If a second quiet time doesn't go somewhere, find a trusted friend with whom to talk. Confessional partners are an ideal choice in such circumstances.

Involuntary Confessions

Several years ago I was invited to speak to a group of public school teachers on the subject of nonverbal communication. We were assembled in a large auditorium. I recall sitting on the edge of a stage with my feet dangling to the floor waiting to be introduced. I was cool and relaxed, having done this many times before. So I thought—until I looked down and observed my feet shuffling vigorously one way and then the other, as if attached to someone else. I had long since learned to pay attention to such bodily behavior in the therapy room, but here before an audience of grade-school teachers, the smell of chalkboards and lunchroom, and the buzz of smaller feet headed to class outside, part of me was back in my own third-grade days, about to write on the board and recite before this assembly of formidable matriarchy.

Years before, I would have ignored my feet, gone back to rehearsing what I was about to say, and suppressed my childlike anxiety in front of all these teachers. Now I had learned to pay attention to what my body expresses beneath my awareness. Deep down I really wanted to bolt, but I had learned some things since third grade. One was to let my feet do the talking for a moment and just listen. "Let's get out of here," they said, not so quietly, "before you make a mistake or don't do well or get a low grade or something worse." I now recognize the anxiety of the Little Performer

(Three) beneath my awareness. I knew I was much better off listening to the Child in me than ignoring his needs. That's preferable to having him act out his anxiety and then struggle to avoid its distraction. I needed to deal with those teachers somehow or "get them on my side," at least in my own mind. So I decided to confess to everybody there what had been going on and use it to introduce the value of paying attention to nonverbal behavior, whether in yourself or others. They laughed with me; the ice was broken, and I became suddenly free to devote my full energy and resources to what I was presenting.

Long before I was thinking about nonverbal behavior confessionally, Freud did. "No mortal can keep a secret," he wrote, "if his lips are silent, he chatters with his fingertips; betrayal oozes out of every pore."* Freud made records of such "symptomatic actions," noting that to the keen observer they often betray everything, occasionally more than one wants to know. I spent a decade in clinical practice developing ways to help people establish awareness of what they were experiencing in their bodies. I quickly discovered, as Freud wryly suggested, that you seldom make friends with those to whom you try to tell the meaning of their actions. I soon gave up "body reading" as well as "mind reading" of any form. I was learning much more effective ways to encourage people to get into touch with their own postures, gestures, and bodily movements, especially incongruent ones like mine that suggest something else is going on beneath the surface of our awareness.

Few of us ever benefit from efforts to ignore or override such secrets, poorly kept from ourselves and others around us who sense them at various levels of awareness. I learned to invite people to pay attention to their bodily experience in various postures, particularly ones that appeared with amazing frequency when they addressed what troubled them most. Each posture had an overriding character. Some were protective with legs and arms tucked tightly over groin and viscera. Others were clearly diminutive as if to make oneself small and insignificant. Still others were ascendant as if to claim dominance and strength, while others were discordant and awkward as if robbed of comfort and gracefulness. Many were passive, suggesting resistance or noncompliance. You get the idea. The point was to encourage people to discover for themselves the dominant trend and describe in their own words how it felt. I found ways to help clients explore a repetitive posture, gesture, or mannerism. One was to exaggerate it to its endpoint by letting the body do more and more, and more of the same. Then one could experiment with finding its polar opposite to try that on for size. For instance, a diminutive posture could be expanded in search of

---

* Freud, Sigmund (1905) A case of hysteria. In A. Strachey (ed.), *The Standard Edition of the Complete Psychological works of Sigmund Freud*, 7:78. London: Hogarth Press, 1953.

the other extreme. Invariably, something new and different was introduced into an existing impasse. I didn't realize it at the time but some bodily or psychomotor parallel to Jung's principle of psychic equivalence seemed to enter the equation. A new and better way of being became a possibility. Sometimes it was there immediately. Sometimes one had to search for an appropriate point of balance along a continuum between the extremes.

My favorite clinical example is Nan, a devout member of a religious order, who was nearing the end of her training as a psychotherapist. She had developed recurrent cramping in her right hand so severe that she had difficulty writing her clinical records. Nan was convinced her "writer's cramp" was an expression of her mounting anger toward others who took advantage of her. Her conscientious efforts were exploited in the center where she worked long hours beyond her contract. But this was nothing new—a compulsion to please others at considerable self-sacrifice went back to early childhood. Banging her right fist repeatedly on the arm of her chair, she defiantly declared she had produced more hours of patient care than any other staff member. She concluded her speech by declaring her freedom from guilt and her resolve to say "no" to whomever she chose.

Nan moved only from the right side of her body as she spoke. On impulse, I asked her to experiment with movement only from her left. She began haltingly, checking her tendencies to return to the right. Suddenly she began to explore with her left hand making broad sweeping gestures. She burst out laughing in delight. Others who were present remarked how free her movements had become and how graceful they were, approaching elegance. Her movement was accompanied by immediate affective relief, her anger disappeared, and a rush of enthusiasm for returning to work followed.

Two days later, quite on impulse, Nan suddenly stopped writing with her right hand and shifted her pen to her left hand. Immediately, the small pinched scribbling of her letters disappeared before the broad sweeping strokes of her fingers. She wrote with ease, without practice or effort, bringing samples of her new handwriting to her therapy group. Only then did she recall being corrected by her grade-school teacher, who insisted she stop using her left hand and follow the prescribed right-handed writing of her day.

Nan's awkward adaptation to right-handedness can serve as a symbol of the countless ways someone might suppress the natural ease and gracefulness in anybody (*any body*). Whenever anyone—be they parent, teacher, authority figure, or peer—fails to recognize the natural rhythm and growth as it unfolds in the development of anybody else, something sacred is violated. The resulting difficulties may lie dormant for years awaiting discovery. Near the end of my work, I wrote the following:

> At the conclusion of this writing, I am filled with a sense of awe at the marvelous wisdom of our bodies in their innate drive toward health and wholeness. I have long been struck by the relationship between what the theologian calls grace and the grace-ful expressions of uninhibited movement and growth we can encourage among people of all ages. In its most profound sense, grace is a gift freely given by the Creator. Our task as creatures is not so much one of learning how to get it or receive it; rather it is one of discovering what we have already been given, opening ourselves to where it has already begun to lead, and gracefully accepting the full lines of our being that are constantly seeking expression and completion.*

Involuntary confessions come from a wisdom at work in our body beneath our awareness. Not only do they claim our attention by overriding lesser concerns that mask what we repress or deny; but they also often signal what we ignore or neglect, begging for a response. Often the problem suggests the solution. Headaches can work this way at times. I have seen them come and go with stress and internal conflict. When we listen to them the way I did to my shuffling feet, they often reveal important messages. When we pay them heed, an added bonus often is their disappearance. As Fritz Perls suggested, at times we need to "lose our mind to come to our senses."

Some therapists have sought to establish a healing presence in the body that awaits such attention. Among them is Eugene Gendlin at the University of Chicago, who developed the theory of *focusing*. He set out to study why psychotherapy is helpful to some people and not to others. He listened to recordings of hundreds of sessions from the beginning to the end of treatment with different therapists and their clients. The therapists rated the success of their work, and psychological testing was used to verify when positive changes occurred. This separated the tapes into two groups of subjects: those who were successful in therapy and those who were not. Researchers listened to the therapists of both groups but found no significant differences. Then they listened to the clients and immediately discovered one important difference between the successful ones and the unsuccessful ones. It was nothing that they learned in therapy because it appeared immediately in their first two sessions. The successful clients invariably slowed down at some point in the conversation and became less articulate, starting to grope for words to describe something they were feeling at the moment. They struggled to express it, lacking the vocabulary to describe their sensations. Often they spoke of experiencing some feeling in their bodies: "Its right here in my chest," or "I have this

---

* Steere, David. *Bodily Expressions in Psychotherapy*, (New York: Brunner/Mazel, Publishers, 1982), p. 298.

funny sensation in my stomach." What distinguished the successful clients was this vague, hard-to-describe feeling that could be associated with physical sensations.

From these findings, Gendlin sought to establish treatment methods that *focused* attention on just such a *felt sense* of bodily awareness.* As with Fritz Perls, Gendlin emphasized the necessity of getting clients "out of their heads" by fixing their attention upon their bodies. Some of his followers even taught focusing methods within the context of spiritual encounter.[†] They believed these techniques overcame two critical issues in spiritual development. First, focusing presented a more holistic approach than ordinary means of prayer and meditation by encouraging one to let go of the mind's strict control and permit some broader wisdom within to speak. Second, focusing took the unique next step of allowing a sense of "me" to emerge as an integral, harmonious expression of some Larger Process. It supported a felt sense of being sustained within the presence of some greater Mystery. I see these approaches to establishing self-awareness beneath the level of everyday consciousness as contemporary expressions of what the writer of the gnostic *Gospel of Thomas* was describing when he had Jesus say, "If you bring forth what is within you, what you bring forth will save you."

Practice

Most people who work with internal awareness today do so with an interest in identifying and cooperating with a healing presence within. The following exercise is designed assist you in contacting this Presence in your confessional practice. I have put it together from a number of sources. They include Fritz Perls' ideas of creating dialogues with whatever troubles us, particularly by owning whatever we experience in our bodies. Some of the methods of focusing are very helpful, and you may find a book such as Ann Weiser Cornell's *The Power of Focusing* full of worthwhile suggestions.[‡] I like Charles D. Leviton's understandings of visualization, hearing, and responding to an internal message, receiving healing energy from within your bodily self.[§] You are encouraged to develop your own hybrid form or ritual as you experiment.

---

* Gendlin, Eugene. *Focusing* (New York: Bantam, 1981).
[†] McMahon, Edwin M. Ph. D. and Peter A. Campbell, Ph. D. *Why We Teach Focusing in the Context of Spirituality* (Unpublished paper from forthcoming book), pp. 1–15.
[‡] Cornell, Ann Weiser. *The Power of Focusing: A Practical Guide to Emotional Self-Healing*, (New York: Barnes & Noble Books, 1990).
[§] Leviton, Charles B. *There Is No Bad Truth: The Search for Self*, (San Francisco: Kendall-Hunt, 1990).

Exercise 2 — Begin with your customary practice of quiet and relaxation. Shut down your Generalized Reality Orientation and all the busyness of everyday concerns. When you are ready to open yourself to your unconscious, permit whatever comes to mind to bid for your attention. Select something of genuine concern, something you have been carrying with you, to emerge in your awareness. It may be some concrete discomfort or sensation, some pain or symptom or stress or issue. Locate the point in your body where you feel this matter as it claims your attention. Embrace it and feel it for what it is to you.

1. Visualize your pain, symptom, stress, or issue as you feel its presence in your body. Give it a shape, a form, or a symbol that permits you to focus attention upon it. When you are ready, move into the pain, consciously owning it and claiming its presence as a part of yourself. Experience yourself as becoming the pain as a messenger bearing some significant and important message for you.

2. Have a conversation with your pain/symbol/symptom. Coyote medicine men would speak to the spirit of an illness and learn what it had to say. Ask questions like: "What do you want me to know?" "What are you connected to?" "What are your terms for my healing?"

3. Receive the message your pain/symbol/symptom has for you. Answer it in whatever way you choose. Don't remove it without receiving and responding to whatever it has to say. Take your time to complete the conversation. Be aware of any change within your pain/symbol as you progress. Some people establish sufficient awareness for it to serve as a biofeedback measuring change.

4. When you have finished, remove the pain/symbol by finding a way to image yourself reaching inside and holding it before you in your hands. Accept it as an important part of your being. Send it your love and comfort. Remain open to whatever may happen to improve its condition.

5. Now set the pain symbol aside. Imagine yourself shelving it for a few minutes. Experience getting it off of your hands. Feel what it is like to be without it. Open yourself to whatever comes when you free yourself from it.

6. Receive into your hands healing energy from your bodily self. Permit this energy to build until it takes some virtually tangible form. What takes shape can represent your constantly active immune system, your instinctive powers of repair, and all your wisdom resting in the unconscious sources of your being.

Let this energy assume some form, such as a liquid, a salve, or a powder, that you hold there in your hands. Allow this healing energy to build within your grasp so as to focus and receive its full presence.

7. Now find a way to apply this healing energy to the place where the pain/symbol was removed. Anchor it within you through the touch of your hands. Fill the emptiness left within through this ritual act of healing so you can return and re-experience it. Stroke the healing energy into your body; rubbing in the salve, liquid, or powder. You can participate in this larger healing Presence whenever you choose. You can permit it to work unencumbered beneath your awareness in its own time and way.

Dreams

Then there is the other third (or so) of our lives we spend asleep. So much goes on there that we either don't understand, ignore, or discount as "just a dream." Who hasn't been rudely awakened by a nightmare and comforted by the grown-up knowledge it was "only a dream"? For some strange reason, organized religion has restricted its attention to the "realities" of waking life. Only now and then do dreamers like Joseph in the Old Testament or Augustine quite a few centuries later concern themselves with the subject. Augustine, you will recall, felt constrained to deal with the unacceptable in his own dreams and ideas that appeared in the dreams of his mother as well.

Early in the last century, an archeologist's dream (of another kind) came true. The Senoi Indians were discovered, a "primitive" tribe that managed to survive into modern times in Malaysia, unspoiled by any contact with the outside world.* Here was a chance to explore the patterns of organizing a culture literally as different from ours as night and day. You see, the Senoi completely reversed our Generalized Reality Orientation. They believed that their waking life was lived in a transient material world that was largely illusory and barren of meaning. The real world was the world of the spirit, the principal manifestations of which were the dreams that broke through to their awareness at night.

So the Senoi set out to organize their conscious daytime life around the realities their dreams revealed to them. In their arid climate, minimal time was required to supply their needs for food by hunting and raising crops. So they had lots of time on their hands. If you grew up in a Senoi family, you began each day by sharing your dreams from the night before.

---

* See Tart, Charles T., ed., *Altered States of Consciousness: A Book of Readings*, (New York: John Wiley & Sons, 1969), pp. 159–167.

Children were included and praised for remembering their dreams, which they learned to analyze at an early age. Every one was taught to believe that guidance for daily living was given each night in the nether world of sleep.

Each morning your family would start the day sifting through everyone's dreams. Yours would be carefully examined for some call to a particular quest in waking life you may have received. If you dreamed of a neighbor, there might be something important to pursue about that relationship. Personal plans for community projects, festivities the following evening, costumes, or particular assignments in other activities were given by the spirit world that appeared in your sleep. When a loved one died, that person remained around in your dreams, staying in touch as long as necessary for your well-being.

Your Senoi community would possess some remarkable features. There was a total absence of crime, warfare, rape, and violence. Your ancestors had learned to live peacefully together for centuries, following the guidance of their dreams, and learning to live them out, so to speak, in waking life. Often a quest for some new element in the life of the community would be envisioned. For example, one tribesman of note was said to have dreamed of a 4-foot blowgun with uncanny accuracy for hunting. This dream led him on a journey that lasted for months in search of a new strain of longer bamboo. In the process, he met and married a wife from a neighboring tribe and returned with this additional prize to be greeted with a great celebration of his successful quest.

The method of dream analysis employed by the Senoi is worthy of our close attention. You were taught to reenter the dream after the fashion of what we call daydreaming. Only a fragment of your dream the night before was necessary. When you began to embellish whatever you recalled, the search would lead to a central figure bearing the message of the dream. Once this figure emerged, it was killed and incorporated into your own being as your food is devoured and digested. Now, for the Senoi, the act of killing was in no way violent or hostile. As in many archaic societies, you killed only when hunting for food. The act of taking an animal's life was a sacred one performed with profound gratitude and deep reverence. To kill and eat was to take into yourself what was vital to your existence, so you killed the central figure of your dream, whether it was an animal, a child, a neighbor, an ancestor, or a god. This you did in the daydream state through which you reentered the dream. Killing was the means whereby you assimilated the gift of its essence and power, and came to understand the meaning of its message. Such an act, rather than signifying an end to life, became the wellspring of ongoing spiritual being in mutual relationship.

On the other side of the world, Sigmund Freud considered dreams to be "the royal road to the unconscious." Jung agreed. As in Walt Disney's *Cinderella*, "A dream is a wish your heart makes when you're fast asleep."

Of course, you have to take into account that not everything in Freud's "id" and Jung's "shadow" is pure and loving and heartfelt. Both contained wishes we would describe as violent, destructive, even self-destructive. Freud thought of the unconscious as a cauldron of seething desires, a bottomless pit of perverse, incestuous cravings (libido), and infantile rage (aggression) when our desires are thwarted. Sleep revealed a burial ground of frightening experiences and instinctual energies, not only toward life and survival but toward death and destruction.

Jung had a different set of dreams, but equally disturbing. In the autumn of 1913, he dreamed of a monstrous flood engulfing most of Europe. He saw thousands of people drowning and the waters turning into blood. He feared he was psychotic when dreams of eternal winter and rivers of blood followed. The next year, World War I broke out, and Jung felt connected in some mystical or mysterious way to humanity in general. He launched into a study of his dreams, fantasies, and visions; as the Senoi, drawing, painting, and sculpting what he recorded. Beneath the personal unconscious, which he shared with Freud, Jung encountered what he came to call the collective unconscious, filled with the accumulated experience of the whole human race.

Jung concluded that as a species, we are born with this reservoir of our collective experience that contains an innate knowledge beyond anything we acquire purely on our own. Although it influences the way we perceive our world, especially our emotions, we can never be directly aware of it. There are experiences that suggest it is there, as love at first sight, a sense of déjà vu (as Yogi said, "all over again"), or an immediate affinity for certain symbols or meanings in myths, fairy tales, and legends. In his own dreams, Jung recorded figures such as a wise old man who appeared as a spiritual guru and a young girl who accompanied him as "anima" or the feminine soul who became his main medium of communication with the deeper aspects of his unconscious. These were archetypal figures that he identified through analyzing common themes in the dreams and fantasies of his patients. They are also found in the art, legends, and mythologies of all civilizations, figures like *the mother, the father, the child, the wise old man,* and *the self.*

Jung decided the *self* that lay at the center of our being is the integrating principle of reunification and healing of the personality. It is often conceived as a point halfway between the conscious and the unconscious. The self is best represented by the figure of the *mandala.* It is the locus of the archetypal presence of the "God within" who works through each individual soul seeking God's goal for us. True self-understanding leads to such awareness.

Practice

The exercise that follows incorporates the ideas we have been discussing and offers a way for you to explore your own dreams as a source of self-understanding and spiritual encounter. It seeks to bring together Freud's understanding of dreams as the royal road to the unconscious with other more expansive views.* It is constructed with Fritz Perls' ideas that our dreams contain an existential message about the unfinished business of our waking life, and also that we are everything in our dreams, which serve as a projection of our internal experience of the world. It preserves space for the possibility of spiritual encounter deep within the self as Jung envisioned it. And it contains the invitation implicit in Senoi dream work to follow your self-analysis with a personal quest in waking life by completing your dream through daydreaming its ending.

Occasionally I meet people who say they don't dream. That isn't possible. We all dream seven or eight times a night. In laboratories for sleep research, we can distinguish periods when the eyes move rapidly back and forth, which has been termed REM (for rapid eye movement) sleep. Subjects awakened in REM sleep report they are dreaming. Everybody has REM sleep, even rats. People who "don't dream" just don't remember their dreams. I think of the "Dreamer" in us as a small child who rushes up with a picture carefully drawn to show us. We can be inattentive, unresponsive, or rude and ignore it, making no effort to take it in. After so long, the "Dreamer" says, "OK, no more pictures," and we cease to be shown our dreams.

So if you "don't dream" or have trouble remembering your dreams, you may wish to make friends with your "Dreamer" or whatever term or metaphor you may have for that part of your unconscious. Ask it as gently as you would a small child to help you remember a dream. When you wake up with recall, keep pencil and paper at the bedside so you make sure it doesn't slip away, jotting down just enough of the fragments so you can reenter it in the morning, as the Senoi. Many a great dream, so vivid when I first had it, has slipped into oblivion a short time later, completely eluding recollection, without reminding notation. With your notes you can always recollect enough to move back under its spell or trance.

1. Set aside some time to work through the meaning of your dream, either by yourself or with others. If you have a confessional partner or group, these steps have proved adaptable to both settings. I have

---

* See Langs, Robert, M. D. *The Dream Workbook.* (Brooklyn, NY: Alliance Publishing Co., 1994); Perls, Fritz. *Gestalt Therapy Verbatim.* (Lafayette, CA: Real People Press, 1969); Steere, David. *Spiritual Presence in Psychotherapy.* (New York: Brunner/Mazel Publishers, 1997, pp. 145–160.

found dream work especially effective in groups where a few persons can enter and participate in the dream with you, somewhat like the Senoi family. If you are by yourself, get pencil and paper for a worksheet that will help you organize your reflections.

2. The Dream Narrative—If you are with a partner or group, tell your listener(s) the dream in the present tense as though it is happening now. If working alone, jot down the skeletal narrative of your dream, just enough to help you recreate its memory and impact. Again, use the present tense and record what you feel during this dream. A worksheet can also serve to preserve your recall until it can be shared with partner or group.

3. Precipitating Events—Now reflect upon the "trigger events" of the day before your dream (or shortly before). Take whatever comes to mind, although no immediate relationship between these narratives and the dream narrative is apparent. Often, the Dreamer in us disguises meanings by associations and encoded themes. I suspect this is to sneak them by our tendencies to deny and suppress from awareness their more troublesome, unacceptable, or unfathomable aspects.

4. Themes—Now sift through the narratives you have accumulated to identify the powerful themes that appear, particularly ones they share in common. These have to do with a certain interlocking relevance to the dreamer's life situation. Some of the more common themes are power, control, conflict, danger, violence, death, sexuality, anger, shame, love, joy, grief, success, identity, limits, desires, fears, illness, wellness, and fulfillment. Confessional partners and group members are often helpful in identifying these common themes, particularly as they come to know you through previous conversations.

5. Related Associations—Having explored the context of your dream, you may wish to open your associations to any related memories or events that come to mind. This permits other narratives to take their place as pearls on a string of meanings your dream may connect. Partners and group members can sometimes suggest something they know about you that fits. This is your dream, however, and only you can determine whether or not something fits.

6. Connecting Themes and Narrated Events—The next step is to connect the Powerful Themes in the Dream Narrative and the Precipitating Events in the steps above. I do not wish to present an example at this point because we are approaching your dream as a uniquely created event. Often, examples serve to suggest some particular way for you to emulate. I choose to leave the possibilities as limitless and open as they really are. I have done this many

times with individuals and groups. The results defy generalizations. Confessional partners and group members may join in the search for relatedness and relevance, but in doing so, they need to be especially careful not to get in your way. Others are most helpful when they can project themselves into your life situation as if to "have your dream with you." This involves leaving one's own perspective (often including gender) and assuming yours, so far as this is possible. More about this in Chapter 13. For now, suffice it to say that we understand one another only to the extent that we can do this. I encourage others present to share their experience of your dream having a mindset something like: "If I were you having this dream, I would think/feel/wonder/want ..." (however they choose to finish the sentence). This frame of reference reflects and honors two crucial facts. I am not you and therefore am able only to imagine what you are really experiencing. And my response is mine, not something you should feel constrained to accept as yours. Take only what fits and adds to or strengthens your own awareness.

7. Neglected Trigger Events—Whether working alone or with others, it is not uncommon to recall some neglected precipitating event at this point, if not before. Now is a good time to check for the appearance of one or more such events in the immediate context of the dream. Normally there is some wonderment on the part of the Dreamer: "How in the world did I forget about that?"

8. Ownership of Major Symbols/Images—We are now ready to establish ownership of the major Symbols/Images in your dream as part of your inner world. Fritz Perls insisted that everything in our dreams is a projection of our self. This part of the exercise provides a powerful means to pursue what Jung called the reunification of the self. Complete at least five to eight sentences that begin "I am ...," describing yourself as each major symbol or image in the dream, including people, animals, monsters, mountains, bridges, and other inanimate objects. Take time to absorb what you feel with each powerful symbol, especially those that you are most reluctant to own. On occasion, you may wish to establish some kind of dialogue between contrasting or conflicting symbols/parts that emerge needing some type of cloture. You can write this, if alone, or pull out the chairs to explore it as we have described with or without the help of others.

9. Cloture—The final step is to bring cloture to your dream through daydreaming its ending in any fashion you choose. Virtually all dreams are incomplete. We awaken in the midst of something,

often with strong feelings and a sense of unrealized fulfillment. Some unfinished business of our waking life dangles before us with all its loose ends—an existential message from deep within our unconscious. You claim full ownership of your dream by exercising your right to construct its ending. Your dream is yours to finish in any way you choose. This is often difficult because it seems either too easy or too difficult. It may seem too easy to day-dream your own ending against the vivid and often harsh realities a dream suggests. We might melt monsters into faithful dogs like Lassie and live happily ever after in our daydreams, but playing with symbols is different from playing with what they represent in real life. That can become really difficult. So do it anyway. Play freely until your heart is content with any and every symbol in your dream. Confessional partners and groups can participate with their own concluding stories. You can listen with your full powers of imagination and creativity for what your own relevant response wants to be, for here your Quest in waking life can take shape in the world to which we all must return.

In Conclusion

Sigmund Freud never wanted to make an important decision without first dreaming upon it. I have seen a number of people who were able to elicit dreams by requesting some message from their Dreamer during the night. Often it comes without our even asking. Have you ever awakened in the morning with the solution to some seemingly unsolvable problem or sudden clarity about something that was a quandary the night before? Not long ago I woke up with a very workable solution for a seemingly unsolvable problem with my computer. It appeared as the result of some night-time mulling by a deeper wisdom in my unconscious than I had been able to produce.

Now for a concluding note about some confessional dimensions of our dreams. They certainly stand near the top of the list of involuntary confessions our unconscious offers for our waking consideration. Edgar Robinson was an English professor at a large university. He presented to others an extraordinary absence of temper or any display of anger, regardless of how large the provocation or injustice. He came to treatment depressed and disillusioned, upset with members of his department, who failed to reelect him as their chairman. His style was to duck conflict at any cost, which no doubt influenced his colleagues' reluctance to vote for him. His timidity with anger was rather obvious to others in his group as they came to know him. Finally one day, Robinson reported an unsettling dream the previous night. He and a friend were walking down the hallway where they taught when a stranger entered the building and began blowing people away with an AK-47. The two of them managed to escape by climbing together up an elevator shaft, but Robinson awakened with a feeling of terror.

The task of owning the powerful symbols in his dream brought Edgar face to face with his unresolved anger. He could own "I am ...." sentences about the hallway: "I am a hallway in the building where I teach. I am crowded with people. I am a passageway for others to go through. I am walked through over and over again. I am hardly noticed by all the busy people on their way somewhere else. I am just used by others to get where they're going." He could own the friend: "I am my friend. I care about me. I'm terrified by the assassin. I am afraid he will blow me away. I must escape and get away however I can." When he came to the assassin with the AK 47, there was a very strong resistance to describe himself as this figure. He had to be urged to try it on for size to see if it fit: "I am the assassin. I am just blowing people away as they come down the hall. I just do it without thinking. Actually, I'm enjoying it—blowing people out of my way. I am smiling. I am angry. Very, very angry at everybody."

When he finished, Robinson was angry. His fists were clenched. His involuntary confession had established a clear awareness of his repressed anger. As in many dreams, a bit of the punster was present in the shaft through which he and his friend escaped. He was tired of scurrying up the elevator shaft with a friend or confidant, fearful of his anger. He would rather give others "the shaft" and return to stand his ground in the hallway. In daydreaming the finish to his dream, Robinson returned to disarm the assassin and restore life to those blown away in the hall. (In our dreams we have such magical powers, even the power to fly.) He decided that the assassin, once disarmed, could become a helpful colleague in the internecine struggles of campus politics, particularly in standing up to conflict. And he, his friend, and the assassin now go off, arm in arm, to cope with such political warfare on his campus as Rick (Humphrey Bogart) and the Police Chief at the end of the film *Casablanca*, saying, "This looks like the start of a beautiful friendship."

Spiritual encounter with genuine aim and purpose often comes disguised in symbols that at first appear anything but relevant. Only as we are able, with or without assistance, to put the dream in the context of our current lives and establish the personal significance of its powerful symbols is its meaning clear. Evelyn reported the following dream. She was crying with a deep flow of tears unlike any she had experienced. They streamed down like gushing water inside her body. Her throat and chest were filled with rocks and stones. The water was accompanied by a rush of wind that swept its currents downward, dislodging everything. The wind and water caused the rocks and stones to break down inside her until they were crushed, pulverized, and swept away. She awakened in tears that brought profound relief. She had to go to the bathroom and accomplished her mission as quickly as possible in order to return and finish the dream. Back in bed, she was able to continue in the dream state until her flow of tears reached a point of satiation. Then she felt a quiet strength come over her, filling the emptiness in her throat and chest.

Obviously, we need to know the context of this dream and the significance of its symbols to Evelyn. Otherwise it is nonsense to us and to her as well. How many of our own dreams have we dismissed as such, leaving them unexplored? Evelyn had done enough dream work previously to do her own analysis, which she reported to the group. Her long and difficult divorce had just become final after 2 years of failing efforts to work out differences with her husband. She struggled to stand up for herself, to be assertive. Often she would choke on her words and feel tight across her chest as though she could not get them out. She had been battling long-standing guilt of "failing in her marriage" leading to the first divorce in her extended family. She also was filled with shame, dreading conversations with friends and colleagues at work who knew and inquired how she was doing.

For 3 weeks afterward, she related more experiences of the newfound quest her dream produced. She no longer lost her voice and choked on her anger, owning and expressing it clearly and reasonably. She had always thought her guilt alerted her to danger and helped her avoid mistakes. Now her guilt and shame had largely disappeared, and she could speak freely with others about her divorce. A different sense of self-acceptance had replaced the choking sensations and tightness in her chest, and she had found her voice. The water represented the quantum of tears in her grief, the rocks and stones the rigid blocking of deep anger and disgust. And the wind? Several in her group wanted to know. Evelyn had her deepest struggle with God, her father, and her conservative church, because she felt all three had conspired to remove her from teaching Sunday School when she became pregnant before a hastily arranged marriage to her ex-husband 22 years earlier. "The wind?" said Evelyn, "That had to be the presence of God."

CHAPTER 13

Forgiveness and Confessional Relationships

"My whole attitude has changed," said Sawsan al-Momen, in Mecca to complete her fourth hajj, "Every time I come here, I become more forgiving. ... I told my husband that we have to be more forgiving and patient with one another."* Forgiveness is the driving force behind full confessional experiences, whether by Muslims, Jews, or Christians. In the next three chapters, we turn our attention to its role. We have seen how an accepting relationship is an essential precondition for confession. Once we gain a sense of self-acceptance, we discover our capacity to accept others. Receiving forgiveness opens the possibilities of forgiving one another and leads quite naturally to the practice of empathic participation in each other's lives.

Confession among contemporary Catholics has been termed a Sacrament of Reconciliation. Mike Rankin, a former student and a Catholic priest, now Executive Director of the Kentucky Association for Marriage and Family Therapy (KAMFT), gave me the topic "Depression and Reconciliation" for a workshop at its annual meeting. The occasion featured Michael D. Yapko, Ph.D., presenting on "Preventing and Treating Depression."

The week before, my wife Margaret and I were returning from a restful visit at Sedona, Arizona, wandering around amid the striking red rock formations and vortexes, soaking up Native American lore and spirituality. We reached Phoenix in our rental car a little late, anxious to find the airport, which somehow eluded us. Suddenly, while urgently scanning signs along the expressway for one pointing the way to our destination, I saw

---

* Faramarzi, Scheherezade. "A difficult spiritual quest during Islam's annual pilgrimage," *The Courier Journal*, Thursday, December 20, 2007, p. 47.

it—there was, a huge black sign with its message accented in white lights: "JESUS CURES DEPRESSION."

I was annoyed but too preoccupied to figure out why. Later, after we had successfully caught our plane, I settled back to check my reaction. I have a number of objections to the people who put up signs like that. First, I didn't know they had such a franchise. I wonder where this leaves people like Michael Yapko and me. Their solution seems to dismiss the hard work of many, many folks. Second, their approach usually involves some form of evangelistic conversion through "accepting Jesus Christ as your Lord and Savior," based upon the premise that Jesus' death on the cross made it possible for our sins to be forgiven. They normally pay little attention to the kind of self-awareness we have been describing or consider the range of relevant responses that serve to complete a full confessional experience. One solution is offered to fit any and all aspects of the human predicament.

Even more disturbing than the franchise claimed by these people is their sweeping disenfranchisement of the rest of the world. Not just Jews and Muslims, but the entire human race beyond Christendom is unentitled to such Spiritual Presence as they share and call salvation. No, the sign is spectacularly unhelpful to most who read it—depressed or not. That's why I was annoyed. Now this forced me to raise the question: what would I do with my own Christian understandings? What would I put on such a sign? In Phoenix or anywhere else? This question presented quite a challenge but it eventually served to help me decide how to end my workshop at the KAMFT and this book as well. So we start with another exercise as you read through to the end. Come up with your own sign to put there in Phoenix, or anywhere else. And compare it with mine at the conclusion.

Forgiveness in Human Relationships

So many things converge when we consider the role of forgiveness in human relationships. To err is human but to forgive is divine. Paul Tillich, as we have seen, described forgiveness as *God's acceptance of us in spite of our unacceptability.* There is something God-like about the ability to accept ourselves and to accept others *unconditionally,* that is, without imposing all the conditions we normally place upon one another with guilt, and shame, and anxious conformity to what is championed as the right way to be. How easily we learn to blame, and denounce, and condemn. How profoundly difficult it is to accept what is wrongful in both ourselves and others, and stay in a relationship. Yet our very survival as human beings may depend upon it.

Whatever else Christians do with Jesus of Nazareth, his life among us is universally associated with forgiveness. Augustine's confessions were filled with affirmations of God's mercy. Among our confessors, even crusty old

Kurt Vonnegut chose to end with his sermon on Palm Sunday, claiming Jesus' idea of being merciful as "the only good idea we have received so far." For Tolstoy, the search for truth led him to abandon any ideas of certainty in correct belief. He came to accept his own uncertainties, while he discovered faith among the poor and common people of the land. These were the very people he had exploited and abused, and he went on to advocate nonviolence and champion their cause. Among our women confessors, Julian of Norwich and Margery Kempe dismissed the medieval preoccupation with sin and judgment, embracing a sense of "motherhood" in Jesus and God as sufficient assurance that we are never disowned. Both insisted nothing we might do can place us outside the pale of our Creator's compassionate care. Elaine Pagels and Karen Armstrong pursued a similar sense of forgiveness, capable of accepting the religious practices of others of different persuasions and spiritual backgrounds. Compassion became the litmus test for good theology. Armstrong insisted that some form of *empathic participation* in the lives of others was the key to her experience of spiritual encounter.

Among our confessors, only Augustine concerned himself with the orthodox emphasis upon Jesus' death on the cross as an atonement for the sins of humankind. He adopted the idea of substitutionary atonement from other early church fathers such as Irenaeus, Origen, and Gregory of Nyssa, who explained its logic by what became known as the *ransom theory*. The idea followed from a common practice in that time of redeeming or "buying back" captives of war from slavery by paying a ransom for their release. Because the wages of sin are death and eternal punishment in Hell and because everyone has sinned and is guilty, Jesus' death was a ransom paid to Satan for his rightful claim upon the souls of all humanity. So God baited a trap for the Devil, sending Jesus of Nazareth, who lived a perfect life, deserving neither death nor punishment, and tricked Satan into releasing all those held captive for this one prize of Jesus Christ, a ransom sufficiently rich to free everyone. Jesus, of course, could never be held in such a place and simply strolled out after his descent into Hell and ascended into Heaven. The ransom theory in some form dominated ideas about salvation in an afterlife within Western Christianity well into the eleventh century.

Many people have difficulty accepting the idea of substitutionary atonement so dear to Irenaeus. To many it seems a strange and unnecessary maneuver for the Creator of humankind to go through in order to extend forgiveness to us all. As seminary students, we traced various metaphors to describe the atonement through different periods of history. In an age of chivalry and courtly honor, there was Anselm's *satisfaction theory*. It went something like this: As Lord and Ruler, God's honor has been offended by our sinfulness. This offense demands some satisfaction on our behalf to restore the obedience merited. No mere human being could render this, so God sent Jesus Christ, His only son, to accomplish what was required on behalf of all humankind. His sinless life of perfect obedience offered an honorable way for God to grant forgiveness to believers.

With the dawning of the age of law, Catholics like Thomas Aquinas and Protestants like Luther and Calvin employed the *courtroom metaphor* discussed in Chapter 5. Because all have sinned, all stand guilty before a righteous God whose sense of justice has been violated. Jesus Christ atones through living a just and righteous life and dying on the cross, paying the penalty for sinners who can now be justified by their faith this was done on their behalf. There are other explanations, such as the *moral influence theory,* that such an act of self-sacrificing love should inspire us actively to restore our relationship to God and engage in acts of meaningful service. In 1931, Gustav Aulen published his classic work *Christus Victor* in which the incarnation is seen as a passion story of Christ entering into human misery and wickedness, thereby redeeming it.[*] To early Christians, this story was not so much a rational theory to be given doctrinal expression as a drama presenting the idea of God's entering human life to triumph over the powers of cruelty, evil, and death. This theory is still widely held today among Eastern Orthodox Christians. By and large, orthodoxy in the Western world has fallen silent about substitutionary atonement except among those who put up signs in Phoenix and other places.

To me, the silence is welcome because it clears the way for us to think about forgiveness from a different standpoint—as something in which we may take part, rather than something accomplished on our behalf. Among Mormons, there is an *empathetic purpose* to Christ's suffering and death. Through him, God participated firsthand in the experience of human pain, illness, anguish, emotional turmoil, and depression "that he may know according to the flesh how to succor his people according to their infirmities."[†] Forgiveness involves caring for others, participating in their lives, extending to another the kind of acceptance upon which confession is based. This notion was also present in the earliest Christian expressions of faith. Even Irenaeus suggested the idea of seeing in Jesus the possibility of a kind of recreation in the human spirit—Jesus becoming what we are so that we could become what he is. Had this idea grown to full stature, a constructive practice of participating in forgiveness such as we are about to consider may have become a dominant theme in orthodoxy as well. Instead of substitutionary atonement, we have an

---

[*] Gustav Aulen. *Christus Victor: An Historical Study of the Three Main Types of the Idea of Atonement.* (Transl. By A. G. Herber, New York: Macmillin, 1997).

[†] *Book of Mormon,* Alma 7:12.

emphasis upon the practice of accepting forgiveness and extending it to one another, a *participatory atonement* if you will.

The Practice of Forgiveness

Extending forgiveness to one another stands at the center of the many compassionate expressions among the world's great religions. Reading the *Koran*, I have been impressed by the many times forgiveness appears as a continuing theme among the faithful. My Jewish neighbors have just celebrated Yom Kippur, the holiest day of the year. It is a day of atonement and forgiveness, of purification and cleansing. It is also a day of reconciliation with others from whom one is estranged, of seeking and granting forgiveness. Among Christians, extending the forgiveness we have received to others is as natural as repeating in the Lord's prayer "forgive us our trespasses as we forgive those who trespass against us." Compassionate participation in the lives of others is an essential part of self-acceptance. Recently the practice of forgiveness has begun to receive attention and research at a level of interest seldom witnessed before.

In 1984, Lewis Smedes published *Forgive and Forget: Healing the Hurts We Don't Deserve,* which has been credited with inspiring a newfound scientific passion to examine forgiveness.[*] Prior to 1985, only a handful of such studies had been undertaken. The next 15 years brought more than 50 research projects, leading the Templeton Foundation to initiate the Campaign for Forgiveness Research to raise an additional $5.5 million to fund further study. Archbishop Desmond Tutu, winner of the Nobel Peace Prize in 1984 as spokesman for the rights of black South Africans, was one among those selected to co-chair it. He was founder and head of the South African Truth and Reconciliation Commission, which actively encouraged forgiveness on a national scale. Former President Jimmy Carter joined him with a vision of restoring compassion as a basic tenet of American government, having helped Israel and Egypt achieve reconciliation through the Camp David Accords. Another co-chair was Ruby Bridges Hall, who, in 1960, as a sixth grader in New Orleans, became the first African American to integrate an elementary school, overcoming the taunts of fellow students. Robert Coles, Harvard Professor of Child Psychiatry, was another. He was so moved by Hall's acts of forgiveness that he made her the first subject of his study of children in crisis. Still another was Everett L. Worthington, a specialist in Marriage and Family Therapy at Virginia Commonwealth, who became a pioneer in developing research in forgiveness and reconciliation.

---

[*] New York: Harper and Row, 1984.

An old Chinese proverb says, "The man who opts for revenge should dig two graves." A rash of studies indicates forgiveness can become a key factor in the health and well-being of individuals, couples, families, communities, nations, and society as a whole.* Research suggests that letting go of anger and resentment can reduce the severity of heart disease and, in some cases, prolong the lives of cancer patients. Studies at the University of Montgomery reveal how psychologically damaging the desire for revenge can become and how forgiveness education may reduce the vengeful mentality behind criminal acts. Dr. Frederick DiBlasio from the University of Maryland is among a number of family therapists successfully employing forgiveness to reconcile couples when other methods have failed. The Templeton Foundation funds research on the effect of forgiveness among at-risk adolescents who have been victims of physical or emotional abuse, Viet Nam veterans suffering from post-traumatic stress disorder and related problems, substance abusers, victims of domestic violence, persons with HIV/AIDS, physically disabled individuals, and survivors of suicide victims. Among the Foundation's international research projects are studies on the role of forgiveness among warring factions in Northern Ireland, two projects analyzing transcripts of hearings by the Truth and Reconciliation Commission headed by Archbishop Tutu in South Africa, and studies in Rwanda where Hutus and Tutsis whose families were engaged in genocidal warfare were assembled in forgiveness groups to promote healing among survivors.

These studies suggest there is promise for scientific/therapeutic concerns and spiritual commitments to merge in promoting what forgiveness may offer to the health and well-being of human relationships at every level. Among the benefits for forgiving others are increased anger control, mutual trust, freedom from control by past events, increased physical health, and improvement in psychiatric disorders. These studies stress that forgiveness is never glossing over wrongdoing, or simply pardoning or condoning, or excusing others by removing the consequences of their actions. Most set forth steps or guidelines in the process of forgiving others. Some form of forgiveness education with measurement of its effects on different populations accompanies most of them.

Robert D. Enright suggests four phases to the process in his study entitled *Forgiveness Is a Choice:*†

Phase 1—involves uncovering your anger by facing it fully, overcoming any fear of exposing your own shame and guilt, stopping

---

* See E. L. Worthington, Jr. (Ed.), *Handbook of Forgiveness* (New York: Brimmer/Routledge, 2005). Also McCollough, M E., Pargamont, K. J. & Thoresen, C. E. (Eds.), *Forgiveness: Theory, Research, and Practice* (New York: Guilford Press, 1999).
† Robert D. Enright. *Forgiveness is a Choice* (New York: Harper and Row, 1984).

yourself from obsessing about your injury or the offender, and assessing any changes the injury has made in your life or world view.

Phase 2—involves deciding to forgive, including an assessment of everything you have been doing that does not work. When you become willing to begin the process of forgiveness, you are ready. Forgiveness is a decision.

Phase 3—is working on forgiveness. You make an effort to understand the other. You work toward developing compassion. You acknowledge your pain and let it be. You undertake some act of kindness toward your offender or devise some way to honor your choice to forgive.

Phase 4—is discovering your release from the "emotional prison" in which you have been. This involves establishing some meaning in your suffering, as well as your own need for forgiveness. This phase is accompanied by a sense of spiritual encounter, realizing you are not in this alone, that there is a purpose for your life, and that through this process you have gained a sense of freedom.

Attention to forgiveness is still growing among the helping professions. The initial impact of the forgiveness studies served to whet the appetite among psychotherapists for further experimentation with its practice. Increasing numbers introduced the concept to their clients in a variety of ways. Terri-Ann Legaree, Jean Turner, and Susan Lollis at the University of Guelph in Ontario (Canada) have compiled a helpful summary of how forgiveness is conceptualized in the literature of family therapy, counseling, and clinical psychology over the 15-year period between 1990 and 2005.[*] Here are some important findings:

1. Seventy-five percent of the books and articles they examined advanced forgiveness as important or essential to our well-being. The use of structured interventions or recommended steps to make apologies and extend forgiveness for past hurts is widely practiced. An educational component teaching steps in forgiving, similar to Enright's, is a frequent part of the treatment program.

2. Other authors are skeptical of common approaches to forgiveness, especially when applied to female victims of childhood sexual abuse. Such efforts can serve to minimize or deny the validity of their feelings, interfere with the survival empowerment process, short-circuit the healing process with a premature cessation of

[*] Terri-Ann Legaree, Jean Turner, and Susan Lollis, "Forgiveness and Therapy: A Critical Review of Conceptualizations, Practices, and Values Found in the Literature," *Journal of Marital and Family Therapy*, April 2007, Vol. 33, No. 2, pp. 192–213.

anger, derail legitimate claims for requital from the offender, or force some unwise effort at reconciliation.

3. Some think it is possible to forgive with no restoration of the relationship. A number of therapists choose to concentrate on forgiving oneself rather than one's offender or perpetrator. Others are reluctant to encourage forgiveness because they feel it circumvents the healing expression of anger. However, most acknowledge that the expression of anger is of limited potential for healing when it is not followed by eventual forgiveness.

4. There is some controversy regarding whether forgiveness involves a voluntary, intentional decision or is a longer process of discovery that cannot be willed. Most stress the notion that forgiveness is a conscious choice, a cognitive event that involves a shift in thinking. This decision can be made without necessarily feeling emotional readiness. Then one can work through lingering feelings of "un-forgiveness" with cognitive and spiritual techniques. Those who hold to a decisional view normally endorse forgiveness as essential to recovery.

5. Others argue that genuine forgiveness comes when one realizes that negative, unforgiving feelings are inhibiting and detrimental, and tend to diminish without a decision to curtail them. Forgiveness is more a by-product of self-healing than a goal of treatment and emerges naturally as one lets go of preoccupation with past wounds and moves on. Although Enright's position is decisional, his steps also evidence some elements of discovery.

6. Enright and others believe that the therapeutic environment leads to a natural choice to forgive. Humane relationships engender a capacity for acceptance. A willingness to forgive is developed through empathy for the offender, humility that sheds one's defensiveness, and awareness of one's own wrongdoing. Then a conscious commitment to forgive follows.

7. Others disagree that cessation of resentment, anger, and vengeance is normally accompanied by an emergent compassion, or empathy, or mercy. They insist upon a distinction between forgiving and reestablishing a relationship with the offender. Reconciliation is not a necessary part of the process, particularly for those who work with victims of sexual abuse. One may let go of the intense emotions attached to such incidents, even surrender resentment, anger, blame, and vengeance, without reconciliation with their perpetrator. What is crucial is completing their release from control by their own negative affect toward the abusing party.

Confession and Forgiveness

What can we add to this emergent practice of forgiveness from our understanding of confession? To begin with, extending forgiveness requires a certain degree of maturity. This is true developmentally. Issues of "fairness" so dear to the latency period of childhood (ages 6 to 11) fall quietly into the background. Forgiveness cannot be governed by rules of any kind. By latency standards, the compelling need to forgive others is blatantly unfair. If I shouldn't do that, then neither should you or anyone else. Forgiving another involves the suspension of fairness in the interest of some higher principle filled with paradox. Forgiveness cannot be required. At the same time, we have to forgive in order to move on. Otherwise, we impale ourselves endlessly upon repetitive pain, resentment, and hurt, as well as estrangement from others whom we must cut off, avoid, or pay back. We are ensnared by a situation in which we have to give up to get, but we cannot set out to give up in order to get. The changes brought by forgiveness involve a much deeper internal response in the way we think and feel about ourselves and the other person.

Forgiveness as Empathic Participation

A *full confessional experience* is sustained throughout by an understanding of forgiveness as empathic participation in the life of another. Honest confession is established by someone conveying this quality of acceptance to us. Forgiveness exceeds any prescribed series of steps or phases through which one may simply "go." We can only accept ourselves when we take the perspective of those in the past who have accepted us despite our unacceptability, let alone find the internal resources to forgive someone else. We are all quick to view our behavior through the eyes of those who taught us to be critical and judgmental. We wriggle frantically to escape the painful grasp of their blame or disapproval through various ways of saying "Not Me," which serve only to subvert our efforts to gain self-acceptance. Only when we can recall (literally "call upon") the perspective of someone who truly accepts us despite everything does honest confession proceed. Sometimes this acceptance must come afresh through the perspective of a person who listens and understands and hangs with us, regardless. Without some genuine access to self-acceptance, confession is irretrievably lost at the level of defensiveness and denial.

Through being forgiven, forgiveness of others becomes a possibility. The experience of forgiving acceptance by others and by God creates a sense of its reality in which we, too, may participate. Without it, we are too busy avoiding genuine self-understanding to muster the energy and interest to understand others. With it, we acquire sufficient awareness to consider the need others have to be understood in the same way. We become free to take their perspective and understand them. This constitutes a crucial step toward *accepting them despite their unacceptability*. Or choosing not to. We will always have a choice because forgiveness can never come as simple obedience to a command.

So the capacity to forgive is inseparably linked to a full confessional experience. It appears among the *relevant responses* we can make in the most dire and depressing situations. It provides compelling opportunities for *spiritual encounter* through active participation in the forgiving spirit of a Presence much greater than ourselves. I began to envision this relationship when I was developing various models for determining how theological understandings and psychological methodology intersect in clinical practice.* In the *Gospel of John*, Jesus is the *logos* or the Word of God who was in the beginning with God, who was God, without whom nothing was made that was made. This Word "became flesh and dwelt among us (literally, "tented," "tabernacled," or "made a home among us") full of grace and truth." At the heart of early Christian faith was this notion that God was present in Jesus Christ and engaged through empathic participation in human life as you and I experience it. The idea of God's choosing this special way to make full entrance into our human perspective had a compelling effect upon His followers.

In 1939, Rollo May in *The Art of Counseling* described "empathy" as a deep state of identification with another person in which we feel our way into that person's presence so fully as to temporarily lose our own identity.† Empathy is different from "sympathy," in which we think to ourselves, "Now, how would I feel if I were you?" while scanning our memory to recall similar experiences. Empathy involves leaving our own perspective long enough to experience the other person "from inside" theirs. The old Indian proverb "Never judge others until you have walked in their moccasins" suggests just that.

We all have a capacity for empathy. Many practices in psychotherapy and the early Christian community converge to embrace this central activity of *empathic participation in the lives of others*. Rollo May was not the only one to recognize the curative force in learning this way to relate to our fellow human beings. The Apostle Paul described an analogous "self emptying" (*kenosis*), modeled after Jesus, as a way for the early Christian community to care for one another. In Philippians 2:7, he urges them to "have this mind among yourselves which you have in Christ Jesus, who although he was in the form of God, did not count equality with God a thing to be grasped, but emptied himself, taking the

---

* David Steere, *Spiritual Presence in Psychotherapy*, (New York: Brunner/Mazel, 1997). See the discussion of the Empathic Model, pp. 161–178.
† Rollo May, *The Art of Counseling* (Nashville: Cokesbury Press, 1939).

form of a servant, being born in the likeness of a human being." Clearly some early Christians thought of themselves as somehow taking part in this "empathic identification" with humankind of God in Christ. Karen Armstrong noted similar themes of *kenosis* or the self-emptying by God in Islam and Judaism.

In the 1940s, Carl Rogers' theory of client-centered therapy appeared on the scene, challenging the predominance of psychoanalytic theory.[*] What he called the therapeutic conditions of *empathic understanding, respect, and genuineness* were established as curative in any form of psychotherapy. If therapists place a high value on the worth and capacity of the person, treat the individual as capable of self-understanding and self-direction, create a relationship of genuine acceptance and warmth, accurately perceive the experience of their client, and respond in a way that communicates understanding of the client's inner world, then clients find it safe to explore the fearful and threatening aspects of their experience, come to a deeper sense of self-understanding and self-acceptance, and begin to reorganize their lives on their own without a continuing need for their therapists. That's client-centered therapy in a nutshell.

Rogers, who studied at Union Seminary in New York, was widely accepted in both the worlds of psychology and theology. Pastoral counselors like Seward Hiltner adopted client-centered therapy as a valid expression of Biblical care. Theologian Thomas C. Oden drew direct lines of parallel between God's activity through the incarnation in Jesus Christ and therapists empathically assuming the frame-of-reference of their counselees.[†] As the state of the art in general grew, so did the emphasis upon the therapists' accuracy in perceiving and understanding what their clients expressed. This was apparent in the stress contemporary psychodynamic approaches placed upon empathic attunement, which involved a similar "self-emptying" of any preconceptions in order to "feel with" others, authenticating their inner worlds, and providing a "holding climate" of safety, sufficient to "contain" the full range of experience they choose to explore. Similar ideas emerged among family therapists like Salvador Minuchin, who insisted upon therapists *joining* with the families they treated, adopting their style, symbols, meanings, pace, and idiosyncrasies. Patterns of empathic participation were particularly evident among systemic therapists who formed reflecting teams to work with families in even more pronounced ways of joining their relational system. More about this presently.

---

[*] Carl R. Rogers. *Client-Centered Therapy* (New York: Houghton Miffin Co., 1951).
[†] Tomas C. Oden. *Kerygma and Counseling: Toward a Covenant Ontology for Secular Psychotherapy* (Philadelphia: Westminster Press, 1966).

Problems in Forgiving

The practice of forgiveness is firmly established within the whole confessional process. It invites and accepts heightened self-awareness. Forgiveness never insists upon some prior or anticipated degree of moral or spiritual achievement. It is simply given in a commitment to join others in search of some relevant response to the situation at hand. It is based upon an awareness of being fully as much in need of acceptance as they are. Only through embracing our own unacceptability can we move beyond preoccupation with our own guilt, shame, and anxiety into accepting relationships with others. Extending forgiveness to one another is as natural as supplying water to someone who is thirsty.

Of course we encounter problems here. We are dealing with a practice that suspends common judgments, notions of fairness, and our usual rules of equity and quid pro quo. In its more difficult situations, instead of getting even with someone who has wronged us, we are searching for some form of reconciliation. And there is that strange paradox that we need to forgive as much as they need to be forgiven. Only then can we get on with our lives free from the distractions of growing resentment or preoccupation with avoidance or revenge. Probably all of us have encountered some version of Captain Ahab's relentless pursuit of the "damned white whale" working self-defeating obsession and destruction in our own lives.

The largest problem is how can we forgive the unforgivable and restore a relationship that has been damaged to the breaking point or beyond? I suspect we all operate with at least three levels of acceptance in mind, whether or not we are conscious of them. I want to present them as three distinct levels of estrangement, each marked by a different degree of alienation and requiring different measures to bring about reconciliation.

Level I: First Degree Estrangement—The Level of Alienation/ Reconnecting. Here the degree of isolation is minimal and the potential for reconnecting is strained moderately to severely. It requires the everyday level of forgiveness we know in lovers' quarrels, parent—child disputes, and misunderstandings among friends. Communication is broken off temporarily. People are "not speaking" to each other. We often overlook how important simple acts of acceptance and understanding can become to our everyday morale and mood. My tennis friends, Fred and Allan, used to have such arguments with each other (both on and off the court) that they went through substantial periods when they were "not speaking." But they and their wives were close friends and they all still went out to dinner together. This required Fred saying to his wife anything necessary to convey to Allan, and Allan's wife returning his response to Fred. This somewhat humorous state of affairs could continue until one of them either relented or made the spontaneous mistake of speaking directly to the other without thinking. Couples can break off communication, often for days; neighbors for longer. All squander valuable lifetime in low-grade estrangement that can breed cycles of resentment, retaliation, testing, sarcasm, "point making," and pseudo-polite distancing. Level I acceptance involves extending some measure of reconciliation either spontaneously or though a gesture such as flowers or saying "I'm sorry." Normally the parties involved can reconnect without significant repair to the relationship. Usually the differences in question will continue until mutual awareness of what is at stake is established and their issues resolved. Otherwise, working or living together drives our differences underground only to reemerge as various games or dramatizations of the unresolved until they are accepted and confronted openly. It is possible for most people to reach a workable level of forgiving acceptance of each other to hold the disruptions of Level I estrangement in tow and good repair.

Level II: Second Degree Estrangement—Breach of Trust. A more severe degree of estrangement follows some action that threatens the mutual bonds upon which a relationship is established. Communication and communion are disrupted to such an extent that it becomes necessary to rebuild confidence in one another. Significant damage has been done, as in the case of marital infidelity, sustained neglect, some betrayal of loyalty, or harmful deception that constitutes a major breach of trust. It is necessary that both parties engage in significant efforts to restore effective conversation, repair the damage done, and reestablish the relationship on a better basis. Some degree of mutual understanding of each other's perspectives is normally involved to overcome estrangement. This usually requires some solid measures of empathic participation in each other's perception of the events involved. Without such a practice of forgiveness, reconciliation at any satisfactory level remains elusive and tenuous. With it, the relationship is often reconstructed in a way worthy of such statements as: "It's the best thing that ever happened to us," or "I wouldn't go back to where we were for anything," both of which I have heard on more than one occasion.

Level III: Third Degree Estrangement—Emotional Cut-Offs. The most profound problems confronting forgiveness are in destructive behaviors that inflict permanent damage to others, as in physical harm, prolonged abuse, violence, rape, predatory sexual behavior, murder, child abuse, and so forth. These tragic events normally lead to some emotional cut-off of the perpetrator in a blind effort to shut out that person and the memory of what was done to one's life. Such occurrences demand radical changes in both the perpetrator and also the victim. Empathic participation in someone else's part in such events strains the limits of possibility. I shall never forget the appearance that a former student, Bill Stith, made in an Ohio courtroom a number of years ago. Two years before, he and his family stopped at a gas station somewhere north of Cincinnati. His son was making a long-distance telephone call when, suddenly, a man they had never seen before burst into the room with a gun and shot him to death. Overcoming his bitterness and grief, Bill urged the court to show his son's murderer leniency, testifying against the death penalty. Such forgiveness despite the other's unacceptability is most difficult when someone continues to live with the perpetrator. It becomes possible only when firm safeguards are in place providing sufficient measures of security to prevent any kind of recurrence. This can permit the parties involved to back up and start over again at Level II.

Practice

Whether we start with the problem of accepting the unacceptable in ourselves or in others, each aspect of forgiveness enables and buttresses the other. Until we can learn to forgive ourselves, we are too preoccupied with our own unacceptability, denying it and blaming others ("Not Me"), to have either the energy or the desire to forgive anyone else. A compassionate life comes with the recognition that others need forgiveness fully as much as we do. Through self-understanding we learn to understand and accept others, and vice versa. The practice of *empathic participation* in one another's lives becomes possible. The following exercises are designed to expand our practice of compassionate involvement.

Exercise 1. Start by assessing where you are with self-acceptance. In your quiet time alone, open your awareness to what you still have difficulty accepting in yourself. Make a list if you want to, just for your eyes. Is there an old, recurrent shame of some kind? Is there something you did or failed to do, or an old guilt, anxiety, or fear that keeps recurring? This time, go farther with it. Address the part of your shadow side that harbors these feelings. Speak directly to it. Listen to what it has to say. Get into another chair for its part in the conversation, if that will help. Commit yourself to accepting and understanding it fully. Respond with forgiveness. If you need help to do this comfortably, think of the most accepting person you know. Say what this person would say to you. If that doesn't bring the cloture you desire, go talk to that person, or your confessional partner, or someone else you really trust. Or, move to Exercise 3.

Exercise 2. Now let's select some person you have trouble accepting. We want to shift from thinking or talking about this person to addressing this person directly. Get out the empty chair if that will help. Most of us have rehearsed a speech we wish we had made or would like to make to someone else. Usually we do it silently, sometimes out loud when driving or alone elsewhere. More often than not, we break off in the middle and fail to finish. We seldom hear what that person has to say or make any attempt to understand him or her. Carry the conversation through to some conclusion. Then consider whether you wish to respond further, either with the exercise or in person. Do you have cloture? Can you say and feel, "I forgive you." Remember, you may need to but you don't have to.

Exercise 3. We considered another practice with the empty chair in Chapter 6. I learned to use it with religious people who complained of being overwhelmed by some sense of guilt or shame. It proved valuable in sorting out their understanding of God's desires in such controversial matters as divorce, abortion, infidelity, and other issues that involve a sense of having done the unforgivable. They were asked to image (or imagine) their God present in the chair, taking any form with which they were comfortable and to have a conversation with this Presence about what troubled them. It usually became necessary to get a second chair for religious figures, parents, and other authority figures whose thoughts, opinions, teachings, and judgments contaminate their "God within." All of us must finally decide for ourselves what comes from our Creator in our own experience and then separate that from whatever we have taken from others who may or may not accurately represent the "aim" or purposes of the God we have come to know.

At times, this is no easy task. Most of us are filled with all sorts of ideas from others who claim to speak for God. Some we may have taken for granted since we were very young. Later we may grow to think or feel or believe differently. But we rarely cast old ideas aside without deep visceral discomfort. Very few decisions about life that matter deeply can we make with absolute certainty, free from doubt of any kind. So when you are really stumped, or overwhelmed, or at an impasse, pull out the chairs and listen to all the voices in your head and heart until a fitting and relevant response takes shape. Remain open to whatever possibilities for spiritual encounter may emerge. If your response feels right, you can see your way through, and it makes sense to you, then, in all likelihood, you have moved beyond your darker side and connected with a Spiritual Presence deep within.

CHAPTER 14

Changing Our Minds

Forgiveness involves changing our minds. In the Preface, I mentioned the growth of the neocortex (your fingers, remember?) around the hippocampus (your thumb), which forms about the age of 2. Our capacity for autobiographical memory is the result of this newly formed circuitry. Now we gain a sense of personal history and begin to process a range of human emotions about it. We can recall past events with fondness or rumination. We can remember others with growing affection and affiliation, or with increasing anger and aversion. We integrate our brains as our neocortex grows around our hippocampus, uniting our left-brain functions of language and logic with our right-brain functions of images, associations, and relationships. Our reptilian brain with its emotional energies governing survival is integrated with our neocortex, forming new patterns of thought, reflection, and understanding.

Our minds grow through what Daniel Siegel called *contingent relationships* in which from childhood onward we have the experience of *being accurately perceived, understood, and responded to by others.* Such conversation is essential for us to develop a full sense of selfhood and a resonant compassion for others. Without this conversation there is isolation and estrangement from ourselves and also from others. Here, what we know about the maturing mind, psychotherapy, and the processes of confession and forgiveness converge to work toward health and well-being.

Mind and Mental Process

We have already considered an *active intelligence* that is constantly at work beneath our awareness. Without thinking, we perspire when we are hot and sometimes when we are anxious with no conscious thought of "cooling down." We catch falling objects by reflex or recoil from a flame before we even have time to think. Our eyes know to blink or shut quite on their own when threatened by a flying object. Every cell in our body knows how to repair itself when injured.

When our family had its close call with that pick-up truck on a Virginia highway, I scarcely had time to think. An intelligence deep within my body mobilized my response with a massive burst of energy. Normal-style metabolism (anabolic metabolism) gave way to its opposite (catabolic metabolism), breaking down tissue to burn for energy. My endocrine system went into an established alarm procedure, shared by the entire animal kingdom, set off in situations calling for "fight or flight." My adrenal glands secreted glucocorticoids, alerting my body to react. My heart raced, my eyes became hyper-visual, my body free in fluid coordination to steer clear of disaster. When the event was over, all these systems intelligently returned quite on their own to a state of normality.

Gregory Bateson carefully distinguished between the *brain* and *mind or mental process*. By the *brain,* he meant the physical brain in the human head, which we can actually remove from the body, dissect in part or whole, and place in a glass jar. By *mind* he referred to a larger mental process that the brain shares with an *active intelligence* at work both inside and outside our skin. *Mind is the mental process involving the flow of energy and information necessary to hold in balance what is required to create and maintain life itself.*

Neuroscientists can establish various parts of our brain in use when we think or interact with others. An electroencephalogram (EEG) can chart the flow of electrical brainwave patterns when energy is being expended. Brain scans show where certain chemicals are consumed or blood flow increased by changes in metabolism. We may literally witness the mind developing in give-and-take with others through *contingent relationships.* We can see how our ongoing experience shapes the brain by altering connections among neurons. Neuroscientist Eric Kandel won the Nobel Prize for demonstrating that when neurons fire repeatedly, the genetic material inside them is "turned on" in such a way that new proteins are synthesized, creating new neuronal connections or synapses. This, in turn, permits the brain to change its internal connections or its memory. We can literally witness people "changing their minds." No wonder Daniel Siegel made such a fuss about contingent relationships.

Bateson saw a similar mental process surrounding us in infinite extension. In Bateson's thought, *mind* became synonymous with this cybernetic system sustaining all that is. Mind is at work wherever we observe this circuitry of feedback loops between too much and too little, serving to balance, conserve, and sustain life on the planet. We have our being in an ever-expanding labyrinth of thermostat-like controls similar to those that keep our bodily temperature around 98.6 degrees F. Bateson was interested in what he called the *difference that makes a difference* in how an ongoing process sustains itself through some sort of self-corrective system. What keeps a woods, a climate, a family, a community, a nation, a planet going. His search was always for this *difference that makes a difference* maintaining that part of our being or environment between all the necessary polarities that govern its continuing existence. All his efforts were shrouded with the mystery of an infinite number of expanding circuits coming together at once to hold the universe on course.

At our house, the grandchildren love a nest of Oriental dolls that we brought back from Russia. The dolls increase in size from a tiny one inside a larger one, inside an even larger one, inside an even larger one, and so forth. Our grandchildren assemble and disassemble this nest over and over again. We know that *Mind* in its larger sense must somehow resemble that nest of dolls, becoming an endless hierarchy of subsystems, any one of which we may call an individual mind. Everything that lives and moves and has its being, from the tiniest amoeba to the farthest galaxy, must somehow be contained within a "doll" of such infinite intelligence and proportion that its very being escapes comprehension.

This "doll" Bateson describes as *Mind* is immanent in the whole process of evolution. In each step, we have to include pathways outside protoplasmic aggregate from DNA in the cell to cell in the body to body in the environment, and so on and so on. He shifts from *mind* to *Mind* in his efforts to describe the magnitude and infinite character of such a *Mental Process*. As we have seen, Bateson the anthropologist/scientist moves over into the realm of ethics and theology. Suddenly all mental processes take on great importance not only theoretically, but also ethically. We can no longer think about "survival" as individuals, or groups, or even nations. We must consider survival within this system of mind-like complexity of circuits bound together by an unfathomable progression of Mental Processes containing it. We may know about it here and there and in part, but it always eludes our capacity to comprehend. Bateson noted that Freud and Jung expanded the concept of *mind* inwards to include the whole communication system within the body—the autonomic, the habitual, and the vast range of unconscious processes. "What I am saying expands the mind outward," Bateson writes, "and both these changes reduce the scope of the conscious self. A certain humility becomes appropriate, tempered by the dignity or joy of being part of something much bigger. A part—if you will—of God."*

---

* Bateson, Gregory. *Steps to an Ecology of Mind* (Northvale, NJ: Jason Aronson Inc.), pp. 467, 468. See pp. 454–471 for a broader discussion.

For 5,000 years, Bateson notes, the Mediterranean religions swung back and forth between thinking of God as immanent and transcendent. In Babylon, the gods were transcendent on the mountain tops. The Egyptian god was immanent in Pharoah, while the Judeo-Christian tradition presents a complex combination of both beliefs. How we conceive of God becomes a matter of profound importance. If we put God outside of creation and its evolution, we may tend to see the world around us as mindless, and therefore not entitled to moral or ethical consideration. We can claim dominion over it as ours to exploit and use as we see fit. We can think of survival in terms of ourselves and our people against the environment and other social units, races, nations, species, and so on.

The good news, according to Bateson, is that we are fortunate enough to live in a world where there is a semipermeable linkage between our consciousness and the totality of Mind. Obviously, the whole of mind cannot be reported in any part. Our limited individual consciousness can never frame within its awareness what is contained within this larger Awareness that encompasses all that is. It is impossible even to imagine some aspect of it in relation to the whole. Despite the occasional glimpses we get of the total systemic character of life, it remains beyond our capacity to know.

In fact, each additional step toward increased consciousness carries our human mind farther away from any consideration of the workings of Mind in its total systemic intelligence. If you think of your conscious awareness as a television screen upon which our mental process can cast its picture, the problem becomes more vivid. What shall we think of at this given time? Only this one thing. That is the only picture we can view on the screen. All else, at least temporarily, must be ignored. To focus our attention, we always settle for some form of limited consciousness. The more we concentrate on this one thing, the more we ignore other aspects of reality, both known and unknown. This is the *tyranny of conscious purpose*. The more we learn one thing, the more we ignore the systemic character of our being, and, in this sense, the more ignorant we become.

As individuals, we are easily blinded to our systemic nature. Purposive consciousness pulls out sequences from the total mind from their self-corrective structure in the whole system that sustains them. Purposive consciousness lacks the wisdom found in guidance by awareness of the total systemic reality. We do not live in the sort of universe where simple lineal control is possible. No part can control the whole to which it belongs. Human beings, as individuals or in the various groupings we form, are always surrounded by the labyrinth of larger systems in which we dwell. Only by humble and wise efforts to participate in directions to which this larger Systemic Presence points can we find our true and effective place and purpose. At best, we can anticipate some encounter with what Whitehead calls *aim* in whatever *actual occasion* we find ourselves. We may choose some form of *empathic participation* in the lives of those around us through accepting ourselves and forgiving others. We may search together for a relevant response to our problems, our offenses, and our differences.

When we recognize this total systemic character of creation, we are guided by a certain mixture of *wisdom and humility*: wisdom, which seeks to correct the ignorance of one-sided consciousness through the constant pursuit of a more balanced knowledge of the whole, and humility, which fully understands the vastness of the Systemic Presence before us that we can never know in full. We recognize the futility of all our efforts to affix concrete blame either upon others or upon ourselves for whatever predicament is at hand. No individual person or group of people can gain total power over the system to which they belong. Recognizing our common and shared complicity in every situation forms a basis for mutual acceptance and forgiveness, which sets in motion any confessional relationship. We stand together with shared responsibility to work things out.

Family Therapy

Bateson became the patron saint of the family therapy movement, providing a foundation for understanding the characteristics of each family's cybernetic system. When there is conflict, members tend to blame each other ("Not Me") and sometimes themselves for what is essentially a systemic pathology. The truth of the matter for Bateson was that such notions are fundamentally arrogant. Either alternative makes the assumption that particular human beings may have total power over the system of which they are a part. There is no first horse on the cybernetic merry-go-round.

I discovered Bateson during our efforts at the seminary to learn to practice and teach family therapy effectively. In the process, we experienced firsthand his understanding of the virtues of *wisdom* and *humility*. In the mid-1980s, we began working with various ways to treat the family system, a natural for pastoral counselors. Soon we were consulting with the Commission on Accreditation for Marriage and Family Therapy Education (COAMFTE). In those days, programs worth their salt were training with the use of a one-way glass through which treatment could be observed and supervised by teachers and peers. We soon found this setting of *live supervision* a vital laboratory in which to explore our perceptions, our prejudices, and our limitations. I have often been asked as the program's first director how to prepare oneself to go through the whole process of accreditation, establishing candidacy, completing self-studies, and enduring site visits by the Commission. Greg Brock at the University of Kentucky once offered to come up and "hold my hand" during one such ordeal. My best training was far and away the 3 years I spent becoming an Eagle Scout. Never since had I been called upon to meet the requirements of so many merit badges. But our greatest learning came behind the one-way glass, where we worked daily to develop the most effective way to help families change for the better and teach a room full of students at the same time. It was here that my own understandings of *confessional relationships, acceptance, and the power of forgiveness* all converged within our mindful efforts to bring our staff up to snuff.

Behind the Glass

Let me take you into our workplace for a moment. We enter the basement of the chapel at the Presbyterian seminary by way of a side door. We have crossed an open courtyard and passed a contemporary metallic sculpture of "the cock that crew" to announce Peter's denial of his Lord before the crucifixion. There, next to the Audiovisual Department, we had constructed a small classroom, one wall of which held a life-size, one-way window into a consulting room rigged with state-of-the-art sound and video capability. We would never put it there again because of the number of conflicts this unholy alliance in the basement struck with worship services, weddings, and organ and choir practice above. Once in the middle of a heated session with a couple, the organ boomed forth the wedding march, causing both partners to exclaim in unison "You'll be sorry!"

Eventually, Seminary President John Mulder, who became an ardent supporter of our work, proclaimed certain hours off-limits for organ and choir practice so that we could record proceedings below unmolested by sudden bursts and strains of sacred music. A staff of two full professors and ten adjunct professors supervised and taught there. The adjuncts oversaw the work of 25 to 30 students in our various practicum sites and joined the team when one of their students presented. We met regularly as a staff to evaluate each trainee's progress. Here in the room behind the one-way glass, all of us labored to discover the most effective family therapy in that setting. There was usually a team of six students and one or two supervisors working together regularly to consult with co-therapists doing treatment on the other side of the glass. We could telephone in various instructions, ideas, or hunches. Normally, the therapists came out at least once, often twice, for consultation with the team. They returned with messages that soon took on profound and mysterious importance as if from "beyond." We worked on making them succinct and to the point.

We were teaching various schools of family therapy in the classroom and our observations, comments, and interventions "from beyond" usually followed one or the other. Structural approaches such as Salvador Minuchin's had us looking for ways to restructure the family to ensure an appropriate hierarchy with parents in charge and cooperating with each other. We worked to establish effective boundaries between family members, respect for differences, age-appropriate conversations, and a climate of mutual support. Strategic therapists such as Jay Haley had us preparing carefully worded directives for the family or paradoxical instructions designed to stimulate various positive changes. The Milan group (Mara Selvini Palazzoli, Luigi Boscolo, Gianfranco Cecchin, and Giuliana Prata) had us practicing positive connotations of everyone's behavior to establish a nonjudgmental context, while looking for an opening to explore how the family was organized. The intent was to send a clear message to the whole family that their problem was meaningful and logical given its context. The enemy is the family game, not a person or a structure. We experimented some with Palazzoli's *invariant prescription,* which called for mother and father to disappear regularly for secret activities that served to strengthen the parental subsystem. And lots of other stuff.

All these approaches were helpful and we sometimes felt successful. At the same time, we found ourselves increasingly dissatisfied with our expanding eclecticism. We began searching for our own unique way of treating families, one that fit our diversity and yet provided some continuity of consultation in its practice. I might add that many of us were increasingly frustrated in our efforts to exercise power and control over the outcome of what we set out to do. The frequent ineffectiveness of our brilliance produced in us some of the *humility* of which Bateson wrote. The Milan group had also read Bateson, and some began to adopt a different way of approaching the family system than their structural or strategic counterparts. Others also became less certain of their ability to determine objectively what was going on in the family or accurately devise schemes and interventions to change it. As their practices evolved, they joined a growing number of family therapists, variously described as "systemic," or "collaborative," or "constructivist," who assigned themselves a much less objective and powerful role in the treatment room.

These *systemic therapists,* as we shall call them, increasingly surrendered their role of authority and expertise to establish a more cooperative, collaborative stance with families they saw. The emphasis was upon mutual discovery of what may alter complex family relationships in a positive direction. As soon as therapists observe a family system or join it in any other way, they become part of that system. A systemic approach championed Bateson's understanding of *wisdom,* reminding everyone that no part can control the system to which it belongs. The best we can do is involve ourselves by rummaging around in its life space in search of some *difference that makes a difference.* True *wisdom* is born out only in some discovery we happen across while honoring the distinct possibility that it may emerge through influences that are unpredictable.

Change appears to follow some alteration in the storehouse of cognitive maps and lenses for looking at life lodged in the "common mind" or "shared mentality" of the family system. Some systemic therapists set out to "bump up against" or "perturb" this shared mentality, offering different descriptions of repeated interactions, stories, questions, hypotheses, or "wonderings," surrendering any impression of superior expertise. Others joined with the family to "co-create" opportunities for a different response or some shift in their common mentality. Some even use the word "hermaneutics" to describe their emphasis on language and dialogue. All meanings and interpretations of life (hermaneutics) are socially built through conversations that establish new meanings, new realities, and new narratives by which to live. The word *hermaneutics* had a strange fit for us there in the basement of the chapel because it was a term frequently used in preaching to describe the task of interpreting a Biblical text. So, upstairs they interpreted the Bible; and downstairs we set out to interpret shared meanings in family life.

A lot of other ideas also began to come together. *Systemic theory* seemed to parallel a *full confessional experience* with a family—creating conditions of heightened self-awareness through an accepting relationship and enabling a common search for some relevant response to what troubles them most. A lot of the language sounded like the language of client-centered therapy or Daniel Siegel's description of *contingent relationships* and the type of *empathic participation* in the family's perspective associated with forgiveness. How would all that translate into a session of live supervision in the chapel basement?

The Reflecting Team

Then I ran into a Norwegian family therapist named Tom Andersen at a conference of the American Association for Marriage and Family Therapy (AAMFT). He was working with what he called *reflecting teams* in Norway with a much more collegial stance toward families than we began with.* Instead of viewing the therapist's work from outside the room via television or one-way glass, the team would quietly take its place in the same room, demystifying their presence. Or the supervisor and team might change rooms, letting the family come over behind the glass and observe them reflecting on the treatment process.

The job of the reflecting team was to offer as many different descriptions of what they had been watching as possible. There was no effort to direct or instruct the family. The discussion would be filled with all kinds of questions, wonderings, differing explanations, ideas, hunches, fantasies—all in search of "openings" for the family to consider. The idea was to provide as many alternatives as possible to the meanings created by the family system that served to perpetuate its difficulties. There were no illusions about

---

* See Andersen, Tom. *The Reflecting Team: Dialogues and Dialogues about the Dialogues* (New York: W.W. Norton and Co., 1991).

arriving at some objective solution. They understood that by joining the family, everyone in the reflecting team was now part of its cybernetics. Their job was to become partners in searching for something to unstick the system or dislodge its grip on everyone. They openly admitted that there was no way of predicting any one or two measures that would accomplish that.

Andersen's idea of the *reflecting team* was to stir up as much curiosity as possible. He believed that a questioning stance is the major contributor to the evolution of living human systems. It was important for the team really to join the family—enough to understand the explanations and meanings governing its difficulties. The team was joining a problem-determined system, firmly tethered to its repetitious dissonance. Andersen had also read Bateson. The reflecting team's job was to search for some *difference that makes a difference*. His idea was modeled after the work of two Norwegian physiotherapists, Aadel Bulow-Hansen and Gudrun Øverberg. Over 40 years, this pair developed a method for treating people who suffer from muscular tension based on the premise that our ongoing breathing cycle, from inhalation to exhalation, corresponds to the movements of all muscles throughout the body. Bulow-Hansen's treatment involved bending selected muscles, creating sufficient pain to simulate an extension of the body parts they manipulated. It was a search for just the right amount of pressure. Too much stimulation would produce additional contraction and even more reduced breathing, while just enough would bend the muscles, deepening breathing and relaxation throughout the organism. Andersen found that helpful reflections to the family followed a similar principle.

Workable reflections upon a family's problem-determined system followed what we came to call the "Goldilocks Principle"—not too little, not too much, just enough. If family members were exposed to an idea that was "too usual," they tended to remain unresponsive. If the reflection was "too unusual," they rejected the idea outright. Only a certain range of reflections proved sufficiently novel to produce some change capable of dislodging the existing system from its stuck point. As Andersen suggested, we have no way of predicting ahead of time what this will be or the exact direction of the changes that follow. This matched the growing humility we had acquired and left selecting a relevant response in the hands of the family.

Systemic Voicing and Dramatization

Andersen's ideas inspired us to experiment with our own unique way of joining the family. It incorporated the kind of *empathic participation* in the family's life we associated with acceptance and forgiveness. Some member of the reflecting team behind the glass was assigned to listen to the conversation in the treatment room from the standpoint of each family member. Each therapist, and occasionally some important figure from the family who might not be present, also received listeners. Twice during each therapy session, the family and the team exchanged rooms, permitting family members to hear someone from the team seated in their chairs describing reactions listening from their point of view. This we came to call *systemic voicing*.

If you were a member of the reflecting team, you had two assignments. First, you were to identify as completely as possible with the person on whose behalf you were listening. This involved empathic participation in their place, giving their part in what was going on as positive a connotation as possible. You gave voice to unspoken and novel expressions of their role in simple language within the "Goldilocks Principle" (Not too cold, not too hot, just right). Second, you made observations about who speaks to whom, what could be said and what could not be said, who may be closer to whom, who may be farther apart, and so on. We soon discovered the most effective way to begin systemic voicing was for the team members to start by stating, "I have been listening from the standpoint of (Name), and I have been experiencing...." After two or three rounds of such voicing, the team would go back behind the glass and the family would return to resume its conversation with the therapists, everyone sharing their reactions to what they had heard. No one was under constraint to accept any particular direction or value one comment over another.

An additional reflective measure soon emerged naturally from this practice of systemic voicing. On several occasions, members of the reflecting team would spontaneously say something to another family member in the middle of their voicing. Then a brief series of exchanges would develop, sometimes involving other team members. We discouraged this at first but soon realized something valuable was happening, especially when we noticed the particular delight on such occasions among family members who were watching. The reflecting team had intuitively begun to model different ways of speaking to each other, going beyond where the family normally stopped. We realized we had before us an opportunity to act out or experiment with all kinds of new family transactions heretofore unexpressed, avoided, cut short, or undeveloped. Suddenly, the reflective process had come to life in search of an interactive experience sufficiently unusual to dislodge what had blocked a more productive conversation in the past.

We called this second kind of reflection a *systemic dramatization*. It is a clear cousin of psychodrama, with which I had worked for a number of years without realizing its relevance for family therapy. Systemic dramatizations were spontaneous and unplanned, a natural product of our team's efforts to join the family system. Each person's behavior was connoted positively and respectfully. From this position, each team member searched for some novel and unexpressed, yet authentic, contribution their character could make to the family scene. Dramatizations could be threatening at times but were normally witnessed by observing family members of all ages with great interest and appreciation. We often found someone from the family eager to telephone in instructions or to "feed a line" to their counterpart on the other side of the glass. One 7-year-old could hardly wait to have "himself" say something to those who represented his parents in the other room, something he had never said before. On occasion, someone would suggest a conversation between two family members, a conversation long awaited but yet to happen. The success or failure of the session depended on the quality of empathic participation by the team joining the family. As one family member put it, "It was like they had been living with us. Once I saw a group of people who could understand us that well, I knew there was some help for us here."

After several months of practice, everyone agreed we had found our own unique way of doing live supervision with a reflecting team. Once or twice during each session, the family and the observing team changed rooms for *systemic voicing* and *systemic dramatization*. We did live supervision twice a week on campus. Off-campus sites without one-way mirrors could do it with small reflecting teams in the room at their own facilities. Sessions scheduled at the chapel were for special consultations with unique and challenging treatment problems from which we could all learn. They served as a forum to which therapists in training and their supervisors could bring the new and the unusual among their clinical problems for broader consultation. I was grinning like a Cheshire cat—until something happened that set in motion the events leading to the next chapter.

Practice

Our experience with reflecting teams proved to have far-reaching applications. Of course we developed these teams in a graduate training program with the luxury of numbers of trainees behind the glass who were eager to learn and free to participate. But how could this be translated into the typical treatment setting where there is one therapist working with a family or a group with no one waiting in the wings to reflect? Then one day I was working with a clinical training group of seven people who had reached an impasse with one another due to conflict between several members. I yearned for the help of a reflecting team. It occurred to me we could form one by asking everyone to move one chair to the right and "become" that person long enough to assume that individual's perspective with as much understanding as possible. We were then in a position to engage in *systemic voicing and systemic dramatization*. I was soon using the same or similar procedures in work with groups, families, and even couples.

Exercise 1: For groups with a small number of members—from four to ten people or so, like a confessional group, or a family, or a therapy group, or a committee—it is possible to form an effective reflecting team without outside help. Members can engage in similar measures of self-reflection by calling time-out, exchanging chairs with other participants, and proceeding with the kind of empathic participation from the other person's perspective we have been describing. I have done it a number of times with families, especially those with older children, asking members to move one chair to the right for *systemic reflection* and *dramatization*, or inviting a "fruit basket turnover" assuming chairs of their choice. Recently, I was privileged to meet a family that had conducted meetings with their two children since the youngest was 6 years old. Each meeting started with the family selecting one member to act as "leader." Now with one daughter age 19 and in college and the other 16, they struggled to sustain their meetings, which became highly conflicted. They responded immediately to a reflecting team experience and worked their way through a number of difficult issues dealing with dating and relationships with men.

Exercise 2: Two-party systems like a couple, or confessional partners, can experiment with empathic participation by changing chairs to experience the other person's perspective. You take your partner's chair and begin sentences, "Listening from your perspective, I am experiencing...." This kind of role reversal is a very effective technique in psychodrama to expand our capacities for taking another person's perspective. Even in the midst of an argument, inventive partners can agree to adopt a simple three-step process:

> Step 1: Establish *empathic identification* through changing chairs and continuing the conversation "as the other person."
> Step 2: Pause for each to do *systemic voicing* of what you experience from the perspective of your partner.
> Step 3: Engage in a *systemic dramatization*, expressing thoughts that may have gone unspoken, ideas or feelings that are sufficiently novel (using the Goldilocks Principle) that the other person might choose to say, as well as anything you would really like to hear.

Then partners switch to their own chairs and continue the original conversation modified by empathic reflection.

You can repeat the process several times at one sitting. There is always the problem of how a two-person system monitors itself. I have seen couples able to do this despite considerable disagreement, even in the midst of exchanges that have become quite heated. Prior contracts can permit either person to call time to consult, separating such interludes from active engagement by rising and standing together to decide the next step. It may take a while to master the practice of such measures. When successful, they appear far superior to methods of fair-fight training that I have been exposed to in the past.

My experience with reflecting teams suggests they are laden with possibilities for spiritual encounter. Dennis Tyner, a rational, engineer type, whose shirt pocket bulged with pens and calculator over his heart, put it better than I. Couples make great reflecting teams for each other in a couples' group. He had just served on a reflecting team for a couple listening from the standpoint of the husband who was locked in a heated debate with his wife over how to parent their rather shy teenage daughter. He managed to express what the husband was experiencing so effectively that the husband co-opted his words to speak in a conciliatory way to his wife. I have Dennis on videotape at the end of the session reflecting, "You know, there is something kind of spiritual about doing this sort of stuff."

CHAPTER 15

The Compassionate Community

So I was grinning like a Cheshire cat. We had arrived and had the accreditation for our Marriage and Family Therapy (MFT) degree program. We had passed all the tests and hit our stride as a staff in teaching and our style of supervision. In short, we were "cooking with gas." And then, one of my best reflecting teams went to hell in a hand basket. Its members simply stopped working well together. There was an air of tension in the room that would not go away. The quality of our work began to deteriorate; our group had obviously become fragmented. We were becoming more dysfunctional than the families with whom we worked. I received a wake-up call that I will never forget.

Steps Toward a Confessional Community

Now I know what happened. For 3 years going through the process of candidacy and accreditation, we had managed to live entirely in the consciousness of our *public story*. We had formed an MFT community, mobilizing itself around manuals, materials, programs, and requirements, honing our "persona" to the standards we had to meet. We had subtly come to believe we actually were what we said we were in the self-studies, polished record keeping, and promotional materials, all conforming to and in compliance with the Commission on Accreditation for Marriage and Family Therapy Education (COAMFTE). And in a very real sense, we were up to their snuff.

But in the process, our *private story* as an MFT community was shoved out of our awareness, left to develop its own life unattended. We had hidden our perennial jealousies and continuing competition for the common good. Interpersonal wounds, inevitable slights and injustices, disputes and differences that accumulate across time were concealed and repressed. Our MFT community was like a newlywed couple fresh from the honeymoon—except now the honeymoon was over.

As its director, I had to do something; so I scheduled a meeting with this reflecting team to determine what was up. It didn't take long to find out. A lot of problems had begun to fester at the level of our *private story* while we managed to hold our *public story* intact. I was about to learn the hard way what I really knew in the first place. All organizations, whether large or small, old or new like ours, cannot live indefinitely at the level of their persona any more than we as individuals can. Sooner or later we have to deal with the effects of what is stirring and accumulating in our private story, which constantly circulates beneath the surface of all our relationships. Life inside institutions is never what it is in the public-relations materials any more than life inside the family fits its descriptions in the Christmas letter.

I had a lot of listening to do. When I did, I learned we were no exception to the problems beneath our public story. Several members of our team told me that our program "sucked." A lot of what they related I already knew, wanted to deny, or tried to ignore. Some of it I wasn't even aware of. There were animosities among several of our better students that simmered and fumed. Two women on my team felt offended by what they considered sexist remarks by a male member. Others sensed a growing estrangement that I had struggled to overcome between one adjunct professor and me. There were conflicts between several practicum students and their supervisor whom they felt had treated them unfairly. There was rising discontent in several classrooms that had gone unattended, marked by minor quarrels and hurt feelings. I won't attempt to describe it all. Much was the gossip, murmurings, and discontent that seems always to accompany troops in the field, the children of Israel in their wilderness wanderings, or our institutional life in general, whether it be in health care, industry, education, or politics.

Obviously, a mounting estrangement had sapped our morale so that it interfered with our ability to cooperate and do effective reflection with the people we were trying to help. The time was ripe for its crescendo, and our relational problems had emerged to claim enough attention to distract us. Recognize any similar problems where you work? What does an educational community of therapists in training, composed of reflecting teams, supervisors, and teachers, do when their relationships get in the way of treating their clients? Organizations of all sizes, even as small as our MFT community, are forced to stop and deal with such problems from time to time. When we do, we have to choose between confronting them openly in the light of day or engaging in various measures that evade, suppress, or ignore their impact. This latter task normally falls to those in authority who must stem the rising discontent with rules and policies and votes held in accord with *Robert's Rules of Order*. The result usually drives private story problems further underground where more alliances are formed, only to emerge at the next opportunity. I realized I had never worked in a setting where these issues were honestly and openly addressed. To me it became a matter of confession. But could a community such as ours openly accept the difficulties we have with one another and search for a relevant response?

Organizational Games

A number of different theorists have described organizational games. There was Eric Berne who advanced the theory of psychological games. He was joined by Palazzoli and other family therapists who insisted that patterns of repetitive behavior learned in one's family of origin were played out at every level of life, ordinarily out of conscious awareness.[*] These patterns appear to be governed by well-developed rules and roles distributed among various players. The assumptions governing such games are held in common, unconscious agreement, ordinarily shrouded with defensiveness, deceptiveness, and secrecy, accompanied by a stubborn emotional blindness to our own involvement (Not Me).

The world Bateson described was just such an infectious labyrinth of systems and sub-systems with semipermeable boundaries. Live energies and influences percolate up and down and around and about from one to another. Every clinician trained in supervision comes to know this phenomenon firsthand. It's called *parallel process*. Analytically trained supervisors often discover a therapist in training doing in supervision what the patient did to them in the treatment session. For example, therapists with a particularly passive patient may present with pronounced passivity in supervision, unaware they are unconsciously "presenting" their supervisor with what they had to endure. Any treatment system can become affected this way. Behind the one-way glass, the father in the family is timid and hesitant to take over and discipline his 16-year-old son. The therapist somehow avoids recognizing this and fails to support the father in asserting himself. The supervisor has difficulty confronting the therapist with the necessity to "take the bull by the horns" and encourage the father to form an appropriate relationship claiming his personal authority. The same problem plays itself out up and down the system infecting each level, technically known as *isomorphism*. By the same token, a successful resolution at the supervisory level may cascade down the treatment hierarchy from supervisor to therapist to father to family members. I started to realize our

---

[*] Palazzoli, Mara Selvini. *The Hidden Games of Organizations* (New York: Pantheon Books, 1986).

whole teaching/learning/treatment community as an MFT Program was just such a living, breathing breeding ground of isomorphic potential. We could become infected and affected at every level. We must somehow succeed in treating ourselves if we were going to treat others effectively.

There is quite a history in psychiatry of experimenting with the development of a *therapeutic community.*[*] In post-World-War II England, J.R. Rees, Director of Tavistock Clinic, began a movement beyond individual treatment to address the problems of group relations. In 1946, Tom Main reorganized the British Army Hospital at Northfield with the aim of full participation by all community members in shaping their daily life. Wilfred Bion led discussion groups focused on the study of their own internal tensions. Main coined the term "therapeutic community" to describe large group community meetings held to discuss the real issues that arose in living together. Siegfried Foulkes introduced ward-based meetings that considered the whole hospital as its current social field of influence. With the help of Maxwell Jones and others, this concept spread to the United States as an attenuated form of therapeutic community called a "therapeutic milieu." Doctors, nurses, attendants, and patients alike participated in larger group meetings, undertaking to create an atmosphere of egalitarianism, permissiveness, honesty, openness, and trust. Patients were seen as responsible for monitoring their own treatment, capable of helping one another, and able to exercise a democratic voice in affairs affecting their common life. Many centers in this country for the treatment of drug abuse have adopted similar concepts.

As with many movements, this notion of a self-reflecting community has received mixed reviews. Wilmer's study claimed that it eliminated the need for any kind of restraint among the 939 patients he dealt with in a psychiatric hospital. Others report limited and more moderate success. Among them was a psychoanalyst, R.D. Hinshelwood, who wrote *What Happens in Groups,* which I found quite helpful.[†] He insists that any group, large or small, will tend to act out the common internal conflicts of its members in some representative external version of their individual problems. He calls these *dramatizations*, not to be confused with our *systemic dramatizations*. These serve as the psychoanalytic counterpart to the psychological games Berne wrote about. In any setting, from an office building to a mental-hospital ward, you will encounter them. When this happens, you have two choices: either you verbalize these conflicts and work them out, or they get acted out repeatedly in one form or another. In Hinshelwood's hospital, everyone from patients to administrators, doctors, nurses, and

---

[*] For a brief summary, see Whitely, S. "The Evolution of the Therapeutic Community," *Psychiatric Quarterly,* 75(3), 233–248, 2004.

[†] Hinshelwood, R.D. *What Happens in Groups* (London: Free Association Books, 1987).

attendants was affected. The alternatives are always between suppressing these conflicts, which tends to stir their internal cauldron among community members for later outbreaks, or facing and resolving them through conversation and communion with each other. The word "communion" is an interesting choice for a psychiatrist.

So what happens in a community that fails to become self-reflective? Someone gets quietly (and sometimes not so quietly) selected to act out some aspect of its unconscious conflicts. Its leadership gets endowed with magical expectations that will inevitably fail as its members split authority figures into good objects and bad objects of their affections. Criticism of one another escalates; meetings go awry with task drift and ineffectiveness, all of which gets acted out in a series of dramatizations to avoid facing their own internal struggles. Community members choose someone to blame or shame, or correct or oppose. Reflecting teams go to hell in a handbasket; professors mistrust one another, feel slighted or ignored; students rebel against assignments and collect evidence of mistreatment and injustice; and directors learn that their programs "suck."

Interestingly enough, the alternative for Hinshelwood is to introduce *compassion* into the system through some form of communal self-reflection that leads to the verbalization of its difficulties and deals openly with some of them. I said "some" because resolving them all is beyond the possible. That was his experience and it certainly was mine. The important thing is for the community to model successful problem solving on some regular basis. Attacking common difficulties together extends hope for communal growth and represents similar possibilities for individual members to work out their own inner conflicts among themselves.

So my graduate program was no different from the rest of the world in its games and dramatizations, despite all my earnest efforts to be a good director. My principle that how you teach should demonstrate what you teach had taken a direct hit, and so had my pride. What right did I have to expect "my program" to be any different? If "my program sucked," it needed to become "our program" in a much stronger way. This awareness came with genuine relief. Now I could surrender my illusions of somehow creating a healthy, game-free organization in which everyone worked together smoothly. Perhaps I could again stop performing and become captain of a winning team. Why not organize around the premise of "physician, heal thyself?" Our first responsibility in teaching family therapy is to create what is curative in our own educational system. Why not move toward becoming a *confessional community*? We certainly had established a state of *heightened self-awareness*. We had begun to *accept the unacceptable* and search for some *relevant response*. Now what do we do?

Bateson's idea that a semipermeable boundary exists between all parts of any working system and between that system and all other systems began to make perfect sense. We live in a giant percolating universe in which the energy of life and change flows up and down all that is, each part involved beyond its orbit with the next and finding its truest being precisely through acknowledging and acting upon this understanding. This is where *wisdom* and *humility* meet. I had just been liberally gifted with the latter. Now I was becoming aware of how genuine wisdom usually follows from humility. I had never been a part of a confessional community like the one I was starting to envision, one that would devote time and energy to confront openly its *private story* with the underground of games and dramatizations it unwittingly harbored. Those in authority always felt forced to undertake various measures to manage the internecine battles, the rivalries, the disputes, the petitions, and the expanded lists of rules and precedents that befell even the sacred system of our seminary life. We could still teach Greek, Hebrew, and theology and graduate Biblical scholars in such a climate, but we could not do effective marriage and family therapy together.

Somewhere in such a system, those in the hierarchy have to take over, hire, fire, dismiss, grade, and graduate classes, doing their best to make things work with those for whom they are responsible. In the process, most hierarchies close the boundary to any two-way assessment of responsibility and operate from a one-up position that can be preserved only by power and control. Governance in this fashion serves to support illusions of the hierarchy's own objectivity, innocence, and superiority. The weight of administration grows and soon becomes increasingly difficult to manage. That's why we as a nation separate church and state, follow a constitution, establish checks and balances in government, and hold elections for public office. No hierarchy can be right all the time, nor can it exercise effective power and control over all the parts of its own system. No matter how tall the hierarchy grows, it is always subject to the influences of those both above and below in this percolator universe of active and ever-present energies.

We were on the right track behind the one-way glass. We had found an effective way to work with family systems. We were simply overwhelmed by the larger system of which we were a part. It finally occurred to me that we had not carried our process far enough. Our MFT program needed some similar form of treatment. We could only be effective supervisors and teachers of practices in which we were also engaged. As director, it was up to me to help develop a structure parallel to this reflecting-team process that could address the problems impacting our system as a whole. What would it be like to organize our efforts as a community to deal with its conflicts and dramatizations? We were talking about some workable form of self-reflection that could serve to help us move beyond our own stuck points. We had learned to join the families we saw with compassionate participation. Perhaps it was time to discover how to join with one another in the same way.

Compassion and Community

I realize now that I was going through a confessional process of my own. I came to recognize I was failing to do my job in some very significant ways. I had ignored conflicts that I knew were causing difficulties. I had failed to resolve significant differences with at least two colleagues and was busily looking the other way to avoid them. I was unsuccessful in helping resolve several disputes between students and staff members. I felt powerless to put an end to growing complaints emanating from the ranks, and I could no longer sustain my futile and ill-founded hope that they would simply evaporate. I had to accept where we were, which meant forgiving myself for being afraid to face up to some glaring errors in judgment and avoidance of the obvious.

Then I had to ask others to join me in the same confessional process. We needed to abandon together our shadowy impulses to engage in blame games and other versions of "Not Me." Where the program "sucked" was neither my fault nor anyone else's, but it was clearly my responsibility to do something about it—no, that's a bit grandiose and part of my problem. I finally was able to decide that it was *our* responsibility—together—to accept the unacceptable in our midst and engage it openly.

I set out with two proposals. First, we needed to do everything we could to de-triangle our program community. Murray Bowen, Mara Palazzoli, and most family therapists place the phenomenon of *triangulation* at the heart of troubles that start in family life and later get translated into organizational games. Triangulation was Bowen's term for people refusing to work out their differences with someone else and carrying their discontent to a third party. The people initiating the triangle not only avoid the conflict, but they also usually blame the other party involved and recruit the third party to side with them. Coalitions get formed that way. People choose sides to compete against one another. In the blame game, everyone loses by forfeiting their shared responsibility to stop being part of the problem and look for a solution. Instead of complaining to you about what "George" did or didn't do, it is my job to accept what I have done and what he has done, and in that spirit of compassion and mutual forgiveness, go work it out with him. That's everybody's responsibility. No more "Let George do it."

Incidentally, this was quite Biblical and should go over big in seminaries and churches, as well as anywhere else. You recall that Adam said to God, "The woman gave the fruit to me." And Eve said, "The serpent beguiled me." It's always somebody else's fault. In Matthew 18, we find a passage dealing with the triangulation problem in the New Testament community, forcing it to develop its own means of self-discipline. My interpretation is a liberal one: If your brother (or sister) sins against you, go and tell him his fault and work it out between you and him alone. If he (or she) listens to you, you have gained a brother (or a sister). If he doesn't listen, take along two or three witnesses; and if he (or she) still doesn't listen, report the matter to the congregation and work it out there. Only if that should fail do you cut off communication and treat this person like a pagan or an outsider. Even then, you still stand ready to forgive and accept him back. But how many times, the apostle Peter wants to know? Not just seven times, Jesus is remembered as saying, but seventy times seven.

The second measure would be to set aside time for the entire community to engage in self-reflection. We would do this regularly for an hour and a half on the first and third Mondays of each month. Our agenda would address concrete problems we encountered in teaching, supervision, and therapy, incorporating as nearly as possible our own approach to family therapy. We would use reflecting teams wherever we could, engaging as many members of the community as possible as participants. We are talking about community meetings that included 3 full-time professors, 14 supervisors and adjunct professors, together with 25 to 30 students—a gathering of 40 to 50 people in the room.

Armed with this idea, I persuaded the full staff to spend a day considering how we could conduct these community meetings. We started with some hypothetical cases to test how we might approach the task. As a case was read, staff members listened from the standpoint of each individual involved, projecting themselves into the roles of students, professors, supervisors, the director, and so on. A representative of each player took the inner circle and discussed the situation, developing the part of each person in the dispute until the full conflict had ripened hopelessly in front of our eyes. Then a reflecting team assigned to listen from the standpoint of each of the protagonists took their chairs to engage in *systemic voicing* and *systemic dramatization* just as we did behind the one-way glass with families we treated. They engaged in the customary practice to accept and positively connote each person's part in the process. They searched for novel observations and experimented with expressing new and different points of view to each other within the "Goldilocks Principle," not too usual and not too unusual. The idea was to perturb the existing system to move beyond its stuck point. Then the protagonists returned to continue their conversation as our families did. The approach proved equally adaptable to our own problems. Before the day was over, we had repeated the process with several live issues involving people in the room. We could also readily add people who weren't present, including students, administrators, even difficult clients, by adding listeners who could participate on their behalf. Somewhere in this experience we decided never again to discuss or evaluate a student without some staff member appointed to listen from that student's perspective and share reactions on that person's behalf. This practice made our conversations assessing students and developing strategies for responding to their learning problems much more effective.

One more step remained—presenting the plan to the students. They were very responsive, although it involved an extra 3 hours a month added to an already-crowded schedule. Now everyone had a voice and a part in the way our program operated. The hierarchy still existed. The director still directed; the teachers kept on teaching and grading; supervisors still oversaw and evaluated progress in training, and students still evaluated their courses and supervision. But now we had a forum to deal with everything from sticky wickets to problems that threatened the well-being of our community. Every other week we met to consider one carefully selected presentation of an issue, conflict, or clinical problem from which we all could learn. It was my job as director to select and arrange some reflective format to engage in constructive conversation about the problem at hand.

During the weeks that followed, our community became quite adept at these meetings. Everyone took part without any formal requirements for attendance. The sessions were videotaped for members to view if they were absent. We discovered more effective ways to work with difficult clinical problems, impasses in supervision, misunderstandings in administrative matters, and snarls in communication. We started with some relevant hypothetical cases involving our own internal difficulties, such as responding to instances of triangulation, rumors, dissension, and coalition. The exercises helped establish standards for de-triangling our program. However, we didn't have to wait long for a severe challenge to the well-being of our community.

The Acid Test

It began with a telephone call from Rudy Hess, director of the Family Counseling Center, which reserved a number of places for our practicum students. It was an important site because of the high quality of Rudy's leadership and expertise, as well as his role as a key member of our adjunct professors. A student from our program had recently interviewed successfully for one of his positions and was ready to start in the fall. Then she learned she was pregnant. The staff at Family Counseling counted heavily on the services of their trainees and decided they had no way to cover her for a leave of absence with the anticipated mid-year birth.

"We can't take her," said Rudy. "That amount of time off would cripple our budget. Our business manager was adamant. No way we can afford to accommodate a layoff like that without adding more staff."

I was stunned. This refusal was contrary to clearly established seminary policies. It was illegal. It would create a crisis for everyone concerned with women's rights, which included virtually everyone involved in our program. "You can't do this, Rudy," I replied. "It will jump rabbits all over the place. Can you imagine what this will do to her—and to morale in the program? There has got to be some other way."

We talked on the phone. And we talked some more. Rudy was over a barrel. The board at Family Counseling adamantly refused to take her. What could they do with her case load? It would disrupt the training program and her own learning as well. It was against their policies. Well, it was also against our policies. How could we do this to a woman? Our faculty and our board would toast us for it. At one point I ventured the possibility that seminary authorities might not tolerate a relationship with a training program that did such things. Rudy responded something to the effect that they could always take their business elsewhere.

I marvel at what happened next. I proposed that we take our differences to the community meeting and use our reflecting process to get beyond our impasse rather than release the series of events that could follow to rumor, innuendo, and uproar. And Rudy agreed to do so, which speaks for the overall level of trust we had succeeded in establishing.

I can describe in general what happened at this meeting, how it was conducted, and its outcome, but the details of who said what to whom were held in confidence among community members and shall remain so now. We started meetings like this by assembling the principal people involved for discussion in the center of the room. Rudy and I took our places along with two students and two other adjunct professors, all of whom were involved in some immediate way with the consequences of the decision before us. The student who had been rejected for the position was on internship at that time and could not attend, so a friend was appointed to participate on her behalf by taking her place in the discussion. My memory has it that another student served as her advocate, also a close friend. The two full professors teaching in the program also took chairs in the center. One other person was selected to represent the role of the business manager at Family Counseling and his interests in preserving board policies. Rudy and I both presented the problem from our perspectives, and we began discussing our reactions in the inner circle. The rest of the community, about 30 in number, observed from the outer circle, but with reflecting team responsibilities that involved assigning someone to listen from the perspective of each of the ten people interacting in the middle.

What made our reflecting teams so effective? First, everyone had learned to develop skills in empathic participation through engaging in *systemic voicing* and *systemic dramatizations* in the classroom and in live supervision behind the one-way glass. We were putting our theories of family therapy into practice with one another in ways that involved everyone in the hierarchy from top to bottom. Any student could listen from the perspective of the director or a professor or a supervisor. In turn, professors and supervisors could assume the perspective of their students with equal vigor. You can imagine the kind of insights that emerged through voicing the feelings you had when you were in the other person's shoes.

You can also imagine how intense the conversation was that morning in the center circle, punctuated by threatening disagreements and a despairing lack of any kind of satisfactory resolution. The more each person spoke, the more hopeless it seemed. This issue could splinter our community in a skinny minute. Then the reflecting team moved into our chairs to voice what they experienced listening from each of our perspectives. How reassuring it was to hear one of my students take my chair and reflect the range of feelings he had in my place. He sensed my anxiety, my anger and frustration, my sense of responsibility, my fear at what this would do to the program that was somehow "my baby" to protect, my concern for the student involved, my worry over the possibility of losing a valuable staff member and practicum site. I also realized how good it must have felt to Rudy and everyone else involved to hear their participation positively and sensitively connoted.

Now the reflecting team began the second part of their job—experimenting with whatever had gone unexpressed or left unsaid, dramatizing new and different possibilities of addressing one another. The *Goldilocks Pinciple*, not too usual and not too unusual, was conspicuously evident in whatever was offered. I remember being amazed at how well everybody understood his/her job. And did it.

Then it was time for us to continue our conversation back in the center. The first round of comments to one another had been both intense and challenging. Now the air had cleared a bit and seemed to have softened with some mutual understanding and compassion for the place in which each of us sat. The next round of discussion was more free and spontaneous, marked by occasional humor. It remained, however, equally inconclusive and gridlocked without any satisfactory solution in sight. Another round of reflection by the observing team followed. Then with the principals back in the center, anyone from the observing circle was given the opportunity to reflect upon what had transpired or stand behind a participant and speak from that person's perspective. Those of us in the center were then free to conclude the conversation with any approach, next step, or strategy we chose.

None of us as faculty or staff was bound to any finding or conclusion. The hierarchy with its respective duties, commitments, and loyalties still remained intact and functioning. But how different this hour-and-a-half community meeting made our jobs seem. Anger and innuendo had dissipated. There was no room for rumors to build and spread. There was a quiet sense of grim solidarity, supported by feelings of sadness and compassion for everyone who stood in disagreement. In a word, there was a clear acceptance of one another despite the unacceptability in our situation, and the bond that held us together had begun to strengthen rather than weaken.

By the time of our next community meeting, the entire crisis had passed. The three full-time faculty members reported on our conversation with the student whose position had been withdrawn. We had talked in a telephone conference, updating her on the meeting, key aspects of the conversation, and its main recommendations, which included our strong apologies for being unable to work out her current placement, together with our commitment to locate a comparable position for her when she returned to campus. Subsequently, she elected to take the next semester off and postpone her studies to a time more judicious for both herself and her husband. A month later, our community had taken the entire incident in stride and moved on to other concerns. Rudy Hess and I remained colleagues and good friends, working together on the MFT staff and sharing tickets to U of L football games until he left for a similar position in Chicago.

Our efforts to establish a confessional community were far from perfect. I could not claim that we were successful in stamping out triangles and dramatizations or other forms of interpersonal conflict and games. Several adjuncts suggested that "my" community meetings with students openly witnessing our dirty laundry and often reversing roles with us served to jeopardize our authority. One supervisor objected, "There are no boundaries."

There were times when these community meetings were threatening to all of us but I never saw them as stripping the hierarchy of any boundaries or jeopardizing its authority. Instead, when properly done, they served to keep our boundaries permeable and everyone more responsible in maintaining the quality of relationships necessary to work together effectively. Impermeable boundaries, although less threatening at times, tend to separate everyone into closed circuits of communication. Differences are driven underground, where they remain an unacknowledged and unexamined breeding ground for trouble. Bonds of shared responsibility to respect others and assist them in doing their job fall by the wayside. Keeping these boundaries permeable invites any system to search for creative measures that can keep forgiveness operational in a troubled community. Our meetings regularly modeled the possibility for every participant to practice acceptance, both of one's self and of others. Students seemed to thrive seeing members of the hierarchy grapple with the same personal conflicts and difficult choices with which they dealt. If anything, these meetings served to inspire and encourage them to work out their own problems, both as individuals and as co-workers.

My experience in these community meetings strengthened my confidence in the effectiveness of a confessional community. Many ideas converged to guide our efforts. Psychoanalyst Hinshelwood's idea of introducing *compassion* into community meetings on a psychiatric ward connected with Karen Armstrong's idea of making *compassion* the litmus test of good theology and its practice. Gregory Bateson's notion of *Mind* undergirding all the *mental processes* at work to form a human community proved to bring about a certain union of the *humility* and *wisdom* he had envisioned. Confession is born in the humility required to accept the unacceptable in ourselves and others, leading to the wisdom of forgiving one another with a compassion that does whatever is required to work out relationships. The *forgiveness studies* underlined the potential for healing both our bodies and our relationships by participating in the practice of what theologian Tillich calls *God's acceptance of us in spite of our unacceptability*. A full confessional experience originates in honest efforts to accept our own darker side with all its estrangement from others and extend this forgiving acceptance to them in search of some form of workable reconciliation.

Practice

A constructive practice of forgiveness requires regular attention to stay influential in the midst of our very human relationships. There are probably as many different ways to approach this task as there are different kinds and sizes of communities. We have only scratched the surface of possibilities. The key is to discover ways to engage in the kind of *empathic participation in the lives of others* we have been describing. Reflecting teams have possibilities in business circles, in committees and task forces throughout education, in quality circle meetings and the like in industry, in similar circles of politics and government, and certainly in committees and study groups in our religious institutions. Language appropriate to the setting is normally available to the inventive and the resourceful.

Exercise 1. Forming a Confessional Community with larger groups like our MFT program begins by recognizing that the possibility for significant self-reflection is always there. On the very limited basis of our experiment at Louisville, I offer the following considerations. Wherever you are, you will be adapting a compassionate way of communicating and problem-solving to your own unique setting, in your own unique way, and in your own unique language.

1. Like any other confessional practice, an interest in your organization will arise from some form of mounting frustration, growing discontent, dissension, or dissatisfaction. Seldom will the energy for such an undertaking flow from smooth times. Energy does build when relationships become sufficiently stressed to interfere with your common purpose.

2. Someone elevated in the hierarchy (of the organization, community, institution, family, etc.) must either initiate or sanction the decision to begin. If the person in charge (director, CEO, pastor, priest or rabbi, owner, boss, etc.) is reluctant or ambivalent, the effort will probably not succeed. Unanimity is seldom, if ever, present anywhere, but a group of committed people with support from the top can succeed in demonstrating to others the effectiveness of reflection.

3. Some compelling theory or belief, if held in common, can serve to sanction the undertaking and sustain expectations and efforts. In our case, this took the form of melding theological understandings, such as confession and forgiveness, with psychological and psychotherapeutic practices such as empathic attunement, systemic thinking, and reflecting teams. Commitments to these concepts helped us launch our program and hold to its course. In a secular setting or one of different religious tradition, I have used more inclusive terms such as "acceptance" instead of forgiveness, approaching the same confessional task in more neutral language. I believe the potential for spiritual encounter is there, whether or not we name it.

4. A gradual introduction of the process to your community meeting will increase the chances for success. We began with considerable previous experience with reflecting teams in family therapy. Yet we were careful to spend time using hypothetical cases while meeting in the larger group, then forming reflecting teams on group supervision of videotapes in clinical work, before tackling internal problems in our working relationships. I have often used videotaped segments of movies to introduce the use of reflecting teams to help resolve impasses. Teams from the audience can take a shot at empathic participation and then reflecting on different ways to resolve the scene with *systemic voicing* and *systemic dramatization*.

5. Workable boundaries around the number of participants in a confessional community are important. Ours was a group of 35

to 50 people. I don't know how many we can engage in such a meeting. I have worked with over 150 people from a church congregation with a similar format and done demonstrations at professional conferences with more than that. I don't know the optimum number for the level of participation and depth of personal involvement we seek. My hunch is that in larger communities, boundaries between working groups, departments, factions, and the like could expand to accommodate as many as 50 or 60 people before some division into cells or subgroups would be judicious. Obviously, the smaller the division, the greater the potential for participation, involvement, and impact.

As far as the rest of our world is concerned, I must leave you with no defined exercises to practice these forgiving principles of acceptance. Perhaps by now you are forming your own vision of some undertaking in the circles of your own involvement. If so, I share your excitement and wish you a strong Creative Presence in your efforts. Of necessity, you will be mapping out your unique approach to your particular situation. I often dream of what our public and political life could be like with a confessional approach to building integrity in our relationships. Could we begin to overcome such contemporary practices as "maintaining deniability," putting our own "spin" on the news, "tampering with the truth," or other means of denying, distorting, or concealing that mark ever-more-sophisticated ways of saying "Not Me" throughout our corporate and political life? Could we find peace and give it a chance?

Exercise 2. If you are yet to construct your own sign to put up in Phoenix or anywhere else, now is the time to do so before you turn the page and read through to the end.

In Conclusion

In conclusion, I must deal with a question lurking in my mind which I know others must share. How can I extrapolate to the rough and tumble world of corporate life or politics at the national level from my limited experience with the concept of a compassionate community in small bodies of people? Isn't it naive to hope that empathic participation in the lives of others has any relevance to the real world of economic crises, warfare, and hand-to-hand political conflict? Suggesting that honest confession with the practice of forgiveness could transform anything in the secular arenas of everyday life requires considerable "audacity of hope," to borrow a phrase from our forty-fourth president. But it isn't a blind hope.

While I was awaiting the hard copy of this manuscript, I picked up Doris Kearns Goodwin's *Team of Rivals* and devoured it.* This masterful study of Lincoln's management of his cabinet during the Civil War contains 121 pages of endnotes documenting the hundreds of books, papers, dairies, letters, news articles, memoirs, journals, and correspondence she consulted. So many of Lincoln's characteristics she describes remind me of the confessors we have studied. I simply must add some parts of Lincoln's *sacred story* here at the end.

Lincoln was a very shrewd politician and the most unlikely of four candidates contending for the presidential nomination at the 1860 Republican Convention in Chicago. Three much better known rivals were competing with each other: New York Senator William H. Seward, Ohio Governor Salmon P. Chase, and Missouri's elder statesman Edward Bates. As a backwoods lawyer, Lincoln could muster no substantial support in the face of the strong following each commanded. So as Illinois' favorite son, he worked his way into the position of everyone's second choice as the three contended one another out of contention. Like the Gingham Dog and the Calico Cat, they sort of ate each other up leaving him still standing.

Lincoln was never without political savvy. Even the Emancipation Proclamation was a brilliant wartime move to discourage Confederate soldiers who counted on slaves to tend their fields and brought them to dig their fortifications. It encouraged the slaves to escape and change sides with the promise of freedom. He was a keen judge of who could most competently fill each position in his cabinet and who could best serve a nation on the brink of a civil war. William Seward was his choice for secretary of state, Salmon Chase became his secretary of the treasury, and Edward Bates was named his attorney general. These three together with three Democrats (Gideon Wells as secretary of the navy, Edward Stanton as secretary of war, and Montgomery Blair as postmaster general) performed their jobs with distinction. None were political cronies or like-minded insiders.

The team of such influential rivals sharpened Lincoln's leadership from every vantage point and tested it as well. William Seward shared Lincoln's commitment to do everything possible to preserve the Union and proved a valuable consultant, even as the president-elect fine-tuned his inauguration address. Several times Lincoln made significant changes at Seward's suggestion. Yet on the day of the inauguration when a congressman spoke of how disappointed a politician friend might be if he failed to receive an appointment in the new administration, Seward exclaimed, "A disappointment! You speak to me of disappointment. To me, who was justly entitled

---

* (New York: Simon and Schuster Paperbacks, 2005.)

to the Republican nomination for the presidency, and who had to stand aside and see it given to a little Illinois lawyer!"*

The brain trust with which Lincoln surrounded himself was composed of ambitious, as well as learned men who would try their self-taught president's authority and patience with incredible challenges to his power. Seward told a German diplomat that the secretary of state was really in charge of the country and the president a mere figurehead. Salmon Chase was so ruled by an unbridled ambition for Lincoln's job that he campaigned broadly for the party nomination behind his president's back as a second term approached. Both Seward and Chase battled for their way and tendered their resignations more than once over some disputed action. In all these crises, Lincoln's inner strength and extraordinary empathic skills held cabinet and country together through our nation's severest challenge.

Doris Kearns Goodwin reflects upon Lincoln's character at a number of points. He had a reputation for melancholy that she regards as an acute sensitivity to the pains and injustices he saw in the world. She describes him as "uncommonly tenderhearted." Walking with a friend, he once stopped and back-tracked a half-mile to rescue a pig they had passed mired in the mud.

Lincoln's explanation: it was to take the pain out of his own mind. Goodwin observes Lincoln demonstrated more than simple compassion. "He possessed extraordinary empathy, the gift or curse of putting himself in place of another, to experience what they were feeling, to understand their motives and desires."[†] She links it with a faculty the philosopher Adam Smith spoke of in which "by the imagination we place ourselves in his situation . . . we enter as it were into his body and become in some measure him."

Whatever his melancholy, Goodwin points out this empathy was an enormous asset to Lincoln's political career. Hellen Nicolay, whose father served as Lincoln's private secretary, suggested this empathic projection of himself into the lives of others was the president's "crowning gift of political diagnosis." His sympathy gave him the power to forecast with uncanny accuracy what his opponents were likely to do. Goodwin adds that this capacity to intuit the inward feelings and intentions of others was manifest throughout Lincoln's career.

So the cornerstone of *empathic participation in the experience of others*, upon which the practice of forgiveness turns, served to guide Lincoln's relationships throughout his presidency. He did not often make mention of his spiritual commitments. Whereas Seward would speak of God's "higher

---

* *Ibid.* p 327.
† *Ibid.* p 104.

law" and Chase of "natural rights" derived from "the code of heaven," Lincoln was hesitant to ascribe certainty of divine guidance to his decisions. He rarely acknowledged the influence of faith or religious beliefs. But Gideon Wells, his secretary of the navy, observed he had a way of submitting the disposal of a subject to a Higher Power and sticking to what seemed to be the Supreme Will. In such cases, Lincoln would announce to his cabinet he was not seeking advice upon the matter at hand.

We have a strong hint of Lincoln's spirituality in his management of Seward's ideas on how he should end his inaugural address. Seward suggested a bid to the southern states for reconciliation as fellow countrymen, speaking of mystic chords from the battlefields and graves of patriots past that could pass through the hearts of all, harmonizing again in their ancient music "when breathed upon by the guardian angel of the nation." Lincoln fine-tuned the mystic music and patriot graves as he suggested, but altered the final sentence to conclude this music "will yet swell the chorus of the Union, when again touched, as surely they will be, by the better angels of our nature." Goodwin notes the difference: "Most significant, Seward's 'guardian angel' breathes down on the nation from above; Lincoln's 'better angels' are inherent in our nature as a people.'"*

Lincoln's *better angel* was constantly active in his management of the cabinet. He accepted each member as he was on the hoof. He forgave Seward's arrogant bid for influence with the German diplomat, gently suggesting he would handle the matter at hand. When Seward declared the country to be without a viable foreign policy, Lincoln faced another bid on his part to seize power. Seward proposed to deflect attention from their domestic crisis by demanding Spain and France stop meddling in the Western Hemisphere, requesting an accounting from Great Britain, Canada, and Russia for their threats to intervene, and even declaring war on any country without a satisfactory explanation. Lincoln responded to Seward simply that if we needed a more aggressive foreign policy, then he, Lincoln, must be the one to frame it. The idea of engineering a foreign war to reunify the Union, widely criticized by historians, did not merit a reply.

Seward was convinced that if they abandoned Fort Sumter the Southerners would be appeased and eventually return to the Union. Lincoln was convinced the fort should be held by the Union and not given to a Confederacy he was loathe to recognize. Seward tried unsuccessfully to negotiate with representatives of the Confederacy without Lincoln's knowledge, when Lincoln refused to meet with them. For weeks, Seward continued to act as though he were the man in charge. This made for a major snarl in communications between Lincoln, Seward, and Gideon

---

* *Ibid*. p 326.

Wells who was secretary of the navy. Lincoln and Wells planned to use the speedy ship *Powhatan* to protect tugs bringing supplies and provisions to the beleaguered Fort in the Charleston harbor. Seward issued orders to use the same ship under different command in Florida. Through an astonishing series of miscommunications, the ship failed to execute either mission. Unsupplied and without reinforcements, a vastly outnumbered Fort Sumter fell to Confederate General Pierre Beauregard and the rest is history. Wells was astonished when Lincoln "took upon himself the whole blame and said it was carelessness, heedlessness on his part and he ought to have been more careful and attentive."* As Wells observed, Lincoln frequently declared that he, and not his cabinet, was at fault for errors clearly imputed to them.

Still Seward continued to battle for control of the ship of state. As the war began, he feared England would not respect the Union blockade simply to feed its own factories. Seward drafted an abrasive memo for Charles Adams to read to Britain's foreign secretary stating the president was "surprised and grieved" that they had an unofficial meeting with the Confederates. No proceedings, said the memo, granting recognition of the Confederacy or breaking the blockade "would be borne." Lincoln rewrote the memo saying the "president regrets" these meetings and no breach of the blockade "will *pass unnoticed*," indicating it was only for Adams' guidance and not to be read or shown to anyone. Once more Lincoln successfully interrupted Britain's momentum for recognizing and continuing trade with the Confederacy by not issuing a threatening message that could have embroiled the Union in a disastrous second war. Seward got the credit as a shrewd secretary of state and began to recognize Lincoln's remarkable abilities. He would soon become Lincoln's most faithful ally in the cabinet and his closest friend across the years they served together.

Lincoln's capacity to forgive and forget eventually won over virtually everyone who knew him. He was able to accept both friend and foe where they were, understanding where they came from, ready to work out their differences wherever possible. When Salmon Chase secretly broke ranks and wrote letters to prospective supporters criticizing Lincoln and urging them to support his nomination in the next presidential election, Lincoln accepted his behavior sensing he was practically addicted to his desire for the office. Chase did a masterful job as secretary of the treasury in gathering and distributing the huge amount of funds required to fight the Civil War. Lincoln both needed and respected this man. That did not mean he would passively tolerate or avoid dealing with such an affront. When one of Chase's letters was published by a prominent newspaper, Lincoln confronted him face-to-face with the copy he had received. At Lincoln's

* *Ibid.* p 344.

urging, Chase immediately abandoned his quest and campaigned vigorously on Lincoln's behalf throughout a number of states. Nor did the incident keep Lincoln from later appointing Chase as Chief Justice of the U. S. Supreme Court where he served admirably for a number of years.

Lincoln, accepting his own failings, readily forgave those around him for theirs. The energy of his compassionate life seemed to radiate to all who met him. It reached the troops in the field as he frequently rode out among them knowing the grave perils they faced. And they cheered him and fought for him. It reached lines of Confederate prisoners he passed by who waved back at him in acknowledgment and respect. Lincoln's compassion for General Lee and his troops led to the leniency with which Grant treated them upon their surrender. He urged General Sherman to let Confederate President Jefferson Davis quietly escape by telling him the story of a teetotaler who refused a drink of brandy, but remarked to his host that if he put a bit in the lemonade prepared for him, while he wasn't looking, he would not object.

Secretary of War Stanton learned that Jacob Thompson, a very troublesome Confederate marauder who swooped down from Canada to inflict damaging raids on the Union, was about to escape to England on a steamer from Portland, Maine. Stanton immediately ordered his arrest, but when he checked with Lincoln, the president issued another of his many anecdotes: "When you have got an elephant by the hind leg, and he's trying to run away, it's best to let him run."[*]

This was Lincoln, melancholy perhaps, but more compassionate and constantly able to project himself into the position of both friend and foe in search of reconciliation. His belief in the *better angels* within the human spirit reflects a profound sense of Spiritual Presence throughout his life. It governed his *practice of forgiveness* with himself and with others. It suggests a belief in something akin to Whitehead's God embedded in the *actual occasions* of life or Jung's God within the *self*. It made Lincoln a lasting symbol of hope for reconciliation between black and white, North and South, nation and nation. When he died of an assassin's bullet across the street from the Ford theater, surrounded by cabinet members, it was Edwin Stanton, his secretary of war, who pronounced his final tribute, "Now he belongs to the ages."[†]

In concluding our consideration of the practice of forgiveness, there is the matter of that exercise you have been working on in the last three chapters. You remember: what sign would you put up in Phoenix or anywhere else in place of the one that reads "Jesus Cures Depression"? I promised you my version of such a sign that would give expression to my own faith

---

[*] *Ibid.* p 733.
[†] *Ibid.* p 743.

perspective as a Christian. Paul's letter to the Colossians (1:19, 20) suggests in simple terms that God was in Christ reconciling the world to himself. Paul goes on to insist we have like compassion for one another; that we forgive each other as we have been forgiven (3:12,13). Now to get this idea onto a sign worthy of our own times may take some doing. I think Paul has it right, and pretty early, too, long before the Gospels, as we've seen. The idea is *God was in Christ reconciling the world to himself.* But how do we get the breadth and height and extent of this Presence into our statement?

Well, first we can do some politically correct editing and substitute *God's Self* in place of the patriarchal use of the masculine "himself." That encompasses the experience of the other half of humankind, including our women confessors who championed the motherhood, empathy, and compassion of this Presence when others did not. Then there is the notion that in Paul's understanding this Presence is so broadly inclusive that people cannot be divided into Greek and Jew, circumcised and uncircumcised, barbarian, Scythian, slave or free and this Presence is *in all*. So God was in Abraham reconciling the world to God's Self, God was in Moses reconciling the world to God's Self, God was in Mohammed reconciling the world to God's Self, God was in Abraham Lincoln reconciling the world to God's Self. And on and on.

Archbishop Desmond Tutu is said to fold his hands together and bow as he is introduced to someone new, making the same gesture he does in approaching the holy table of the Eucharist upon which are placed the elements at the sacrament of the Lord's Supper. When asked why, he responds, "I do this in recognition of the Presence of the Holy One in them." Now we have the sign:

GOD IS IN YOU AND ME RECONCILING
THE WORLD TO GOD'S SELF

Index

DAT